Politics and
International Relations   GENERAL EDITOR
of Southeast Asia   *George McT. Kahin*

Burma: Military Rule and the Politics of Stagnation
   by Josef Silverstein

Malaysia and Singapore: The Building of New States
   by Stanley S. Bedlington

The Army and Politics in Indonesia
   by Harold Crouch

Indonesian Foreign Policy and the Dilemma of Dependence:
   From Sukarno to Soeharto
   by Franklin B. Weinstein

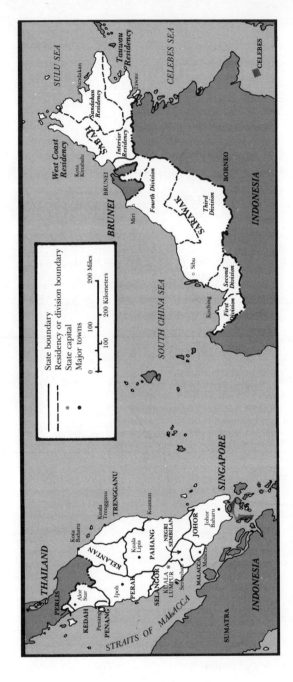

Malaysia, Singapore, and Brunei

Malaysia and Singapore

The Building of New States

STANLEY S. BEDLINGTON

Cornell University Press | ITHACA AND LONDON

First published 1978 by Cornell University Press.
Published in the United Kingdom by Cornell University Press Ltd.,
2-4 Brook Street, London W1Y 1AA.

International Standard Book Number 0–8014–0910–1 (cloth)
International Standard Book Number 0–8014–9864–3 (paper)
Library of Congress Catalog Card Number 77–3114
Librarians: Library of Congress cataloging information
appears on the last page of the book.

Contents

Foreword

That broad area lying between China and India which since World War II has generally been known as Southeast Asia is one of the most heterogeneous in the world. Though it is generally referred to as a region, the principal basis for this designation is simply the geographic propinquity of its component states, and the fact that collectively they occupy the territory between China and the Indian subcontinent. The fundamental strata of the traditional cultures of nearly all the numerous peoples of Southeast Asia do set them apart from those of India and China. Beyond that, however, there are few common denominators among the states that currently make up the area except for roughly similar climatic conditions and, until recently at least, broadly similar economies and economic problems.

The political systems presently governing the lives of Southeast Asia's 300 million inhabitants have been built on considerably different cultures; the religious component alone embraces Buddhism, Confucianism, Christianity, Hinduism, and Islam. Except in the case of Thailand, the politics of all these countries have been conditioned by periods of colonial rule—ranging from little more than half a century to approximately four—each of which has had a distinctive character and political legacy. Even the nature of the Japanese wartime occupation, which covered the entire area, varied considerably among the several countries and had different political consequences. And after Japan's defeat, the courses to independence followed by these states diverged widely. Only through revolutionary anticolonial wars were two of the most populous, Indonesia and Vietnam, able to assert their independence. Although the others followed routes that were peaceful, they were not all necessarily smooth, and the time involved varied by as much as a decade.

Moreover, subsequent to independence the political character of these states has continued to be significantly affected by a wide range of relationships with outside powers. In a few cases these have been largely harmonious, attended by only relatively minor external efforts to influence the course of local political developments. However, most of these countries have been the object of interventions, covert and overt, by outside powers—particularly the United States—which have been calculated to shape their political life in accordance with external interests. Thus the range of contemporary political systems in Southeast Asia is strikingly varied, encompassing a spectrum quite as broad as the differing cultures and divergent historical conditionings that have so profoundly influenced their character.

This series, "Politics and International Relations of Southeast Asia," stems from an earlier effort to treat the nature of government and politics in the states of Southeast Asia in a single volume. Since the second, revised edition of that book, *Government and Politics of Southeast Asia*, was published in 1964, interest in these countries has grown, for understandable reasons especially in the United States. This wider public concern, together with a greater disposition of academics to draw on the political experience of these countries in their teaching, has suggested the need for a more substantial treatment of their politics and governments than could be subsumed within the covers of a single book. The series therefore aims to devote separate volumes to each of the larger Southeast Asian states.

Presumably one no longer needs to observe, as was the case in 1964, that the countries treated "are likely to be strange to many of our readers." But even though the increased American interaction with most of the countries has clearly obviated that proposition, many readers are still likely to be unacquainted with their earlier histories and the extent to which their pasts have affected the development of their recent and contemporary political character. Thus all these volumes will include substantial historical sections as well as descriptions of the salient features of the present social and economic setting. In order to provide as much similarity of treatment as is compatible with the range of cultures and political systems presented by these states, the authors will follow a broadly similar pattern of organization and analysis of their political history, dynamics, and processes. This effort to achieve some basis of comparability may appear rather modest, but to have attempted any greater degree of uniformity would have militated against the latitude and flexibility required to do justice to the differing characteristics of the political systems described. All the books are to be written by political scientists who have lived and carried out research in one or more of the countries for a considerable period and who have previously published scholarly studies on their internal politics.

Although each of these volumes will include a section on the foreign policy of the country concerned, the increased importance of Southeast Asia in international relations that transcend this area has suggested the need for the series to include a few books focused on the foreign relations of its major states. As is true elsewhere, the foreign policies of these countries are heavily influenced by their own domestic politics; hence all contributors to the volumes that are concerned primarily with international relations are also specialists on the internal politics of the country, or countries, about whose foreign policy they write.

In addition, the series will include some in-depth treatments of particular aspects of the politics of the major states of the area. In these cases the focus is on an element of central importance in the political life of the country concerned, the understanding of which helps illuminate its government and politics as a whole.

In this study of the government and politics of the states of Malaysia and Singapore, Stanley Bedlington has brought to bear an unusual combination of academic training and professional field experience. He served in the British Colonial Administration from 1948 to 1957 in the Federation of Malaya and from 1957 to 1963 in North Borneo/Sabah. He then turned to an academic career and carried out eighteen months of research for his doctoral dissertation in Singapore (1970–1972), and continued with his study of Malaysia and Singapore as Research Associate in Cornell

University's International Relations of East Asia Project. He is now the Foreign Affairs Political Analyst for Malaysia, Singapore, and Indonesia in the U.S. Department of State.

GEORGE McT. KAHIN

Ithaca, New York

Preface

It is said that all wars are fought with obsolete weapons; certainly it is my experience that books on current affairs are partially composed with obsolete material. Events rapidly overtake the written word, predictions go awry, assessments need reappraisal—all before the book can be published. Since I first started writing this work, for instance, my feelings about the Association of Southeast Asian States have become more positive, the threat posed by the Malayan Communist Party and its guerrillas has receded, and the September 1976 general election in Singapore showed a continuing and almost overwhelming belief in the ability of the People's Action Party government to provide adequate goods and services for its citizens. Generally, however, the basic theme of this book—the efforts of the two young and quintessentially pragmatic states of Malaysia and Singapore to construct a political identity and a new type of citizen—remains constant.

Many groups in newly independent states resent criticism of their performance, particularly by Westerners and their frequently culture-bound norms. In these days when libertarian ideals are giving way everywhere to rule by the military and other coercive forces, and when as a consequence problems of human rights form part of basic United States foreign policy, leaders of the Third and Fourth Worlds urge that the actions of these countries be considered within the framework of their own problems and their own cultures. I do not agree with this argument, since the debasement of human dignity and other principles of human freedom are not conditional, but the records of Malaysia and Singapore compare well with those of the rest of the world. (Detention without trial in Malaysia and Singapore, for example, is no worse than detention without trial in Northern Ireland.) The form of democracy in Malaysia and Singapore is strongly tinged with authoritarianism, which no matter how benevolently applied infringes upon some political freedoms. There is in both states, however, a real dedication to the improvement of the quality of life for all their peoples. It is in this context that I hope my analyses, and criticisms, will be read.

This book has been written from two vantage points: first, from long experience as an officer in the British colonial service and, second, from academic knowledge gained at universities in the United States. From the first, and earlier, experience, I had learned that many British colonial servants had a genuine sense of service, that despite the inequities of colonial rule (especially ethnic divisiveness and economic exploitation), many British were devoted persons with genuine feelings of affection and sympathy for those over whom they held sway. Many of the values they held, and the institutions they helped build, still exist in postindependence countries: Malaysia and Singapore are no exceptions.

From my academic training, I came to appreciate the limitations of my colonial experience. Fluency in a few languages often leads to an intellectual arrogance that assumes a thorough knowledge of the peoples and their customs. I was fortunate enough to have my weaknesses exposed by many teachers, colleagues, and fellow students who tried, goodness knows, to remedy them. In particular, I am grateful to George McTurnan Kahin of Cornell University and editor of this series, who has been a constant stimulus for new ideas, new values, and new directions, as well as a generous friend to whom I owe a great deal. My gratitude goes also to many others: Cyril Birch and Daniel Lev, who at the University of California at Berkeley did much to foster my undergraduate growth; Benedict Anderson and David Mozingo of Cornell University; Josef Silverstein of Rutgers University and formerly director of the Institute of Southeast Asian Studies in Singapore; and my dear friend George Appell of Brandeis University. In Southeast Asia, Chan Heng-chee of the University of Singapore, Lee Poh-ping of the University of Malaysia, Goh Kian-chee of Singapore, and Sharom Ahmat of the Universiti Sains, Penang, gave me many insights into local events, as did countless other Malaysians and Singaporeans. No person other than myself, of course, is in any way responsible for inaccuracies and other flaws to be found herein.

I would like to extend grateful thanks to Betty Nanatonis of Smith College, who painstakingly typed the original manuscript; to James Twiggs, editor at Cornell University Press; and to Trudie Calvert, who with patience and expertise edited this book. My wife Anne is responsible for its being written at all. She taught for a living to allow me to write for pleasure, and otherwise provided me with the mental and physical sustenance necessary for the endeavor. My gratitude and love for her are constant.

Finally, I must thank the Woodrow Wilson Fellowship program, the Foreign Area Fellowship Program, the Lee Foundation of Singapore, and the Southeast Asia Program and the International Relations of East Asia Program of Cornell University, which at various times generously provided funds.

STANLEY S. BEDLINGTON
Washington, D.C.

Abbreviations

Abbreviations of Political Organizations

General

ASA	Association of Southeast Asia
ASEAN	Association of Southeast Asian Nations
CCP	Chinese Communist Party
KMT	Kuomintang: Chinese Nationalist Party
PRC	People's Republic of China
SEATO	Southeast Asia Treaty Organization
SRV	Socialist Republic of Vietnam

Peninsular, or Western, Malaysia

AMCJA	All Malayan Council of Joint Action
DAP	Democratic Action Party
DMW	Department of Malay Work
FMS	Federated Malay States
GRM	Gerakan Rakyat Malaysia: People's Movement of Malaysia
IMP	Independence of Malaya Party
KMM	Kesatuan Melayu Muda: Union of Malay Youth
KRIS	Kesatuan Ra'ayat Indonesia Semenanjong: Union of the Peninsular Indonesian Peoples
MARA	Majlis Amanah Rakyat: People's Trust Council
MCA	Malaysian (previously Malayan) Chinese Association
MCP	Malayan Communist Party
MCP(M–L)	Malayan Communist Party (Marxist-Leninist)
MCP(R–F)	Malayan Communist Party (Revolutionary Faction)
MDU	Malayan Democratic Union
MIC	Malayan Indian Congress
MNLA	Malayan National Liberation Army
MNLL	Malayan National Liberation League
MNP	Malayan Nationalist Party
MPAJA	Malayan People's Anti-Japanese Army
MRLA	Malayan Races Liberation Army

MSC	Malaysian Solidarity Convention
MTUC	Malaysian Trades Union Council
NF	National Front
NOC	National Operations Council
PETA	Pembela Tanah Ayer: Our Country's Avengers
PI	Partai Islam: Islamic Party
PMIP	Pan-Malayan Islamic Party
PPP	People's Progressive Party
PUTERA	Pusat Tenaga Ra'ayat: People's Central Force
RMPF	Royal Malaysian Police Force
UMNO	United Malays' National Organization
UMS	Unfederated Malay States

Eastern Malaysia
  Sabah

BERJAYA	Bersatu Ra'ayat Jelata Sabah: United Peoples of Sabah party
BNBCC	British North Borneo Chartered Company
SANYA	Sabah National Youth Association
UNKO	United National Kadazan Organization
UPKO	United Pasok Kadazan Organization
USAP	Union of Sabah People's Party
USIA	United Sabah Islamic Association
USNO	United Sabah National Organization

  Sarawak

BARJASA	Barisan Ra'ayat Jati Sarawak: Sarawak Native People's Front
NKCP	North Kalimantan Communist Party
PANAS	Partai Negara Sarawak: Sarawak State Party
PBB	Partai Pesaka Bumiputera Bersatu: United Sons of the Soil Party
PESAKA	Partai Pesaka Anak Sarawak: Sons of Sarawak Party
SCA	Sarawak Chinese Association
SNAP	Sarawak National Party
SUPP	Sarawak United People's Party

Singapore

CCC	Chinese Chamber of Commerce
CEC	Central Executive Committee
ISD	Internal Security Department
KMS	Kesatuan Melayu Singapura: Singapore Malay Union
NTUC	National Trade Union Council
PAP	People's Action Party

PEKEMAS	Persatuan Kebangsaan Melayu Singapura: Malay National Union of Singapore, also known as SMNO
PF	People's Front
SPA	Singapore People's Alliance
SPUR	Singapore Planning and Urban Resources group
SMNO/SUMNO	Singapore Malays National Organization, known before 1963 as SUMNO, or the Singapore United Malays National Organization; SMNO is also known by its Malay acronym, PEKEMAS
UNF	United National Front
WP	Workers' Party

Abbreviations of Newspapers and News Magazines

FAM	*Foreign Affairs Malaysia* (Kuala Lumpur), published by Ministry of Foreign Affairs
FEER	*Far Eastern Economic Review* (Hong Kong), weekly news magazine
MM	*Malay Mail* (Kuala Lumpur), daily newspaper
NCNA	*New China News Agency* (Peking), the official Chinese news organization
NN	*New Nation* (Singapore), daily newspaper
NYT	*New York Times* (New York), daily newspaper
SH	*Singapore Herald* (Singapore), daily newspaper, closed down by the Singapore government in 1971
ST	*Straits Times* (Singapore), daily newspaper, now published as two entirely separate dailies in Singapore and Kuala Lumpur. The Kuala Lumpur version is now known as the *New Straits Times*.

PART I

MALAYA AND SINGAPORE BEFORE 1945

1 | A Common History

Introduction

The governments in Malaysia and in Singapore today, and the political configurations that inform them, have been shaped by common historical and geographical forces. The social, economic, and political realities of the present can be understood only in the light of these shared experiences; the emergence of Malaysia and Singapore as sovereign political systems, or states, occurred in the recent past with the separation of 1965 (indeed, between 1963 and 1965, Malaysia and Singapore were components of one single state), and even now events in one country invariably have repercussions in the other. For this reason the two countries have been included in this one volume, and events in both before 1945 will be treated within the same historical framework. Thereafter their progress toward becoming distinct political entities will be charted separately, although the interplay of events and of similar environments will necessarily result in much overlap. Both states can be included in the newly emerged "Third World"; both have embarked upon ambitious programs of rapid social and structural change known collectively as state building. In Malaysia and Singapore, this process centers upon the domesticization (if not the eradication) of an abiding set of ethnic conflicts and will be the focus of this study.

Malaysia extends over an area of approximately 130,500 square miles and is divided into two distinct regions detached from each other by 400 miles of the South China Sea. The first region, Western Malaysia, comprises what used to be called the Malay Peninsula, stretching from the Thai border in the north to the Straits of Johor overlooking the island of Singapore in the south.

The second region, Eastern Malaysia, is composed of two former British colonies, Sarawak and Sabah, on the island of Borneo. These two Borneo territories, between which lies the tiny but important sultanate of Brunei, occupy a long, narrow strip on the northwest coast of Borneo. Distances are important since they often tend to divide: Kuching, the capital of Sarawak, is 600 miles to the southeast of Kuala Lumpur, the federal capital in Western Malaysia, while Kota Kinabalu (formerly Jesselton), the capital of Sabah, lies some 540 miles to the northeast of Kuching and over 1,000 miles from Kuala Lumpur. The Republic of Singapore, suspended at the tip of the Malay Peninsula, possesses a land area of only 225 square miles (when the tide is out, its residents joke) and is separated by a stretch of water less than a mile wide from the Malaysian state of Johor to the north. The seas off Singapore are speckled with numerous small islands, some of which belong to the neighboring Republic of Indonesia. The whole area of Malaysia and Singapore is, in a real geopolitical sense, of vital strategic significance.

History before the Arrival of the West

Southeast Asia is generally portrayed as lying at the confluence of Indic and Sinic cultures, which together with the residues of strong indigenous influences impart to the area a distinct and peculiar flavor. No single cultural strain is pervasive; each has contributed its individual piquancy to create a singular if syncretic fusion. This process is important to the understanding of Malay culture, for present-day Malay values are compounded of a sometimes contradictory admixture of pre-Islamic custom, the purer precepts of Islam, and Western influences. The shaping of Malay values has been profoundly affected by these conflicting impulses.

The peopling of Southeast Asia, including what is now Malaysia, is shrouded in mystery and lingering controversy, but we may assume that it was effected by waves of migration from the continental north. The descendants of the earliest of these waves, known generically by the Malaysian government as "*orang Asli*," the "original people" or aborigines, still live on today. These people are of the greatest interest to the ethnographer; except for a brief flirtation with Malayan Communist Party (MCP) guerrillas in the deep jungle during the "Emergency" era, they have never been a significant political force and will not play a role in these pages. The present-day Malay and the non-Muslim Malay-types of Sabah and Sarawak are regarded as the true natives of Malaysia and are called together "*bumiputera*," or "sons of the soil." The arrival of the forefathers of these *bumiputera*, the most important of the migratory waves and called by the ethnographers Mongoloid Indonesian or Proto-Malay, probably occurred between 2500 and 1500 b.c. in an area covering the Malay Peninsula, most of the Indonesian archipelago, most of the Philippines, and Taiwan.[1]

The first recorded history of a distinctly "Malay" political unit is that of Langkasuka.[2] Some confusion exists regarding the exact location of this riverine society. Modern interpreters assume that it occupied the area of what is now the Thai Malay province of Patani, centering around Songkhla (also known as Singgora) in southern Thailand. The next significant Malay political network to emerge was Srivijaya, which arose as a loosely knit commercial empire following the decline of Funan (now modern Cambodia) in the seventh century. The political heart of Srivijaya was at Palembang in Sumatra, and the empire encompassed "a confederation of trading posts on the fringe of the primeval forest," including large sections of Sumatra, the Nicobar Islands, the Isthmus of Kra, and Kedah. For some five centuries this Malay Buddhist empire commanded the trade network of island Southeast Asia, levying tribute from ships plying between India and China and dominating the interisland trade with widespread, near piratical menace. The strategic position of Srivijaya athwart lines of commerce flowing between India and East Asia through the Sunda Straits and the Straits of Malacca stimulated jealousy and rivalry from kingdoms in India and in Java. Military attacks from both sides were mounted, and although Srivijaya was able, for a short time, to maintain its hold on Sumatra, its other possessions were dissolved. In the fourteenth century Srivijaya and its dependencies were vanquished by Majapahit, the last of the great Javanese Hindu

1. Richard O. Winstedt, *The Malays: A Cultural History* (London: Routledge & Kegan Paul, rev. ed., 1950), pp. 10–11.
2. Paul Wheatley, *The Golden Khersonese* (Kuala Lumpur: University of Malaya Press, 1961), pp. 252, 298.

states, and Sumatra and the Malay Peninsula fell under this latter empire's dominion and cultural influence. One of the areas brought under Majapahit's sway was Tumasik, later to become Singapore, but the island, with the rest of the Malay Peninsula, was soon wrenched out of Majapahit's grip by an aggressive and expanding kingdom of Siam, whereupon, around 1400, the ruler of Tumasik (a prince originally from Palembang and the consort of a Majapahit royal princess) fled north to found the state of Malacca. Thereafter the influence of Hindu and Buddhist cultures on the inhabitants of the Malay Peninsula declined rapidly, to be replaced by the religion of Islam, whose proselytizing philosophy and jurisprudence pervades and motivates every aspect of the daily lives of its adherents.

The presence of the Malay Peninsula within these great Southeast Asian Hindu-Buddhist empires and within the Malacca sultanate that followed enabled elements of a common culture to be diffused around the islands and coastal areas of Southeast Asia, giving rise to what today is often called the Malay world—an area that includes the Malay regions of southern Thailand and the southern Philippines, most of Indonesia, Borneo, the Malay Peninsula, and the Malay population of Singapore. The early states of Langkasuka, Srivijaya, and Majapahit constituted the cultural foundations upon which the Islamic sultanate of Malacca arose to dominate Malay cultural values and to shape traditional patterns of Malay politics for centuries. The proud nationalism of the Malays of modern Malaysia finds its inspiration in the history, myths, and legends of these stirring times, generating an awareness of being a Malay that transcends the mere political borders of the twentieth century. At the same time, the syncretism of Buddhism, Hinduism, and an indigenous animism, when overlaid with the more rigorous and demanding creed of Islam, has left a legacy of cultural ambivalence that still haunts the state builder and the modernizer. Visionaries of the left and the right working for a Greater Malaysia or a Greater Indonesia, encompassing in one political unit the whole of the Malay cultural world, strident Malay ultranationalists, custom-oriented traditionalists, and reform-minded Muslims, tread yet the boards of this historical past. A Singapore Malay poet, living now in Kuala Lumpur, epitomizes the burgeoning sense of greater Malay nationalism abroad today in Malaysia:

"Malaya-Indonesia"
a poem
by Usman Awang
A Welcome to Pak Djuanda and his Delegation

That bridge of history reaching over the Malacca Straits,
Recreates in a unified chant our emotional oneness.
Live again, spirit of Majapahit and of Srivijaya!
Meet again, Laksamana Tun Tuah and Patih Gaja Mada!

That song, for so long embosomed within us
Behind bars, in its prison of the *ancien regime*,
Is the song of one blood throughout the annals of time,
Entwining us together in the new spirit of Asia-Africa.

One beloved language, our inheritance, bears witness;
Our countenances, our characters, are carved in common descent.

We are as one in the Great Archipelago,
And on our homecoming journey we search
For imprints which conjoin ourselves, our entities,
With a promise of peace and comradeship as an eternal symbol.[3]

The implications for the course of regional cooperation within the "Malay" countries of Southeast Asia and the tension thereby imprinted on the process of building a multiethnic, tolerant society within Malaysia itself (and within Singapore), are obvious.

The Coming of Islam and the Significance of the Malacca Sultanate

The establishment of Malacca at the very beginning of the fifteenth century signifies the nascence of a Malay system of values and politics that has persisted down to the present, even though the sultanate itself proved ephemeral. (It lasted slightly over one century—from 1403 to 1511—before collapsing under the onslaught of the West.) Although some Islamic influence had reached the Malay Peninsula by the mid-fourteenth century, it did not become a vital force until it was adopted and propagated by the first Sultan

3. Reprinted in Oliver Rice and Abdullah Majid, eds., *Modern Malay Verse* (Kuala Lumpur: Oxford University Press, 1963), p. 24. Translation is my own.

of Malacca, originally known as Paramesvara but later to become Megat Iskandar Shah after his conversion from Hinduism to Islam, and by his heirs. The rapid rise and expansion of Malacca immediately upon its founding can be ascribed to its geographical location as a natural center of trade between East and West and to the vacuum of power following the demise of Srivijaya and the increasing decay of Majapahit. Under these conditions the sultanate flourished less as a trading center than as "the site of a vast fair where . . . the products of China and the Far East were exchanged for those of Europe."[4]

Concomitant with Malacca's success in the world of commerce was its role in the dissemination of Islam. Pahang, Trengganu, Patani, Kelantan, and Kedah in the peninsula, many areas of coastal Sumatra, and the state of Brunei in Borneo (then much larger in size and influence than the existing sultanate), all were converted to Islam because of trade connections (which marched hand in hand with a missionary zeal), family linkages, or sheer force of arms. The adoption and the propagation of Islam was at once a religious experience and a political force, for as well as introducing a vital and integrating philosophy to the Malays it also secured the entrance of Malacca into the "*ummat*" of Islam, a great religious (and often political) "community" stretching from the Middle East through India to Southeast Asia. As D. G. E. Hall reminds us, it thereby brought powerful allies and became a unifying weapon against outside encroachment, at first against Siam and later against the West.[5] Another historian suggests that the arrival of Western explorers (specifically Portuguese) in the fifteenth century was one of the most vital ingredients in the spread of Islam as a reaction to this alien incursion.[6] It might be posited, in fact, that the strength of Islam in the Malay Peninsula ever since its establishment there has often ebbed and flowed in relation to the onset of foreign influxes upon Malayo-Muslim culture.

The character of Islam that reached Malacca was a compound of

---

4. D. G. E. Hall, *A History of South East Asia*, 3d ed. (London: Macmillan, 1968), p. 212.

5. Ibid., p. 213.

6. J. C. van Leur, *Indonesian Trade and Society: Essays in Asian Social and Economic History* (The Hague: W. van Hoeve, 1955), p. 113.

the orthodox and the mystic. With the orthodox Sunni missionaries of the Shafi'i school came Sufi mystics, often more successful than their orthodox brethren because of their capacity to tolerate pre-Islam custom and belief that were anathema to orthodox Muslim tenets. To this extent, Islam in Malaysia does not reflect the degree of orthodoxy obtaining in other, more rigid Muslim countries; pre-Islamic *adat*, or custom, is still able to exert legal sanction on Malayo-Muslim behavior despite pressures from an often contrary corpus of Shafi'i jurisprudence. (*"Hidup di-kandong adat; mati di-kandong tanah"* [7] "Alive we are swathed in custom; dead, in the earth"—is a Malay proverb the truth and restraints of which continue to exercise Muslim reformers.) R. O. Winstedt has described the tension inherent in the clash of orthodox theology and popular Sufi mysticism: for the former "God is in heaven," while the latter begins with animist underpinnings and thereafter "inclines towards a pantheism that finds Him closer than the veins of one's neck." [8] One present-day Malay intellectual has suggested that Islam in Malaya was propagated largely by adherents of Sufism, by unschooled Shaykhs lacking any knowledge of rational science, whose leadership qualities rested "on devotion rather than intellect." This writer further suggests that Sufism has had and continues to have a demonstrable influence on Malay political and social life; it is an integrating force, strengthening communal bonds as it enables men and women to rise above themselves, and yet, because of popular and widespread misinterpretation, it evinces "eschatalogical tendencies which . . . [represent] formidable impediments towards economic and social progress." [9]

The other important legacy of the Malacca sultanate lies in the establishment of a prototypical indigenous Malay political tradition that has been followed, with certain changes, by other Malay states in the peninsula. As a result of the Malacca tradition, a hierarchical

7. A. W. Hamilton, *Malay Proverbs* (Singapore: Donald Moore, 1955).

8. Winstedt, *The Malays*, p. 38.

9. Syed Naguib Al-Attas, *Some Aspects of Sufism as Understood and Practised among the Malays* (Singapore: Malaysian Sociological Research Institute, 1963), Parts B and C. See also M. A. Rauf, *A Brief History of Islam with Special Reference to Malaya* (Kuala Lumpur: Oxford University Press, 1964).

system emerged in which the sultan came to embody the source of all prestige and the legitimizer of Malay values. His person represented, in symbolic form, the unity of the state, the fountainhead of Malay secular tradition, and the defender of the Islamic faith. But the sultan was rarely the sole controller of power within the state. In real political terms, he was often a mere first among equals, with a number of territorial or district chiefs lower down the hierarchy of prestige. Collectively the chiefs possessed more power than their sultan, but because of the ever-present fear of outside attack, together with the necessity to transact their trade within a unit broader than their own small district fiefs, they rarely tried to usurp total power; rather they carefully contrived a symbiotic status quo with the sultan, under which the chiefs were enabled to govern their districts without interference from above (at the same time deriving legitimacy from the sultan) while the latter surrounded himself with the pomp of the court and the prestige of his office without fear of subversion from below. Because his power was limited, the sultan had no need for an elaborate statewide administrative machinery, but he did appoint various ministers and administrators, many of whose honorific titles remain today to attest to the legitimacy and the continuity of Malay political rule.[10] From the Sultan, these notables, and their numerous kin arose a hierarchically based ruling class, ascriptive and aristocratic, from which the Malay value system distilled its directions for several centuries.

For the Malays of today the Malacca sultanate symbolizes their golden, heroic age. Films, poetry, novels, and plays often take their themes and inspiration from the history and legends of the Malacca court. The *Malay Annals (Sejarah Melayu)*, well known to generations of Malay schoolchildren, were written during the Malacca period; underneath this work's historical descriptions, its legends, and its mysticism lies a strong sense of political ideology stressing "the subject's unquestioning loyalty and submission to his king, and his avoidance at all costs of the unforgivable sin of

10. *Mentri Besar* (chief minister), *Temenggong* (sometimes a chief minister, sometimes a chief of police and troops), *Bendahara* (state treasurer), *Laksamana* (admiral, or commander of state forces), and *Shahbandar* (harbor master and collector of taxes) are titles still extant in certain Malay states.

derhaka: insubordination or treason."[11] One Malay educator, Syed Hussein Alatas, has suggested that out of the Malacca sultanate and its recorded history can be traced a continuity of what he calls "psychological feudalism," a cluster of phenomena that includes a Malay subject's absolute loyalty to his ruler, while permitting him to escape—through flight, never through defiance or challenge—inequities imposed upon him by forced labor and corrupt officialdom.[12]

Thus there evolved two distinct (and largely mutually exclusive) classes: a ruling class formed by the sultan, the aristocracy, and the chiefs, and a subject class, composed of the masses of Malay peasantry. Political cohesion in the typical Malay state, as J. M. Gullick has demonstrated, rested on the relationship between the peasantry and their immediate overlords, the territorial chiefs. Such a relationship was compounded of a mixture of "loyalty and a cynical awareness of [the peasantry's] own helplessness in the face of oppression" and was buttressed by a common God and a common set of customary beliefs—all sheltered by the symbolic canopy of the sultan as the protector of their welfare, spiritual and temporal.[13]

Until the arrival of the British, the peasants lived mainly in coastal and riverine areas situated on the east and west of the peninsula. (The mountainous nature of the interior and the density of its rain forest meant that communications followed the lines of rivers and the coastline; the only links between east and west were by long sea journeys.) The peasants lived in small hamlets and villages, known by the term *kampong*; the larger villages had a resident *penghulu* or headman. The *penghulu* became the intermediating authority between the peasants and the chief and

11. P. E. de J. de Jong, "The Character of the *Malay Annals*," in John Bastin and R. Roolvink, eds., *Malayan and Indonesian Studies* (London: Oxford University Press, 1964), pp. 235–241.

12. Syed Hussein Alatas, "Feudalism in Malaysian Society: A Study in Historical Continuity," *Civilisations*, 17, (1968), and, by the same author, "Religion, Culture and Social Change," *International Yearbook for the Sociology of Religion*, 5 (1969), section entitled "Some Comments on Islam and Social Change in Malaysia."

13. J. M. Gullick, *Indigenous Political Systems of Western Malaya* (London: University of London Press, 1968), chap. 8.

was generally responsible for the maintenance of peace within his area, for organizing corvée labor, and for contributing men and money to the chief's defense forces. Appointed nominally by the sultan by seal of authority, in actuality the *penghulu* owed his primary loyalty to the local chief; he came from a leading family in the *kampong* and traditionally (but not always) inherited the office from his father.

Theoretically, a codified system of law existed in each Malay state, compiled by learned scholars and deposited in the sultan's palace for that dignitary's dispensation. But no judiciary was ever appointed, and the district chiefs administered their own form of justice unimpeded by any restraint other than their own sensitivities. The imposition of fines by the chiefs and the sequestering of property from their subjects were the major methods of revenue collection; often the means employed were arbitrary and capricious. For these and other reasons, from the time of the Malacca sultanate until the British forward movement in the 1870s, Malay settlements were of a transitory nature, whole villages folding their possessions and moving on in the face of oppression and internecine warfare. There were few incentives to improve the land and increase the crops in order to accumulate capital; the harvesting of surplus crops and the acquisition of possessions of substance would provoke confiscation by the chief on the flimsiest of pretexts.

The indigenous political organization that emerged from the continuity of the Malacca cultural tradition is of vital import for an understanding of the present. First, it marked the foundation, for the first time, of a major Malay political unit on the soil of present-day Malaysia, thereby providing a tradition of Malay political hegemony (the appearances of which were carefully preserved later by the British in the person of the various sultans) imparting legitimacy to the existing political system. The pattern of indigenous political culture established by the Malacca sultanate has thus given an aura of legitimacy to its successors on which to erect a federalized state system rather than one central political authority. The obligations of unswerving loyalty to the sultan and to those in authority under him that were impressed upon the Malay peasant's notion of ideal behavior have persisted to modern times, stifling, until the turbulent years after World War II, active participation in politics, the practice of which was better left to the ruling class.

Second, the Malacca era saw the firm establishment of Islam in most of the peninsula—an Islam in which pre-Islamic *adat* beliefs lay underneath a more orthodox Muslim theology. Because the sultan was defender of the Muslim faith (a sacred function owing much to the Hindu ideal of a god-king), a structured religious hierarchy was never allowed to develop, insofar as the sultan, devoid of any central administrative machinery and possessing few other financial and human resources, was not strong enough (or perhaps willing enough) to create a statewide religious organization penetrating into the districts and villages of his territorial satraps. Religious control and dissemination, therefore, were more often than not left in the hands of village personages appointed by the villagers themselves. These men generally possessed no qualifications other than religious devotion and, in some instances, the fact that they had completed the haj pilgrimage to Mecca. Thus the directions were laid out for a future course of religious conservatism (some Malay reformers would say obscurantism).

The Coming of the West
The Portuguese and the Dutch

The Portuguese presence in Malaya had few long-lasting effects except in the important realm of religion. For whatever reasons the Portuguese embarked upon their maritime conquests in Southeast Asia—whether because of commercial competition or a hell-fire Catholicism or both—they found Malacca an easy target to subdue; the sultanate fell to the attackers in 1511 after only five days of resistance. Imbued with an anti-Islamic fervor acquired from earlier conflict with the Moors in Morocco and elsewhere in North Africa, the Portuguese thereafter found themselves engaged in an anti-Muslim crusade for the control of the spice trade (pepper, cloves, nutmeg, and cinnamon). This century of Portuguese presence in the Malay archipelago, based in Malacca, saw a series of bloody wars and sieges, pitting Muslim against Muslim against Catholic, as the Westerners constructed an always insecure commercial empire in the region. But the demise of the Malacca sultanate did not signify an immediate end to Malacca's influence, as the sultan and other members of the ruling dynasty escaped to other areas in the peninsula (Johor, Perak, and Pahang) to establish new regimes or strengthen old ones. Because of the fragmented nature of Malay political power in the archipelago, the Portuguese were able to sustain a position that would otherwise have been untenable. Finally, however, the threat of Portugal, especially the intolerance of its missionary zealots, brought a stronger religious and cultural unity (in Islam) to the area if not a more coherent political association. In sum, the early Portuguese successes were ultimately negated by the indigenous opposition they succeeded in arousing—and by the coming of the Dutch.

The Dutch, unlike the Portuguese, were not fired up with any great religious fervor and proselytizing ardor, preferring, for reasons of trade, to utilize existing traditional tribute and commercial patterns. Indeed, the first Dutch siege of Malacca, in 1606, was conducted with Malay support on the basis of a Dutch-Johor treaty. This first attack failed, but in 1640–1641 a stronger assault, led by Dutch troops with Malay support, was successful. Once in control, the Dutch proved as commercially rapacious as their Portuguese predecessors, but their main legacy lay in their tolerance of local rule and tradition, a practice to be followed by the British who succeeded them. It should also be noted that the Dutch era in Malaya saw the breakup in several Malay states of indigenous dynasties and their replacement by more enterprising and adventurous Bugis chiefs.

Toward Intervention: British Activities to 1874

The British influence in the peninsula had both qualitatively and quantitatively far greater impact on the native peoples than that of either Portugal or the Netherlands. The two latter powers were content to control trade and other forms of intercourse from small centers of power, but the British ultimately moved to establish their dominion on a broader territorial base—although their first objectives did not envision any such acquisition of territory and the imperial subjects that went with it. By the end of the eighteenth century the British were drawn into the Malay Peninsula and the archipelago generally by dint of their stake in India and China, for strategic as well as commercial purposes. In 1785 the island of Penang was acquired by Captain Francis Light of the East India

Company from the sultan of Kedah in return for assistance and protection against the sultan's enemies,[14] and in 1786 a trading port was opened. In 1819, Sir Stamford Raffles, despite massive criticism from his superiors in India and London, founded the port of Singapore by capitalizing on intrigue and conflict between two rival Malay rulers. British policy toward Penang and Singapore was marked by a desire to turn both ports into cosmopolitan trade centers, "marts of the East."[15] To further this mercantilist policy commercial houses were founded in the two ports, immigration and settlement were encouraged, and Malays, Chinese,[16] Indians, and Europeans began to arrive in substantial numbers. Trade and the profits therefrom grew rapidly, and by the middle of the nineteenth century a considerable amount of capital had been accumulated. In 1824 an Anglo-Dutch treaty was concluded, clearly defining British and Dutch spheres of interest and making the Malay Peninsula, including Singapore, the exclusive preserve of the British. In 1826, Malacca, Singapore, and Penang merged into a single administrative territory, known after 1830 as the Straits Settlements.

14. The enemy was, of course, Siam, which later annexed Kedah. The British defaulted in their promise, failing to extend any real aid to the sultan in his struggle against an expansionist Siam.

15. Rupert Emerson, *Malaysia: A Study in Direct and Indirect Rule* (New York: Macmillan, 1937), p. 74. Prior to the arrival of the British, both islands were sparsely inhabited, Singapore in particular having lost all trace of her former importance as Tumasik. In 1800 a stretch of land opposite Penang, to be known as Province Wellesley, was acquired by the British.

16. A number of Chinese were resident in Malaya prior to British intervention. The sparse indices of history point to the existence of a "practical relationship" between the rulers of China and the indigenous chieftains of the Malay Peninsula from around 400 to 1450 (the approximate date of the arrival of the Europeans), with the avowed intent of maintaining trade ties between China and island Southeast Asia. (See O. W. Wolters, "China Irredenta: The South," in *The World Today,* 19 [December 1963], 540–552, and also Victor Purcell, *The Chinese in Southeast Asia,* 2d ed. [London: Oxford University Press, 1965], chaps. 2, 26, 27, and 28.) The influence of these early Chinese contacts on the course of Malayan history is difficult if not impossible to assess, but certainly the descendants of early Chinese settlers in Penang, Malacca, and Singapore—known collectively either as the Straits Chinese or, somewhat pejoratively, as the "Babas"—came to play an important part in Chinese leadership after World War II in Malaya and Singapore. Eminent figures like Sir Cheng-lock Tan and his son Tan Siew-sin had an impact on Chinese and Malayan politics far beyond that which the size of the Straits Chinese community might have warranted.

Until the mid-nineteenth century the British government adhered to a policy of Liberal laissez-faire in the peninsula, and although British and other European commercial interests had penetrated into the Malay states—the discovery of large tin deposits in the west coast region having become a vital factor—political intervention was eschewed. But by the 1870s new imperialistic forces marched to a different, more arrogant beat. Rivalry among the British, French, and Dutch was exacerbated by forward movements into Indochina and Indonesia by the French and Dutch, and public sentiment at home in Britain was aroused by feats of arms in India; thoughts turned to the taking up of the "White Man's Burden" in far-off, heathen lands portrayed by Rudyard Kipling and his fellow jingoists. These lofty ideals were, of course, underwritten by a hardheaded mercantilism that had scented the profits to be made from the exploitation of the peninsula's resources. The combination of great power antagonism, pressures from commercial interest, and Victorian imperialism at home forced a reappraisal of policies toward the Malay Peninsula, which had, in effect, become the hinterland of a flourishing Straits Settlements.

British Policy after 1874 and Its Consequences

In the meantime, in the Malay states themselves the times had become parlous indeed. Petty warfare between Malay chiefs, brigandage in the Straits of Malacca, and violent conflict between rival Chinese secret societies[17] had wrought an advanced state of political decay and social instability. European and Chinese merchants from the Straits Settlements applied persistent pressure on the British government for some form of intervention on the mainland that would provide protection for their substantial investments there. These worthies had dabbled in the internal affairs of several of the Malay states,[18] but by the early 1870s the situation had become acute. In late 1873 the policy of nonintervention was reversed, and in 1874 an agreement was signed by British officials

17. Large numbers of Chinese had been imported into the Malay states by Malay chiefs and foreign entepreneurs to work in the tin mines.

18. See Khoo Kay-kim, *The Western Malay States, 1850–1873* (Kuala Lumpur: Oxford University Press, 1972), chap. 8, "Straits Merchants and the Peninsular Wars." The states concerned were Perak, Selangor, and Negri Sembilan.

and the major chiefs of Perak. Known as the Pangkor Engagement, the agreement became a political instrument that served as a model for British intervention and control in other Malay states. A new sultan of Perak, acceptable to the British, was installed and provision made for the appointment of British officials (the chief of which was called the Resident) to the court of the sultan for the express purpose of advising the latter on all matters of state apart from those pertaining to Malay custom and the Islamic religion.

The niceties of this model agreement[19] masked the reality of effective British rule, for colonial officials rapidly instituted a centralized, authoritative government bureaucracy. Pax Britannica was introduced, based on British legal doctrine modified by the Indian experience, alongside the customary and religious courts of the sultan. Taxes were collected, fines levied, criminals punished as, after some initial resistance, stability returned to the land. In 1896 the four Malay states of Selangor, Perak, Pahang, and Negri Sembilan were joined in an association called the Federated Malay States (FMS), a move designed further to centralize the administrative process. In 1909 the Federal Council was created in Kuala Lumpur (the federal capital) at the behest of European rubber interests who had long been chafing at what they perceived as excessive authority vested in the civil service. (The Federal Council was also an early attempt to resolve the contradictions posed by the autonomy of individual states vis-à-vis the authority of the Resident-General of the FMS in Kuala Lumpur.) The official British rationale behind the Federal Council Agreement was that the council would restore to the sultans some of their lost power, but in fact it simply institutionalized what had long been a reality. The sultans sat in the council as ordinary members, but their influence was largely nullified by the countervailing presence of private-sector European and Chinese capitalists. In sum, the Federal Council Agreement paid lip service to the fiction that British authority in the FMS flowed from the sultans, but in all truth "the influence and powers of the State Councils and Residents de-

19. Other Malay states that succumbed to this form of British intervention were Selangor, Pahang, and Negri Sembilan. State councils were set up in each state to maintain the appurtenances of nominal Malay rule and also to legitimize the British presence.

creased in proportion to the increasing efficiency and uniformity
under the Federal Government until the Sultans lost all semblance
of independent rule."[20] The Federal Council Agreement did mark
the first attempt at constitutional government in Malaya, even
though it was a colonial creation spawned to further colonial ends.
The FMS, too, underwritten by the Federal Council Agreement,
brought together for the first time several Malay sultanates in
administrative and political unity, starting a tradition of cooperation and conflict that has persisted to the present.

At the same time a divergence in development arose in the
peninsula because of a different set of relationships between Britain and the other Malay states. Apart from the four states in the
FMS, five others (Johor, plus Perlis, Kedah, Kelantan, and
Trengganu, which had gained their freedom from Siamese suzerainty in 1909 because of British pressure on Siam) refused to
participate in a single centralized political entity and became
known, in a strangely negative sense, as the Unfederated Malay
States (UMS)—a term with connotations of collectivity not borne
out by circumstances. Each of these five states operated more or
less independently of the others; they worked together only when
they sensed an impending assault from Kuala Lumpur on their
semiautonomous status. Each unfederated state entered into treaty
agreements with Britain as the "protecting power"; each sultan had
a British adviser (not a Resident as in the FMS) accredited to his
court and a small number of British officials at lower levels of the
state machinery. The unfederated sultans retained a greater degree of autonomy than did those in the FMS, but their states were
not "developed" politically and economically to the same extent as
those in the FMS. The political situation, as outlined briefly here,
obtained with few structural changes until the outbreak of war with
Japan.

Apart from the creation of new political structures, the British
period in Malaya and Singapore from 1874 to 1942 saw the construction in the Malayan west coast states of a completely new
society, outside of which most Malays remained frozen in time,

20. See Chai Hon-chan, *The Development of British Malaya, 1896–1909* (Kuala
Lumpur: Oxford University Press, 1964), chap. 1, "Federation."

embedded in their own traditional value system and untouched, by and large, by the new economic and social forces. The presence of extensive tin deposits and the introduction of rubber as a commercial crop around the turn of the century meant that labor had to be found to exploit these natural resources. The Malay population was neither large enough nor willing enough to desert their rural havens to provide the necessary human energy to satisfy the demands of the European and Chinese capital investors and entrepreneurs, who had to turn, perforce, to sources outside Malaya. Of the immigrant groups brought in to remedy this deficiency in the labor market, the most numerous and most significant were the Chinese, who came from the southern provinces of China chiefly as indentured laborers but also as merchants, shopkeepers, and wealthier entrepreneurs. The next group in size comprised the Indians (using this term loosely to include all persons originating from the Indian subcontinent), who poured into the country in tens of thousands, again mainly as indentured laborers, to work on the rubber estates, on the railways, and for the government on the roads and other public works. The Malay population, too, increased substantially with the arrival of thousands of Malays from Sumatra, Java, and other islands in the archipelago. The imbalance in population figures created by this immigration is dramatic. Prior to the British intervention in 1874, the total population of Perak, Negri Sembilan, and Selangor has been estimated at seventy thousand, almost entirely Malays. By 1901 the composition and numbers of the population in the FMS (including Pahang as well as the aforementioned three states) had changed as indicated in Table 1.

Table 1. Population increase in the FMS between 1891 and 1901

	Number	Percentage increase
Malays(ians)	312,456*	34.9
Europeans	1,422	98.3
Eurasians	1,522	169.8
Chinese	299,739	83.4
Indians	58,211	188.8

* Including some 20,000 aborigines.
SOURCE: Chai Hon-chan, *Development of British Malaya*, p. 127.

The new economic system introduced by virtue of British intervention flourished. The new towns and cities of the west coast region—Taiping, Ipoh, Kuala Lumpur, Seremban, and many others—as well as the Straits Settlements (the exception was Malacca, which slumbered on and became known by Europeans as "Sleepy Hollow") were fast transformed into industrious, prosperous commercial centers, preponderantly Chinese in population, where a Chinese compradorial system worked alongside European business houses amid surroundings administered with quiet efficiency by British colonial officials. In the countryside European and Chinese tin mines and rubber estates operated alongside Malay smallholdings and rice fields increasingly thrust into an economic limbo (even as they were introduced to a new monetary system). Only in the Unfederated Malay States—Johor less than the others—did Malay life styles and Malay values remain dominant.

For decade after decade there were no disturbances, no riots, no revolutions to ruffle the warm, placid face of Malaya. Why should this be so? Why should the Malays, whose homeland it was and who had been carefully if paternalistically excluded from the new economic hustle and bustle and the profits that accompanied it, remain quiescent when confronted with this mammoth disruption? The answer lies in the nature of British policies, which were designed to mollify and in part to co-opt the ruling class, while keeping the Malay peasantry physically and psychologically down on the farm.

The Malay ruling class found the transition to British rule not too difficult a pill to swallow. After two small pockets of resistance had been vanquished immediately after British intervention (the British euphemistically called such resistance "rebellions"), the Malay territorial chiefs were quietly pensioned off, in amounts approximate to their previous income. Many were subsumed into the British administrative system and their sons given the opportunity of being educated at one of the English-language schools established in the FMS and the Straits Settlements in preparation for entrance into the elite strata of the civil service. The position of the sultans was strengthened to a level far greater than they had enjoyed before, when they were obliged to share power with the chiefs. Each sultan was now assured of an adequate fixed income from the civil list, enabling him to maintain an elaborate court and build imposing palaces; in short, the dignity and prestige of the sultans were enhanced by their entrance into the British imperial club, with all its pomp and splendor. So although the secular authority of the sultans had declined to the point of inconsequence, outwardly British officialdom paid due deference to their persons and preserved the fiction of their status as rulers. In addition, the sultans and their state governments accrued to themselves real power in terms of control over religious affairs and matters affecting Malay custom. As one study has remarked, "What the protectorate system protected most of all was the shape and structure of traditional society, from the top down."[21]

Except for an immeasurably improved sense of security and stability, the Malay peasantry derived little material benefit from all the changes taking place around them. No longer had peasants to fear the depredations of rapacious district chiefs, or the savagery of pirates when they went fishing; the erstwhile transitory character of their lives settled down into stable rice-growing and fishing-village patterns. The educational system in particular, as well as other elements of British policy, isolated them in rural enclaves outside of the fast-flowing, turbulent mainstream of colonial society. Yet they remained passive, if not altogether happy, under British rule. Their instinctive, almost instant sense of loyalty to the sultans (some of which ultimately rubbed off onto their British overlords) was reinforced by the punctilious deference extended by the British to their rulers, whom they now saw clearly as the protectors of their faith and their *adat*. A more equable system of land tenure was introduced and a number of Malay "reservations" opened up as further gestures to the safeguarding of Malay rights. Yet in the final analysis the Malay peasantry did not enjoy any substantial socioeconomic progress, but remained immured in a separate and unequal, if tranquil, social system.

Meanwhile, in the different world of the cities, the tin mines, and the rubber estates, the economy continued to boom and more

21. D. J. Steinberg et al., eds., *In Search of Southeast Asia* (New York: Praeger, 1971), p. 191.

immigrants poured into the country. Urbanization proceeded apace, with the composition of the towns and cities being mainly Chinese (approximately 70 percent) together with numbers of Indians. Those Malays who came to urban areas were employed chiefly in the lower levels of government service; where they did arrive in substantial numbers, as in Singapore and Kuala Lumpur, they lived isolated in their own urban *kampongs*, so that while they were in the city they were never of it. For these Malays, urbanization was not a force for social change in any real sense, and like their brethren in the countryside they remained largely unassimilated into the new, modern society.

The British in Borneo: To 1946

The history of the British Borneo territories of Sarawak and North Borneo (later to become Sabah) is described separately inasmuch as it does not fit into the political pattern that evolved on the Malay Peninsula and in Singapore. Indeed, until the end of World War II both territories remained anachronisms, mutations of history on the fringe of the imperial world, perpetuating a form of private colonialism totally unlike latter-day British colonial rule. The island of Borneo is regarded as either the second or the third largest island in the world, depending upon one's loyalties. The former British-controlled territories, including the sultanate of Brunei, occupy only a relatively small portion of the island, stretching from the Sarawak border fifty miles to the west of Kuching in the extreme northwest of Borneo, to the Sabah border with Indonesian Borneo at Tawau in the northeast—a coastline well over one thousand miles in length. Most of the population is concentrated in coastal and riverine areas, and until the 1960s few of the towns and cities were connected by road. Communications today are still limited, the easiest means of transportation being by aircraft, the most common by sea and river. Although Sabah and Sarawak are situated on the same landmass, prior to and during the British presence there was little political and economic intercourse between the two; they were administered separately under different sets of policies.

Both Sarawak and North Borneo were further removed from Indic influence than was the Malay Peninsula; both areas were hardly touched by the Indian customs brought to the Malayan scene by Indian traders and settlers, and they remained unaffected by the Buddhism and Hinduism of Srivijaya and Majapahit. Although there was much trade between Borneo and China from time to time, Chinese influence has remained minimal until recent years. The dates of the advent of Islam are, as ever, disputed, but the Islamicization of the coastal areas probably occurred in the early fifteenth century. The date of the founding of Brunei is also shrouded in the mists of historical argument, but certainly the sultanate was a flourishing political unit when Portuguese from Malacca visited there in the fifteenth century.

Strengthened by the spread of Islam in that century, Brunei thereafter expanded its realm (especially in the sixteenth century) along the west coast of North Borneo and up several of its rivers. On the other coast (in the north and west of present-day Sabah) the sultan of Sulu exercised a vaguely defined suzerainty. Sulu is a state based in the Southern Philippines, marking the northernmost limit of the expansion of Islam (the arrival of the Spanish in Manila in the sixteenth century prevented any further forward movement). Under the Sulus, too, piracy and slavery were rampant to a far greater degree of oppression than in Brunei.[22] Naturally there was much commercial and social intercourse between the coastal peoples of North Borneo and their counterparts in the southern Philippines and in Sulawesi (Celebes).

Sarawak. Sarawak encompasses 48,250 square miles of territory, including swamp, dense rain forest, and rivers. Its border with Indonesian Borneo, or Kalimantan, was, like those of many states in the Third World, sketched out by imperialistic voracity and competition and bears no relation to the reality of ethnic groups, representing merely the arbitrary divisons of conflicting Dutch and British interests. Sarawak fell under direct (if unofficial) British control in 1841, yet not until the end of World War II, in 1946, did it become an actual British colony. What happened in between was a singular admixture of adventurism and privately motivated paternalism known as the White Rajahdom of Sarawak, a period in

22. See K. G. Tregonning, *A History of Modern Sabah: 1881–1963* (Singapore: University of Malaya Press, 1965), chap. 10, "Slavery."

which rule over the country devolved upon one British family, the Brooke dynasty. The first rajah, James Brooke, arrived in his own private armed yacht off Borneo in 1839, a young English adventurer with a small armed force looking for private fields to conquer and profit from. He found and, in true colonial fashion, took advantage of a civil war in process between two factions of the Brunei sultanate. Brooke assisted the Brunei ruler in extinguishing the rebellion and in return was appointed in 1841 to the governorship of Sarawak proper, then a small province near present-day Brunei and controlled by the latter. Thereafter he concerned himself with the suppression of piracy and incipient rebellion and with restoring the realm of the person he perceived to be the rightful sultan of Brunei—with some encouragement and assistance from the British Royal Navy.

For these endeavors the sultan ceded to Brooke the full sovereignty of Sarawak and he became its first rajah. His attempts to bring the territory within the ambit of the British Empire were unsuccessful,[23] and, a disappointed man, he bequeathed an impoverished, independent state to his nephew Rajah Charles Brooke in 1868. Charles was successful in acquiring further territory by purchase from Brunei, and in 1888, Sarawak was afforded formal British protection, even though its internal affairs remained the private province of one man, Rajah Charles Brooke—who for almost fifty years governed Sarawak "somewhat in the spirit of an English gentleman managing his country estate."[24] Charles's son, Rajah Vyner Brooke, who succeeded him in 1917, ruled in a less forceful, more placid manner until the Japanese landed. In 1946, Vyner abdicated, despite much opposition from local Malays, and ceded Sarawak to the British government as a Crown Colony.

The century of Brooke rule in Sarawak inevitably left its imprint on future political and economic configurations. When James arrived in 1839, he found Muslim Malays clustered in numerous

23. The British government refused to move officially into Borneo at this time because of pressure from British radicals in Parliament who had become aware of "the inhumanity and inexpediency of the anti-piracy policy." See Nicholas Tarling, *A Concise History of Southeast Asia* (New York: Praeger, 1966), p. 129.

24. Robert Pringle, *Rajahs and Rebels* (Ithaca, N.Y.: Cornell University Press, 1970), p. 4.

settlements along the coast and a short way up several of the rivers. As Tom Harrisson has suggested, these Muslims were in all probability not migrants from Malaya and elsewhere who had settled in Sarawak (as several previous writers have implied); rather, they were local indigenes who had been converted by Arab and Persian traders, among others. (Harrisson estimates that Islam first came to northern Borneo in the early fifteenth century.) Because of the pre-Islamic indigenous origin, Harrisson further points out that the Sarawak Malays (certainly those of the southwest) "are, in genetic and other origins, often much closer to some still pagan Bisayas or lately Christian Iban, than to their political brothers and leaders in West Malaysia."[25]

Thus, in the centuries prior to Brooke's landfall, there was considerable interaction between Sarawak Malays and non-Muslim indigenes, particularly the Ibans (sometimes called Sea Dyaks, or Dayaks, a term the Ibans find opprobrious). The latter, residents of the interior, fiercely individualistic and often warlike, acknowledged, albeit tentatively, coastal Malay leaders as their overlords, sometimes acting in the name of Brunei, sometimes not. Contact between the Ibans and Malays was maintained in a series of gradations from the animistic[26] Iban hinterland to the Malay-controlled coast, with a middle ground in between where both groups intermingled for purposes of trade and other matters of mutual concern. (It should be remembered that during the whole of this period there were no Chinese and no Europeans to interpose themselves in the way of this symbiotic Malay-Iban relationship.) The term Malay was not in common usage; people designated themselves solely by their district of origin, although the Islamic religion did act as a distinct boundary defining each community. Other cultural differences were marked by the presence of a Muslim stratification system (an upper class of royal and religious aristocrats and chieftains and a lower class of peasants and fishermen) as opposed to the nonhierar-

25. Tom Harrisson, *The Malays of South-West Sarawak before Malaysia* (London: Macmillan, 1970), Appendix II, "The Advent of Islam," pp. 648–651.

26. They are often called "pagan" in the literature. I decry this usage, with its pejorative connotations. The Iban were not "unenlightened heathens" as the *Concise Oxford Dictionary* defines the term "pagan." They were (many still are) animists, possessing a strong sense of soul and life after death.

chical nature of Iban society. Malay upper classes also controlled the patterns of trade, there being no value conflict at this time between membership in the aristocracy and in commerce.

The Brooke rajahs did not allow this state of affairs to be preserved for long. In order to establish control over the new state and build at least a sense of legitimacy, the Brooke government needed to restrain, if not to subdue, the unruly ebullience of the Ibans, whose wanderlust, love of internecine warfare, and pursuance of head-hunting had led to much instability in the realm. After a series of inconclusive military campaigns against Iban groups, the rajah decided upon a policy of physically (and psychologically) separating Malays from Ibans in those intermediate areas already described, erroneously believing that Iban "piracy" was stimulated by Malays to whom they owed nominal overlordship. Christian missionaries contributed to the evolution of this policy, hoping that the removal of Ibans away from Malay-Muslim influence would pave the way for Christian proselytizing activities. A rigid policy of segregation was pursued, in which Malay villages were relocated away from the Ibans. The Malays did not object strenuously to their enforced resettlement because a parallel policy was adopted by the Brookes that assiduously protected Malay *adat* and the Muslim religion and served to revivify the Malay prestige system. Malay native chiefs, many of whom had some semblance of education, were necessary to man the lower echelons of the bureaucracy and so were subsumed into government service, often in positions of limited dominance over the upcountry animist Ibans.

Another far-reaching element of Brooke policy pertains to Malays and their involvement in trade. As already mentioned, prior to Brooke's advent on the Borneo stage the Malay ruling class actively participated in trade, an area of endeavor that, almost by default, they had come to dominate. Such participation ran foul of British intentions in two ways: first, the rajah required a pool of educated Malay native officers to ensure the smooth operation of government (the human resources from which these were to be drawn was limited) and second, the British upper-class ethos of the time viewed with disfavor the overlapping of the two functions of ruling and trading. A good governor could not soil his hands by engaging in the demeaning act of trade. Quite possibly the second reason was a philosophical rationale, ex post facto, emerging out of practical expediency; in any case, henceforward Malay involvement in affairs of trade diminished rapidly. Those Malays who were unable to find a place in the government service were exhorted to become farmers and small planters.

To fill the hiatus caused by Malay withdrawal from trading activities, the Sarawak government attracted to its shores substantial numbers of Chinese. Previous Chinese contacts with Borneo had been considerable, though restricted to trading relations. Several small Chinese agricultural settlements had been established just prior to James Brooke's arrival; their industriousness and progress had impressed the first rajah, and he saw them and future Chinese immigrants as a potential source of revenue.[27] After the first Brooke was established, several thousand Chinese came over the border from Dutch Borneo, where they had been subject to severe local oppression; some years afterward they mounted a bloody rebellion against the rajah, captured the capital, Kuching, and forced James to escape by jumping into the river. But the rajah's Malay and Iban subjects remained loyal, and with their aid the rebellion was suppressed. The pace of immigration for some time thereafter was turgid, and those Chinese who remained kept quietly unto themselves. The second rajah, Charles, realizing the need for agricultural development, eventually brought more immigrants from southern China as farmers, a large group of Christian Foo-chow settling in paricular at Sibu, where they have lived as an important, individualistic community ever since. A further impetus to immigration was provided by the introduction of rubber and the high price of pepper, and thousands of Chinese entered the country in the years immediately before and after World War I. Because of an inefficient, understaffed administration, problems over the granting of land to the newcomers soon became acute. Inadequate survey procedures and the confused nature of traditional native landholdings led to violent clashes between Chinese and Ibans, as eager Chinese settlers hacked down large tracts of Iban jungle. These particular land problems were eventually resolved, but many Chinese were obliged

27. Victor Purcell, *The Chinese in Southeast Asia*, 2d ed. (London: Oxford University Press, 1965), pp. 366–367.

to remain on temporary occupational land permits only, a vexed question even to this day. The question, then as now, as Robert Pringle defines it was one "of accommodating large numbers of Chinese farmers in a country of shifting cultivators."[28]

In summary, the policy of the three Brooke rajahs was one of functional separation of the three major ethnic groups, Malays, indigenous non-Muslims, and Chinese. Most of the Malays today live as farmers (rice, sago, and now rubber) and fishermen in the coastal lowlands and swamps, finding their avenues of social mobility through the ranks of the government service. The non-Muslim indigenous peoples are chiefly residents of inland, upriver longhouses (although many Ibans, quintessentially a mobile people, have broken out of this pattern and reside in the river deltas), shifting cultivators and hunters turning in recent years to the planting of rubber smallholdings. Many of these non-Muslims have also gone into the government service, especially the police and the Sarawak Rangers (a military force). The Chinese control trade and the distribution of produce, plant rubber and pepper, dominate the towns and cities, and operate the profitable timber industry. To understand the present it is important to remember that the Brooke regimes pursued a rigid policy of reinforcing ethnic particularities, where possible restricting the several groups to separate geographical locations. As Pringle has shown

the end result of this blend of conscious policy and unconscious attitude was to stimulate, with all the enormous weight of official prestige, awareness of ethnic affiliations; to encourage people to think more in communal terms and less in terms of geographic location, which had been the traditional focus of loyalties in the atomized and chaotic world of pre Brooke Sarawak. . . . It is fair to say that a Government which viewed people in terms of ethnic groups and encouraged them to do the same naturally if unwittingly stimulated the communalization of tensions and disputes of all kinds.[29]

Sabah. British North Borneo, the present-day Sabah, came into being, as far as its territorial boundaries are concerned, as an artificial Western creation, representing lines drawn on the map

28. Pringle, *Rajahs and Rebels*, p. 313.
29. Ibid., pp. 301–302.

without any recognition of the extent of ethnic particularities. Like those of Sarawak, the inhabitants of Sabah came from the mainland of Asia in a series of prehistoric migratory waves, belonging to "a branch of the dolichocephalic Indonesian race prevalent in this part of the world. . . . They are thus racially closely allied to most of the inhabitants of the surrounding islands."[30] Thus the Dusuns (to be called Kadazans after "independence"), Muruts, and coastal Muslims of today are racially the same stock, even though their cultures and languages have diverged over the years. It may be hypothesized that the original migrants settled on the coastline and in the river estuaries and then were driven inland by succeeding waves of peoples, perhaps more aggressive and urgent than their predecessors. The peoples of the interior lived secure and isolated in their mountainous, jungle-clad redoubts until the arrival of the first Westerners, although those on the periphery of their forest retreats were often subject to slave raids and piratical forays carried out by coastal Muslims from the sultanates of Brunei and Sulu. These inland hill folk of North Borneo have never been as aggressive and as warlike as their Iban brethren in Sarawak, and their contacts with the coastal Muslims historically have been based on oppression and fear. There has never been a middle ground where the hill peoples mixed with the coastal Muslims as equals, such as obtained in Sarawak.

Prior to the arrival of the Europeans there was no single political organization in North Borneo. The coastal areas over which Brunei and Sulu exercised separately at least nominal overlordship consisted of a number of villages and settlements, each controlled by a feudal chief and a headman—the latter called a *pengiran* (Brunei) or a *panglima* (Sulu)—each extending varying degrees of loyalty to his sultan, not linked to each other by any form of sultanatewide system of administrative cohesion, and each exerting a high level of local autonomy. The animistic peoples of the rivers, hills, and mountains of the interior remained untouched by the coming of Islam; these North Bornean montagnards lived clustered together in hilltop

30. Lee Yong-leng, *North Borneo: A Study in Settlement Geography* (Singapore: Eastern Universities Press, 1965), p. 16.

villages and longhouses, troubled by their own internecine warfare and head-hunting, and never subjected to any overall system of political leadership.

North Borneo's primary contact with the British was in 1761, when an agent of the East India Company concluded a treaty with the sultan of Sulu in which the latter granted permission for the establishment of a trading station in return for protection from Spanish encroachment. In 1773 the station was opened on the island of Balambangan, off the Kudat Peninsula, but a combination of piracy, long endemic to the region, and mismanagement brought about its demise and abandonment in 1775; an attempt to revive the station in 1803 was unsuccessful. Next the island of Labuan, in the Brunei Bay and now part of Sabah, was acquired by the British from Brunei in 1846, in return for the Royal Navy's help in the suppression of piracy. Administered first by the Brookes, Labuan became a British colony proper in 1907 and thereafter was administered by the Straits Settlements.

Strangely enough the first major effort at colonial settlement was attempted by an American trading company working out of Hong Kong. The company obtained a concession in 1865–1866 from Brunei to set up a settlement on the river Kimanis on the West coast. A small acreage of crops was planted, but disease and lack of capital brought an abrupt end to the endeavor very shortly afterward. A decade or so later, a more ambitious attempt was embarked upon to open up the country for commercial exploitation. In 1877 and 1878, a mixed group of British entrepreneurs and traders, plus one Austrian aristocrat, obtained substantial grants of territory from the sultans of Brunei and Sulu, acquiring a total of twenty-eight thousand square miles of coastal lands stretching some three hundred miles from Kimanis on the west to Tawau on the east. A company was formed to operate this extensive concession; the British government, mindful of the strategic position of the area and of competition from other imperialist powers, granted a Royal Charter to the company in 1881, and the British North Borneo Chartered Company (BNBCC) was born. During the two succeeding decades, the BNBCC annexed, sometimes by force, further stretches of territory by incorporating the semi-independent Bru-

nei fiefdoms that existed amid the company's new-found possessions.

The whole country was sparsely populated at the onset of the
Chartered Company's rule; an estimated fewer than one hundred
thousand persons lived in a density of five per square mile.[31]
Large-scale agriculture and mineral exploitation, on which the
BNBCC was to base its economic hopes, could not be conducted with
such scanty human resources; the pool of labor had to be increased.
Following extensive exploration of the coasts and the interior,
government stations—for the company soon became, in effect, a
government—were constructed in Kudat, Sandakan, Lahad Datu,
Tawau, and other places. Kudat was made the first capital in 1881,
but it was deemed not to have commercial potential and the capital
was moved to the new and bustling settlement of Sandakan in 1883.
Tobacco was planted, the export of birds' nests (for the famous
Chinese soup) and other jungle produce was stimulated, and inducements were extended to bring new immigrants into the country. Advances to these newcomers (mainly farmers from southern
China) were offered, supplemented in many cases by land grants
that were to be worked to repay the advances. Thousands of
immigrants flocked to this new frontier, and the labor market soon
became saturated; many Chinese could not be absorbed and had to
return to their homeland. For example, when Sandakan was
founded in 1878–1879, only two Chinese were in residence there,
but by 1883 over three thousand had moved in.[32] Large numbers of
Indonesian Malays, especially Javanese, also arrived in the first two
decades of the twentieth century to work as laborers on the rubber
and tobacco plantations and with the timber companies. Most of
these Chinese and Indonesian immigrants moved into the west coast
area, where a railway had been constructed,[33] although some did

---

31. Ibid., pp. 21–25.
32. Purcell, *Chinese in Southeast Asia*, p. 375.
33. The railway, built by the BNBCC between 1896 and 1900 in a fit of optimistic
grandeur, proved to be a noble failure. I lived at the end of it for almost two years,
and had underneath the glass top of my desk the following poem, written by a
despairing, cynical planter several decades previously (little having changed in the
intervening years):
"Along the metals all rusted and brown

venture to the Darvel and Dowie bays on the east coast as well as to the thriving port capital of Sandakan. Most of the Chinese and the Indonesian immigrants remained in the coastal plains, intermingling in the same geographical locations (unlike Sarawak and Malaya). The Chinese worked at first as laborers, as well as providing the infrastructure of trade in the villages and towns, but many soon moved to open up their own land for planting. Many Chinese intermarried with the non-Muslim indigenes of the coastal plains, as today's large and vigorous Sino-Kadazan population demonstrates. The Javanese and other Indonesians worked mainly as laborers, although, like the Chinese, many eventually moved away from the estates and plantations to open up land and establish their own villages. Most married into the families of local coastal Muslims, and they have by now all been assimilated into the local Muslim population. The latter continued to grow some wet rice and coconuts, fish, engage in coastal trade and, with the educated non-Muslims of the coastal plains, enter the junior grades of the government service. The hill peoples continued for the most part in isolation; freed from the practice of head-hunting they became more settled and engaged in wet-rice and swidden agriculture. Many were recruited into the Armed Constabulary, whose ranks they later dominated.[34]

In short, although disadvantages later would accrue to the future state of Sabah from an open-door immigration policy and a system that concentrated economic power almost entirely in the hands of nonindigenous European and Chinese entrepreneurs, at the time

---

Thunders the mail to Jesselton town.
See how the sparks from her smoke stack shower,
As she rushes on madly at four miles an hour.
Sometimes she stops at the top of a ridge,
Sometimes she halts for a broken down bridge.
Sometimes she finds the track washed away,
And postpones her advance 'til the following day.
Beaufort to Jesselton, tour of delight
Taking all day, and most of the night,
Screeching on wildly, recking not fate,
Making up time, she's two days late.
Along the metals all rusted and brown,
Thunders the mail to Jesselton town."
34. Corporals, sergeants, and inspectors who retired from the police were often appointed as native chiefs and became important units of government control.

tranquillity and stability settled over the land under the ministrations of a benevolent if hardly beneficial (to the indigenes) Chartered Company government. Piracy was diminished—although it continues to erupt periodically even to this day—slavery abolished and head-hunting suppressed, and an atmosphere of pleasantly lethargic serenity soon prevailed. The Chartered Company as a financial endeavor was rarely profitable to its Court of Directors and shareholders in London. Except in the small number of towns that grew up, attempts at social improvement were minimal. The Chartered Company governed its best by governing least, and malaria, beriberi, tuberculosis, and other diseases remained endemic in the countryside,[35] education was vestigial, and communications (apart from the railway) were poor. Many of the company's officers were efficient and dedicated servants of the country, but they were stretched too thinly on the ground, profits were too marginal, and financial resources were too limited to afford them any chance of promoting the cause of social progress. North Borneo remained, however, by any standard one of the most peaceful, friendly, and beautiful countries anywhere in the world.[36]

As in Sarawak, administrative patterns followed the Malayan model, with a strong central authority in the person of the governor in the capital, from whom power was emitted in concentric rings to Residencies (two in number, each with a staunchly authoritarian Resident) and thence to districts (several to each Residency, each under a district officer possessing formidable authority and responsibility within his own district). A Legislative Council, appointed by the governor from the ranks of official and unofficial (that is, nongovernment) luminaries, "advised" the governor and provided some outlet for complaints and suggestions from planting and commercial interests; in reality, however, the council did little more than grant the good government seal of approval to the governor's policies.

In the countryside the Residents or the district officers appointed

35. One strain of malaria, for instance, was imported by Javanese immigrants and proved devastating to the indigenous Muruts.
36. My prejudices are showing here, but read Agnes Newton Keith's novel *The Land below the Wind* (London: Michael Joseph, 1939) for a perceptive account, from a Westerner's standpoint, of prewar Chartered Company days.

senior native chiefs and native chiefs to act as headmen in a system of village administration. The powers of these chiefs, who ultimately became salaried officials, were prescribed in law, but were vaguely and often broadly defined in practice. One of their main functions was to safeguard native rights and traditions (to this end they conducted their own native courts with real if minor magisterial authority), but generally they came to identify more and more with the policies of the government as exemplified in the person of the district officer; thus they generally failed to articulate to the government the true sentiments and aspirations of the rural populace. In several districts, too, Muslim native chiefs were appointed in authority over non-Muslim natives because of their greater level of sophistication and education, which frequently led to misunderstanding if not downright exploitation.

Chartered Company rule, then, with that of the Brooke rajahdom, can be characterized as one in which peace and stability were introduced to a newly created territorial state; the population was considerably increased by the flow of immigrants from outside; modern, colonial methods of government were imposed slowly in an atmosphere of paternal tranquillity: socioeconomic development was fitful and ineffective; indigenous political activity, such as nationalism, was unknown; and native participation in the higher levels of government, both on a state and local basis, was nonexistent.

The Twentieth Century and the Stirrings of Nationalism: Malaya and Singapore before 1945
British Educational Policies

The rise of an elite class of Malays educated in English-language schools played a major role in the birth of an incipient Malay nationalism, which was ultimately to adopt a conservative course. By the early twentieth century it had become increasingly obvious to the British rulers that not enough Malays in the FMS[37] were being trained or educated for the middle and upper echelons of the

37. The situation was different in the UMS, where many Malay administrators did hold positions of authority.

government service. The Malayan Civil Service was, with few exceptions, the exclusive preserve of a British administrative elite (known to cynics as the "Heaven Born"). No Malays had acquired qualifications that would have enabled them to enter the professional or technical fields. In 1903, therefore, a new policy came into being. The Malay Residential College was established in the royal capital of Perak, Kuala Kangsar, along the lines of a British "public" school (it became known as the Malay Eton), where Malay boys[38] could be trained on British lines and be exposed to upper-class British values so that they could be painlessly absorbed into the administrative service. Other Malay students from less exalted stations in life (the college tended to cater to the sons of the aristocracy) entered other English-language schools, all of which were situated in the major cities. Poorer Malays living in rural areas—the bulk of the Malay population—had no access to secondary education, although in any case their traditional conservatism, which made them highly suspicious of the values disseminated by non-Islamic educational institutions, and their distrust of cities[39] would have prevented them from enrolling in English secondary schools. Malay-language secondary schools at this point in time did not exist.

British policy generally in the years before World War II was motivated by two imperatives: first, to maintain the traditional structures of indirect rule, and, second to impart a degree of education to the majority of Malays (excluding the privileged elite) that would keep them happy—almost a symbolic gesture—in their rural retreats, while producing a flow of native subordinate officers to man the lower levels of government service. Sir George Maxwell, chief secretary in 1920, explained the rationale behind the government's policy: "The aim of the government is not to turn out a few well-educated boys; rather it is to improve the bulk of the people, and to make the son of the fisherman or peasant a more intelligent fisherman or peasant, and a man whose education will enable him to

38. Education for Malay girls was completely disregarded in deference to the wishes of Malays themselves.
39. Many of the English-language elite schools were operated by various Christian organizations, and the majority of Malays feared that their sons might be converted to Christianity.

understand how his lot in life fits in the scheme of things around him."[40] Clearly, such a myopic policy would keep most Malays firmly outside the new and aggressive world that was evolving around them and in no sense could contribute to any concrete socioeconomic change. The sons of Malay royalty and other privileged Malays were able to acquire an English education, a process that set them further apart from their fellow, less fortunate Malays, who, residing in the rural areas, were not able to avail themselves of the opportunities offered by the English schools in the towns, even if they had wanted to do so. One writer, D. J. Radcliffe, has described how two different worlds emerged in Malaya before 1940: one consisting of modern urban centers connected by an effective communications system, and the other of isolated, rural Malay enclaves. Contact between the two worlds was marginal, and the British educational policy reflected their separateness: "The educational system as it developed was directly governed by this situation, for the English schools and secondary schools were designed to provide the educated manpower required . . . while the vernacular schools were designed to strengthen rural resistance to changes from without."[41] The vernacular schools were run by the government (they also existed, though fewer in number, in the UMS) and offered secular education in the Malay language, normally for a period of four years. Designed to give Malays some literacy in their own language, they suffered from undertrained teachers and poverty of facilities. But they did reach a substantial number of Malays: in 1920 in both the FMS and the UMS a total of 46,000 Malay pupils attended 757 Malay vernacular schools.[42] Unfortunately, all too many of them dropped out before the four-year period of instruction was complete to drift away to the often obscurantist religious schools, and all too few of them ever went on to an English secondary education. The British steadfastly refused to allow English to be taught in the vernacular schools, and one Malay leader commented bitterly on the

40. From the FMS *Annual Report, 1920,* quoted in D. J. Radcliffe, *Education and Primary Development in Malaya, 1900–1940* (Washington, D.C.: U.S. Department of Health, Education and Welfare, 1968), p. 20.

41. Radcliffe, *Education,* p. 28.

42. W. R. Roff, *The Origins of Malay Nationalism* (New Haven: Yale University Press, 1967), p. 128.

quality and meaning of Malay education: "In the fewest possible words, the Malay boy is told 'You have been trained to remain at the bottom and there you will always remain.' Why, I ask, waste so much public money to attain this end when without any vernacular school and without any special effort the Malay boy could himself accomplish this feat?"[43]

A similar picture emerged in Singapore, even though as a large urban center it offered a plenitude of secondary education for those who wished to avail themselves of the facilities. A number of Malays did, of course, enter the English secondary schools—far more, proportionally, than in Malaya—but the vast majority did not. Why should this be so? The answer must lie both in the nature of British policy toward education of Malays and in the latters' attitudes toward secular education. As in Malaya itself, colonial policy provided free vernacular education in the Malay language for all Malay pupils, but once again the purpose was to develop a singularly Malay school system and not to produce an elite stratum of English-educated Malays who might become estranged from their own society.[44] (In fact, as already remarked, this is what happened generally to those Malays who attended the English schools.) Most Malays were reluctant to send their children to English schools for fear of religious conversion; many (but not all) held the traditional Islamic belief that the world of materialism should hold no attraction for the true believer, who should instead concentrate his or her worldly endeavors and studies in preparation for the life hereafter, the *akhirat*. This aversion to Western education served to strengthen colonial policies; many Malay schools were closed down and the Malay Teachers College abolished. The isolation of most Malays inside the confines of their own residential communities also fostered backwardness in education. Singapore, of course, had long since emerged as a bustling, modern city port, but from the days of Raffles, Malays congregated

43. Quoted in Sharom Ahmat, "Singapore Malays, Education and National Development," in Sharom Ahmat and James Wong, eds., *Malay Participation in the National Development of Singapore* (Singapore: Eurasian Press, 1971), p. 7.

44. Zahoor Ahmad, "Malay Education in Singapore," in T. R. Doraisamy, ed., *150 Years of Education in Singapore* (Singapore: Teachers Training College, 1969), p. 107.

in urban *kampongs* (the term is for a Malay village community; in Singapore the urban *kampong* rapidly became a ghetto, in the popularly accepted sense of that word), and although for social and occupational reasons Malays frequently ventured into the outside world, they returned at night to a *rus in urbe* environment, where traditional, rural values still flourished to insulate them against the pull of secular blandishments.

In Malaya and in Singapore vernacular education reinforced the bonds of cohesion within the Malay community by instilling a sense of Malay identity through the use of Malayan Malay standard language, so that the children of the many Malaysian immigrants were able to look upon themselves as Malays rather than as Bugis, Javanese, Menangkabau, and the like. But this integration, as Radcliffe has remarked, was "at the same time exclusive as regards Malayan society, the multiracial society developing in the peninsula."[45] The same circumstance occurred in Singapore, and in this island and in Malaya the result was that the overwhelming majority of Malays were unprepared to compete in a society in which a knowledge of English or of Chinese was a prerequisite for success. The consequences, as we look today in our rear-vision mirrors, were disastrous.

Reform and Tradition: Contradictions in Malay Society

The early days of the twentieth century saw the emergence of religious reform movements in Malaya and Singapore that eventually entered the political stage. Prior to this time Islam as a vital social force had become almost moribund, exercising only the minimum of social sanctions.[46] If one accepts the premise that to most Malays Islam represents virtually the totality of Malay culture—certainly it is the hub around which Malay life revolves—then clearly religious reform was a sine qua non on which to base other much-needed social and economic improvements. But until the end of the nineteenth century, religion had been left largely in the hands of conservative, even obscurantist, religious figures who

45. Radcliffe, *Education*, p. 56.
46. See Radin Soenarno, "The Political Attitudes of Malays before 1945," *Journal of Southeast Asian History* (Singapore) March 1960, 1–28.

often buried its true philosophy beneath centuries of pre-Islamic beliefs and superstitions.

In the face of an aggressive external environment that was producing rapid change all around them, Malays had no other recourse but Islam to offer them emotional and spiritual solace and hope for the future. From 1906 onward a number of Malay religious periodicals ventured militantly into the field of social criticism. A loosely structured group of Malay reformers emerged, to become known as the "Kaum Muda" or the "Young Group." Their attempts to introduce a new system and new styles, including the dissemination of modern secular training and of religious instruction, led them into a collision with a group of older Malays—the "Kaum Tua" or "Old Group"—entrenched in strong positions in the established religious hierarchy and in the Malay traditional aristocracy and nobility. British officials, mindful of the provision of the Pangkor Engagement that insisted upon noninterference in Malay religion and custom, made no attempt to intervene in the controversy, and the Kaum Tua, from its position of traditional power and authority, was able to slow down the pace of reform. This Old Group saw religious innovation not for what it was—long overdue social reform—but as a threat to traditional authority and its values.

By the mid-1920s, as William Roff has demonstrated effectively,[47] the adherents of the Young Group gradually became politicized as they realized the futility of their efforts at reform; they can be described as protonationalists, although their movement never accrued to itself any pan-Malayan organization capable of stimulating genuine popular participation. Many of its leaders emerged not from the ranks of the English-educated but from Malay-educated youths who had gone on to the Middle East for more advanced religious training; there in the great Islamic centers of learning they had been immersed in the rising tide of anticolonialism and pan-Islamicism that was beginning to mount in the Arab world. Transferred to a Malayan context, this pan-Islamicism came to be identified with pan-Indonesianism, the unity

---

47. Roff, *Origins of Malay Nationalism*, chap. 3, "Kaum Muda—Kaum Tua: Innovation and Reaction."

within one political entity of all the Malayo-Muslim peoples of Southeast Asia. The movement was protoleftist as well as protonationalist.

Nevertheless, the English-educated Malay elite formed the first Malay organization with a political potential, partly in response to the efforts of the reform movement. In Singapore in 1926, a group of English-educated Malay bureaucrats, journalists, and teachers banded together to form the Kesatuan Melayu Singapura (KMS, or Singapore Union of Malays), a move originally designed to counterbalance the influence of the wealthier, bourgeois non-Malay elements of the Muslim population such as Arabs and Indians. While the KMS was itself an elite group (its vice-president was a descendant of a former sultan of Johor), its purposes included the furtherance of the interest of poorer Malays in Singapore as well as the promotion of Malay socioeconomic progress generally. Its efforts in this direction met with failure, largely because (a) most of the Malay population of the time had not yet attained that stage of consciousness of their plight (or, conversely, had been conditioned by their culture to accept their lot) that might have led to a more militant and enthusiastic participation, and (b) the KMS leaders, who were an English-educated, bureaucratic, and professional elite, had neither a base of support in, nor lines of communication to, the bulk of the Malay populace.

In 1937 the Malay Union movement spread into peninsular Malaya, and branches were formed in Malacca, Penang, and in the FMS (there was no activity in the UMS). In August 1939 a pan-Malayan conference of Malay Unions, including representatives from Singapore, was held in Kuala Lumpur; a follow-up meeting took place in 1940, but all other scheduled events fell prey to the exigencies of the Japanese war. Perhaps the most tangible consequences of the Malay Union were the establishment of urban Malay land reservations in Kuala Lumpur and Singapore. The underlying concept of the reservations was the hope that Malays living in the cities would build their own houses, surrounded by their own compounds, fruit trees, and animal pens, and thus create Malay urban enclaves and nurture the gentleness and simplicity of traditional Malay culture. Other Malay areas sprang up around these reservations, and today they stand as complex cores of Malay sentiments and values, with significant and negative implications for the growth of multiethnic tolerance. Politically the Malay Union was the precursor of the first Malay political party, the United Malays' National Organization (UMNO), formed after the end of World War II. Kesatuan Melayu leadership, although reform-minded and oriented toward genuine social progress, was essentially of a conservative hue, an offshoot of the English-educated and privileged class. The movement remained embedded, though less so in Singapore, in feudal social structures exemplified by Malay royalty and nobility that staunchly supported the Malay Union. A further inhibiting factor was posed by the compulsion for English-educated Malays to seek employment in the government bureaucracy (they were almost totally excluded from the private sector, apart from a few journalists and lawyers) where, once they were so employed, the dynamics of their work situation imposed necessarily conservative constraints on their capacity to lead their fellow Malays in radically new directions. The process was reinforced by the nature of colonial policy, which assiduously cultivated and respected Malay traditional customs, atrophied the quest for fundamental change, and thereby instilled a high degree of resistance to any foreign ideology.

Despite the disadvantageous environment represented by a conservative and politically intolerant colonial regime, Malay left-wing politics entered the Malaya-Singapore scene. In 1937, Ibrahim Yaacob, a graduate of the Sultan Idris Training College,[48] and Ishak Haji Mohammed, formerly of the Malayan Administrative Service, founded the Kesatuan Melayu Muda (KMM, the Union of Malay Youth). During his stay at the Training College, Ibrahim had been exposed to Indonesian anti-Dutch nationalism, and his intention in establishing the KMM was twofold: first, to throw off the encumbrances of colonial rule, and second, to bring about a united "Melayu Raya"—a Greater Indonesia or a Greater Malaya—banding together in one political movement all Malay Muslims in Southeast Asia. Most KMM leaders originated in the peasantry and lower

48. This Training College was devised to train young men and women from the Malay peasantry as teachers in the Malay language; they were then to go back into Malay rural areas to teach in vernacular schools. The college soon became a seedbed for young Malay nationalists and radicals.

classes and graduated from the vernacular schools of Malay rural areas. They faced insuperable odds, for in addition to attracting the unfriendly scrutiny of British officials, they operated in a Malay society still deeply attached to Malay traditional authority, not yet ready for any radical departure from the old established order.

In the days immediately preceding the outbreak of World War II, the KMM published several articles and editorials containing strong criticism of British colonial rule, and in 1940 many of the group's leaders and members were placed under detention. At its height in the prewar years the KMM was never able to attract more than a few hundred members; the organization's radical ideology, as vaguely defined as it was, could not compete with the more comfortable status quo to which most Malays subscribed. Perhaps the lack of a strong Malay left wing in the 1930s, a period when Malay society was mired in socioeconomic stagnation, deprived Malays of exposure to an ideological and organizational driving force that might have led them in new, less apathetic directions, promoting value change more in consonance with the changing world around them. The KMM re-emerged after the end of the war, but its efforts then met with little success, as will be demonstrated.

Chinese and Indian Nationalism

Whatever form incipient Malay nationalism assumed, it was clearly directed inward, within the Malay world. Chinese and Indian nationalism in the 1920s and 1930s, conversely, looked outward, toward the mother countries. As early as 1906 a branch of a Chinese revolutionary group was set up in Singapore to further the cause of Sun Yat-sen in his attempts to overthrow the Ch'ing dynasty in China.[49] The subsequent revolution in 1912 saw the founding of the Kuomintang (KMT) in China, and branches of the KMT were formed in Malaya and Singapore shortly thereafter; much assistance, mainly financial, was given to the KMT by Chinese resident in the latter territories. In 1927, when Chiang

49. Dr. Sun himself lived for various short periods in the Straits Settlements in the first decade of this century.

Kai-shek imposed a firm KMT government in China, Sun Yat-sen's "Three Principles of Government" were adopted as the official state credo. The first of Sun's three tenets is important to an understanding of the early manifestations of Chinese nationalism in Malaya and Singapore, for it reaffirmed the principle that all Chinese, no matter where they might be, were of one race and one nation and that the propagation of an intense Chinese nationalism, directed toward China and the efforts of the KMT, was to be a major weapon in the fight to save China from foreign and imperialist exploitation.

Chinese living in Malaya and Singapore under colonial rule had no reason to owe any emotional allegiance to the British,[50] and few attempts were made to suggest that they invest such loyalty; the KMT cause was therefore a natural focus for an ever-present ethnocentricity. For the first time in a century or more, Chinese everywhere had reason to feel a renewed sense of pride in their homeland. This new self-respect was mirrored in the Chinese school system in Malaya and Singapore, which evolved and was allowed to conduct itself with only minimal interference from British education authorities. Virtually all Chinese-language schools were operated by the Chinese community on its own, teachers and textbooks were imported from China, Chinese culture was stressed and indigenous culture ignored, and a Chinese nationalism was fostered to the exclusion of all local considerations. Indeed KMT activities in the region gave pause to the colonial regime, and as KMT-inspired anti-imperialist propaganda spread, resulting in several anti-British demonstrations, the government moved quietly to suppress the organization.

50. The exception was the Straits Chinese community. These "Babas" possessed British citizenship and traveled on British passports; in the main they retained pro-British attitudes. Many Straits Chinese grew up speaking only English and/or Malay, although they tended to cling tenaciously to Chinese customs. As Purcell has stated (*Chinese in Southeast Asia*, p. 248), they constituted a form of "local aristocracy," a breeding ground for future political leadership. Essentially conservative in character, in the period after World War II the Straits Chinese imparted a stabilizing influence on an otherwise volatile Chinese community. Their intimate knowledge of the Malay language and culture enabled the Babas to bridge in part the gap between Malays and Chinese, and to this extent Straits Chinese leaders like Sir Cheng-lock Tan and Tan Siew-sin were more acceptable to the Malay leadership, and indeed were themselves more sympathetic to the Malay socioeconomic plight.

Events in China had inevitable repercussions in Malaya and Singapore. Chiang's purge of the Chinese Communist Party (CCP) from the ranks of the KMT in 1927 resulted in a similar split among Chinese in Southeast Asia, and the Malayan Communist Party was born. Attempts had been made by Indonesian Communists led by Tan Malaka in 1924 to introduce Communism into Malay, but these efforts failed because of a demonstrable Malay apathy. During the period of KMT and CCP cooperation between 1923 and 1927, Communist agents from the Far Eastern Bureau of the Comintern based in Shanghai were infiltrated into the Malayan Revolutionary Committee of the KMT, where they operated without hindrance until the KMT-CCP split. The Communist Party that rose out of the ashes of the latter period was first called the Nanyang Communist Party (the South Seas Chinese Community Party) and embraced Thailand as well as having connections with Indochina and Indonesia. In 1929 the Comintern reorganized the Nanyang Communist Party, establishing the MCP proper concurrently with party groups in other Southeast Asian countries. Thus was the KMT-CCP split reflected in Chinese society in Malaya and Singapore. The MCP found its supporters mainly in the ranks of the trade unions, together with many teachers in Chinese-language schools and other radical intelligentsia. The KMT, on the other hand, found its sustenance in the wealthier bourgeois, in shopkeepers, compradores, tin-mine owners, and the like, although Chinese-language schoolteachers were also well represented. The causes of both the KMT and the MCP were given a tremendous boost after the outbreak of Japanese hostilities directed against the Chinese mainland.

As did many Chinese, Indians in Malaya before the war generally still considered their true home to be their motherland. Their interest in politics was defined not in Malayan terms but by events in India, where the anti-imperialist nationalist struggle was welling to a full intensity. While no Indian political organizations as such were formed in Malaya or Singapore, several interest groups emerged that had political potential. Laborers on the rubber estates and elsewhere organized themselves for the purpose of negotiating with employers in order to further their often appalling working conditions, and in their pioneering militancy can be discerned the seeds of the powerful postwar trade-union movement. In general, however, Indian nationalism in the 1930s was not concerned with internal politics in Malaya and Singapore, but confined its interest to the more dramatic scenarios being enacted in the mother country.

It is obvious that nationalism in prewar Malaya and Singapore varied greatly in significance from community to ethnic community, each of whose activities were conducted on separate, isolated levels. The merest handful of Malays and Indians had connections with the MCP, but otherwise a sense of a Malayan or a Singaporean nationalism, crossing ethnic boundaries in search of mutual ideals, simply did not exist. Most Malays viewed Chinese and Indians as interlopers, transitory figures with no role to enact in local politics, no fealty to invest in Malayan soil. The shape of postwar politics was beginning to emerge.

The Japanese Occupation: The Races Draw Further Apart

Japanese forces landed on Malayan soil in December 1941. Despite numerical inferiority in military strength, the Japanese imperial army fought its way swiftly down the peninsula to Singapore, and on February 15, 1942, the British forces surrendered in one of the great military debacles in modern history. This disaster was not merely a shameful defeat for British arms; it signaled the first lowering of the Colors of British imperial might, the beginning of the end of colonial rule. The Japanese concept of a "Greater East Asia Coprosperity Sphere," with which they had hoped to draw peoples of Asia together under an anti-Western banner, eventually failed dismally because of brutal excesses perpetrated against Asian populations, but nevertheless for many Asians World War II effectively destroyed the myth of European invincibility and superiority.

Japanese policy in Malaya and Singapore was colored by experiences in the war against China, which had raged on for many years. Toward the large Chinese populace in the peninsula they exhibited ruthlessness and ferocity—an attitude exacerbated by the growing strength of Chinese resistance. Despite a plethora of Chinese-organized anti-Japanese activity before 1941, only the MCP was prepared organizationally to resist the Japanese when they arrived.

The party's commitment to the united front against Fascism enabled it to obtain some little military assistance and training from the British army and thus to form a small nucleus of armed guerrillas, called the Malayan People's Anti-Japanese Army (MPAJA). Upon the fall of Singapore in February 1942, the MCP and its guerrilla wing immediately went underground, living in jungle encampments, constantly harassed by the Japanese army, but always drawing emotional succor and logistic support from the Chinese community. Toward the end of the war British aircraft dropped arms, supplies, and a few British liaison officers by parachute, and the MPAJA was able to build itself into a substantial, well-armed, and well-trained guerrilla force.[51] The United States atom-bomb attacks on Hiroshima and Nagasaki forced a premature surrender by Japan (upstaging a scheduled British and Australian invasion of Malaya that might have restored some of the myth of colonial superiority), and MPAJA units were deprived of the opportunity to mount a sustained, coordinated attack against the occupation forces. Undoubtedly in the latter days of the war the focus of the MPAJA's efforts had changed from a short-term anti-Japanese policy to long-range preparations for the overthrow of British colonialism, but in any case the end of the war saw MPAJA forces intact, maintaining strong ties to the Chinese population, and, as the only organized and armed force abroad in the land, poised to take whatever action MCP leaders decreed. Above all, most Chinese, fully conscious of their role in the vanguard of the anti-Fascist struggle (certainly when compared to the efforts of non-Chinese), were fortified in their view of themselves as a prideful, distinct ethnic community.

Malay reaction to the Japanese presence was different. Japanese attitudes toward Malays were based on cooperation rather than repression, realizing that the civil administration of Malaya and Singapore could not easily be conducted without active Malay

51. The MPAJA never embarked upon any large-scale military activities against the Japanese army of occupation. Nevertheless, the very presence of the guerrilla body gave concern to the Japanese, causing them to station troops in Malaya who might have been deployed on other battlefields. For a fascinating account of the MPAJA during the wartime period, see F. Spencer Chapman, *The Jungle Is Neutral* (London: Chatto & Windus, 1951).

participation. Malays in government service were given increased authority and promotion opportunities. In 1943 district advisory councils were formed in Malaya, composed mainly of Malays—some appointed, some elected—and an increased sense of participation in government was engendered. In 1943, too, the Japanese adopted a policy toward the Malay sultans roughly comparable to that of the British, and Malay acquiescence, if not active enthusiasm, toward the occupation forces was ensured. (Many Malays wholeheartedly opposed the Japanese in several areas, performing gallantly in guerrilla groups organized by Malay and British officers who had been parachuted into Malaya.)

The small Malay left wing actively cooperated with the Japanese, no doubt under the influence of events in Indonesia. Even prior to the landings in 1941 the Japanese had established contact with the KMM, and after the British surrender KMM detainees were released from prison, enabling them to resume political activities. At first KMM members cooperated with the Japanese, reportedly as a cover for more clandestine endeavors, but in mid-1942 the Japanese moved to proscribe the organization. Proscription did not lead to further sanctions against the Malay left, however, as the Japanese needed as much support as they could garner. Malay left-wing cooperation continued with the formation of a Japanese-sponsored group called PETA (Pembela Tanah Ayer, Our Country's Avengers), an armed militia under the command of Ibrahim, now a Japanese-appointed lieutenant colonel. Documented history for the wartime period is sketchy, and the scope of Malay activities is difficult to trace. Radin Soenarno states that KMM members had secret contacts with the MPAJA and with the MCP and that the group's secret purpose was to help administer the coup de grace to the Japanese when the time came.[52]

Another development that had some effect on Malay nationalism was the Japanese decision to combine Sumatra with Malaya and Singapore under one administration. Some increase in cultural communication between these territories ensued, but in 1944 the Japanese reversed their policy and Sumatra was severed off under a separate administration. Ibrahim Yaacob and his PETA

52. Soenarno, "Political Attitudes."

followers seized upon the opportunity in 1944, following Japan's promise of independence to an indigenous Indonesian government, to press their own claim for independence within this future Indonesian state. In 1943, just before the Japanese collapse, Ibrahim formed a new group, a successor to the KMM, called Kesatuan Ra'ayat Indonesia Semenanjong (KRIS, or the Union of the Peninsular Indonesian Peoples), to further this goal; shortly afterward discussions were held in Taiping with the Sukarno-Hatta Indonesian independence delegation. When the British returned in September 1945 the movement disintegrated; most of the KMM-PETA-KRIS leaders were imprisoned, and Ibrahim and his close associates were compelled to flee to Indonesia. Nevertheless, the activities of the Malay left wing during the Japanese occupation were significant to the extent that, after the war, a new Malay political movement arose from its ashes, the Malayan Nationalist Party (MNP), which was later to have a close association with the MCP. In the final analysis, however, the impact of the Malay left wing on the masses of the Malay peasantry during the war caused no residual reverberations.

Many Indians, too, collaborated with the Japanese, seeing in them the means whereby the British raj could be driven out of India. (Again, as with the Malay community, substantial numbers of Indians resisted the Japanese in various ways, at dire cost to themselves.) The Japanese saw the Indians in Malaya and Singapore as a potential fifth column for use against the British in India and Burma; a number of branches of the Indian Independence League were opened throughout the peninsula and in Singapore, under Japanese auspices. The Indian National Army was formed, and, with the arrival of S. Chandra Bose in Singapore in 1943, a provisional Indian government-in-exile, called Azad Hind, was established. As the war progressed Japanese-Indian relations became strained, and thousands of Indian laborers and others were sent to work on the Siamese so-called Death Railway. After the war pro-Japanese Indian organizations were disbanded and their political influence demolished: only a heightened level of political awareness remained.

The effects of the Japanese occupation on the relationship between the various ethnic communities, especially between Malays and Chinese, were ominous. The atom bombs that disintegrated the Japanese military regime and foreshortened the ending of hostilities in the Pacific were dropped by an American aircraft, and although the British were able to recover control over Malaya and Singapore, they did so without a fight; the myth of their military supremacy that, no matter how far removed, had always under-written the British presence in the region, was never reimposed. The occupation afforded educated Malays an opportunity to par-ticipate more intensively and with more real responsibility in the affairs of government, resulting in increased Malay self-confidence. Apart from the small and relatively uninfluential Malay left wing, no militant or rigidly ideological Malay nationalist movement emerged to threaten the postwar British administra-tion, but Malays would no longer be so quiescent, so pliable, under British colonial rule. The moderate Malay leadership sailed un-scathed through the stormy years of the Japanese interregnum, gaining a new awareness of itself and of Malay potential in the postwar world.

Malay identification with the Japanese oppressors, particularly the activities of some Malay detectives and informers, aroused bitter reactions among the Chinese resistance movement and its supporters. In the one-month hiatus between the Japanese sur-render and the return of the British, Malay-Chinese hostility erupted into violence in several states, and scores of people were killed in interracial clashes and rioting. For the Chinese commu-nity, the middle-class leadership of the KMT was totally eclipsed by the MCP and the MPAJA, which, with their superior organization and greater level of dedication, emerged from the jungle into Malayan towns and villages actually to perform for a while, in many areas, the functions of government until they were compelled to give way to the returning British. Relations between the Malay, Chinese, and Indian elites, most of whom had been educated at the same English-language schools and shared many of the same values, remained free and easy, as they had in prewar days. But contact between Malays and Chinese at a lower level, carefully guarded and kept to a minimum by British policies before De-cember 1941, rose to a new level of exposure, most of it adversary, by the occupation experience. Malaya and Singapore would never be the same again. The soaring rhetoric of the United Nations Atlantic Charter, promising self-determination for the peoples of the world and trumpeting the demise of colonial domination, found appreciative ears in many sectors of the population.

The Borneo territories of North Borneo and Sarawak did not remain untouched by the depredations of war, even if they were not so affected by ethnic conflict. But the towns of North Borneo in particular were destroyed by Allied bombers, and in this country and in Sarawak substantial numbers of the populace entered wholeheartedly into the anti-Japanese resistance movement. Unlike those in Malaya, however, the resistors were not led by an internal political group such as the MCP, but were organized ab initio by Australian and British officers introduced into the area either by submarine or by parachute and operating from home bases much closer to Borneo than the Allies were to Malaya. In 1943 a combined force of Chinese, local Muslims, and some other indigenous persons rose up against the Japanese and annihilated the small garrison in Jesselton. Retribution was not long in coming; the Japanese army dealt terribly with the local inhabitants. Chinese in Sarawak, too, resisted the Japanese from time to time, and toward the end of the war other segments of the population, especially the hill people of the interior, were trained into formidable guerrillas by Commonwealth officers.[53] Again, unlike Malaya and Singapore, British Borneo was liberated directly by Allied troops: Australian forces landed in June 1945 to defeat the Japanese and receive their surrender before the atom bombs exploded in Japan. Two of the reasons why North Borneo and Sarawak were less prepared emotionally to struggle against British colonial rule may have been, first, that British forces were never defeated in Borneo (there were none to defeat when the Japanese landed!) and, second, that Allied forces vanquished the Japanese army in battle before the dropping of the atom bomb, liberating in a real sense the oppressed and starving population. In any event, no political organization espousing the cause of nationalism emerged in Borneo for many years to come.

53. For accounts of wartime Borneo, see Tom Harrisson, *The World Within* (London: Cresset Press, 1959), and, by the same author, "The Chinese in Borneo, 1942–1946," *International Affairs*, 26 (July 1950).

PART II

MALAYSIA

2 | The Rising Tide of Ethnic Consciousness

*After the War: The Malayan Union Experiment and
the Emergence of Indigenous Politics*
  The Malayan Union

For a number of years before the war the British government had been exercised by the unequal pace of development in the various Malay states, particularly the Unfederated Malay States, and by other anomalies posed by the fragmented nature of the political system in Malaya and Singapore. During the course of World War II the Colonial Office in London formulated plans that would bring together the FMS, the UMS, and the Straits Settlements in one centralized structure, a system of government that would promote administrative efficiency and economic progress. The proposed changes were intended to provide a foundation for the construction of a "modern" state, free of the anachronisms of indirect rule, and thus a prerequisite, in the judgment of the British, for future independence.

After 1945, with the advent to power in Britain of the Labour Party (in a Britain perhaps less pro-Malay because of wartime relations with the Japanese), plans to implement the new proposals were ushered in with the publication of a White Paper[1] that also included two significant departures from previous British policy. First, Singapore was to assume the status of a Crown Colony, severed from the other two Straits Settlements of Penang and

---

1. Great Britain, Colonial Office, *Malayan Union and Singapore: A Statement of Policy on a Future Constitution*, Command 6724 (London: H.M. Stationery Office, January 1946).

Malacca that were now to be included in the new and separate Malayan Union; and, second, citizenship requirements were amended to give every person born in Malaya or Singapore, regardless of ethnic affiliations, equal rights to a common citizenship.

The Malay community thought it would be adversely affected by every provision in the new Malayan Union scheme. Indeed, to many Malays it seemed as though Malaya could no longer be considered to be the land of the Malays. The dangers to their erstwhile "special position" as the rightful heirs to the country were apparent: first, the position of the sultans would be eroded to the point where their symbolic status as the sovereign rulers would be rendered even more meaningless by abolition of their control over religion and Malay custom; second, the principle of equal rights for all would mean that Malay special privileges (as ineffective in real terms as these had been) would be eliminated; third, and most important in long-range terms, the granting of equal citizenship rights to non-Malays born in Malaya and Singapore implied that when free elections were held as a prelude to (and after) independence, the resultant non-Malay participation in the affairs of the country would pose an abiding threat to Malay political hegemony. The narrow majority held by the Malay community in terms of population percentages added to their fears.

In October 1945, Sir Harold MacMichael was sent to Malaya to negotiate new agreements with the rulers concerning their status under the proposed Malayan Union. Using questionable methods of persuasion,[2] MacMichael was able to compel the rulers' signatures on a new set of treaties. Malay reaction to this series of events and its implications for their future was unexpected (by the British government) and severe. Although the Malayan Union was officially established on April 1, 1946, and a British governor installed, it did not remain in being for long. Early in 1946 the first Malay political party was formed specifically to fight for the rights imperiled by the Malayan Union plan. This new party's name was the United Malays' National Organization, and it brought together

2. It is doubtful whether the sultans appreciated the meaning of what they were signing. See the British parliamentary debates in Hansard during this period for criticisms of MacMichael's policies: *Parliamentary Debates—Commons* (5th ser., Vol. 420, 1945–1946).

English-educated and Malay-educated Malays. The former group led the party and gave it its articulation, but Malays from the vernacular schools joined in large numbers—schoolteachers were especially active. Prewar British policies had brought about a split in Malay society; postwar British policy unwittingly brought the two together again, at least politically. Malays throughout Malaya and Singapore showed a surprising militancy compared with their previous apathy and acquiescence. Demonstrations, rallies, and public meetings were held in the countryside and in the towns, uniting almost all the Malay community in an impressive show of strength behind the sultans and the UMNO. The Malays were not alone in reacting adversely to the Malayan Union. Retired British colonial servants and some British commercial interests lobbied in Britain for the repeal of the Malayan Union provisions, while the situation in Malaya itself grew tense as ethnic antipathies, Malay versus non-Malay, worsened. In May 1946 a British parliamentary mission was sent to Malaya to investigate the matter, listen to representations from the various protagonists, and make recommendations to the British government. In July 1946 a decision was made to replace the Malayan Union by a federal system of government in which some power was returned to the sultans and the position of the Malays generally was returned to its special status. Malaya was to be given back to the Malays, if only politically.

The Malay left wing was quick to seize upon the imposition of the Malayan Union as a natural issue. After a short spell of imprisonment, KMM, PETA, and KRIS leaders were released from detention, and the KMM was reformed by Dr. Burhanuddin, who was to become a focal figure in Malay left-wing and ultranationalist activities. The dividing line between the left, at least rhetorically committed to a multiethnic socialism, and the ultranationalists, a rightist group whose goals determinedly focus upon the promotion of exclusively Malay interests, if necessary at the cost of the non-Malays, sometimes is blurred. Normally the ideology of both groups stands in diametric contrast, but the objectivity of the Malay left has in the past been influenced by the subjective knowledge that Malays remain socioeconomically retarded. Thus Malay leftists can at times be ignited by the same fierce awareness of Malay rights as the ultranationalists, obviously to the detriment of interethnic cooperation. In such cases, the left makes its attacks and bases its appeal within the framework of the Malay community alone, criticizing the allegedly feudal structure of the Malay social hierarchy as the source of the ills that bedevil progress. Yet another blurring ingredient between the two groups stems from the fact that many adherents of both factions have tended to be recruited from the Malay vernacular and religious schools. In October 1946 another Malay left-wing group, the Malayan Nationalist Party, was founded. Shortly thereafter the two organizations merged under the presidency of Dr. Burhanuddin under the title of the MNP. Behind the banner of the Malayan Democratic Union, (MDU), a very loose coalition of leftist organizations including the MCP, the MNP and its Malay adherents tried to rally the Malay population in an attempt to overturn the anti-Malay provisions of the Malayan Union. Once again, however, the Malay left was thwarted in its efforts by the newly formed UMNO, which, like its predecessor, the now defunct Kesatuan Melayu, was based on a more acceptable Malay traditional leadership combined with broad elements from other strata of Malay society. The UMNO was thereby enabled to enjoy the support of the vast majority of the Malay population in the struggle against the Malayan Union proposals, and the left-wing leadership could find no disaffected constituency on which to construct a power base. The MNP, as a political movement, was able to exert little influence on the Malay masses either in Malaya or Singapore. Left-wing labor unions in Malaya and Singapore tried to organize ideologically across ethnic cleavages and appointed some Malays to high executive positions. According to one scholar, left-wing trade unionism did have some influence on the more radical Indonesian Malays then resident in Singapore, but leading Malay leftists were unable to acquire any personal power base or following, especially since no trade union had an overwhelming Malay or Indonesian membership.[3]

Non-Malays, too, were active in opposition to the Malayan Union scheme. The non-Communist (but vaguely Marxist) MDU, formed in 1945, spoke out strongly when the British plans were an-

3. Michael R. Stenson, *Industrial Conflict in Malaya* (London: Oxford University Press, 1970), pp. 131–132.

nounced. Other organizations, including the Malay left as well as some Chinese moderates, joined with the MDU in December 1946 to form a broad political coalition to be known as the All Malayan Council of Joint Action (AMCJA). Almost immediately the Malay group broke away from the AMCJA to set up their own coalition, the Pusat Tenaga Ra'ayat (PUTERA, the People's Central Force). Still cooperating with the AMCJA, however, the PUTERA persuaded the coalition to forward to the British a set of counter-proposals for a new federal constitution to include Singapore that would provide for several specifically pro-Malay measures as well as granting equal citizenship rights for all. After the demise of the Malayan Union, the AMCJA-PUTERA coalition tried to arouse a pan-Malayan (as opposed to Malay) brand of nationalism that would unite all races behind a common set of anticolonial goals and, at the same time, would present a political alternative to the UMNO.[4]

They failed dismally. For reasons discussed above, the Malay community—by far the most politicized at this time—preferred that the more conventional leadership of the UMNO with its own brand of Malay nationalism lead the struggle for its rights, and still adamantly opposed any form of common Malayan citizenship. The Malay left, too, although cooperating with the AMCJA, found the relationship tenuous; many left-wing Malays found an emotive nationalism clouding their ideologically based rationality, thus precluding a wholehearted commitment to a multiethnic left. The Chinese and Indians, while fearful of the militancy of Malay nationalism, had for the most part little experience in Malayan and Singaporean politics (their prewar political endeavors had been directed outward), and their response to the AMCJA-PUTERA call to action was lukewarm. Finally, the AMCJA-PUTERA group had been joined by several obviously Communist or pro-Communist organizations and individuals and thereby attracted

4. See Gordon P. Means, *Malaysian Politics* (London: University of London Press, 1970), chap. 7, "The Radical Nationalists 1945–48"; K. J. Ratnam, *Communalism and the Political Process in Malaya* (Kuala Lumpur: University of Malaya Press, 1965), chap. 5, "Party Politics"; and M. N. Sopiee, *From Malayan Union to Singapore Separation* (Kuala Lumpur: University of Malaysia Press, 1974), for accounts of these complicated maneuvres.

close British surveillance—unwanted attention that further repelled public support.

In sum, the ill-fated and ill-timed Malayan Union proposal fell
victim to the unexpected strengths of Malay nationalism and to the
inability of non-Malays to organize politically in support of the
British plan (which, if successfully implemented, would have given
non-Malays equal citizenship rights in addition to the privileged
economic status their elites already enjoyed). The Malays themselves at long last had formed a genuine if communal political
party, the UMNO, and thenceforward were assured of a major
voice in determining the future directions their homeland would
follow. While failing to acquire the status of first-class Malayan
citizenship, non-Malays began to think of their own political interests in a purely Malayan context; shortly after the demise of the
Malayan Union, non-Malay political organizations such as the
Malayan Chinese Association (MCA) began to emerge.

The Federation of Malaya Agreement, 1948

The Federation of Malaya was inaugurated on February 1, 1948,
by virtue of the provisions of the Federation Agreement, 1948.[5]
The new political system represented, in effect, acquiescence to
Malay pressure as it related first to the "special rights" of the
Malays, second to the constitutional position of the sultans, and
third to the granting of qualified or limited citizenship to non-
Malays. Yet it was not a complete victory for Malay nationalists.
Although the sultans were to retain the powers, rights, and pre-
rogatives they enjoyed up to 1941, they were to do so within a
framework of strong central authority emanating from the British
High Commissioner, working through a federal executive council
and a federal legislative council based in Kuala Lumpur. The FMS,
UMS, and Straits Settlements were abolished as political units and
replaced by a new federation of nine Malay states together with
Penang and Malacca, each with its own state executive council
(advisory) and council of state (legislative). Singapore remained a
British Crown Colony and was separated from the peninsula in an
absolute political sense. In the new federation, the status of the

5. See Federation of Malaya, *The Federation Agreement, 1948* (Kuala Lumpur:
Government Press, 1952).

rulers was strengthened somewhat by the establishment of a Council of Rulers, which was to meet regularly under the chairmanship of one of their own, a sultan to be elected by the rulers themselves. Among other powers, the Council of Rulers was required to approve changes in the immigration laws—another means of safeguarding the Malay position.

The rights and powers of the states were carefully prescribed in the agreement in an attempt to limit conflict between the center in Kuala Lumpur and the various components of the new federation. Malay nationalists pressed vigorously for strong states' rights to act as bastions of Malay privilege against the encroachment of non-Malays. State governments, following the formula delineated in the Pangkor Engagement, remained autonomous in all matters pertaining to Islam and Malay custom and in other areas not specifically reserved to federal authorities; in most major fields, however, and despite Malay pressure, the federal government exerted the ultimate authority over the states. In this sense the new concept of federalism, as opposed to the outright concentration of power at the center in the form of a union, was made more palatable to Malay sensitivities, yet many of the centralizing features of the Malayan Union were retained. For non-Malays (whose claims for equal citizenship and equal rights were only passively articulated at this embryonic stage of pressure-group politics) once again a compromise was arrived at so that citizenship could be acquired through a lengthy process of application and qualification. Automatic citizenship was granted to all Malays, and restrictive immigration procedures were introduced to keep down the rising numbers of the non-Malay population. The Malayan Union, which had contained a formula whereby a common Malayan identity might have emerged in time, had been unable to withstand the pressures of ethnic nationalism. The Federation of Malaya admittedly was a compromise and therefore did not provide long-range solutions, in this case to the problem of containing or domesticizing ethnic conflict.

The Emergency: 1948–1960

The MCP's decision to enter upon a period of "armed struggle" in early 1948 resulted in the imposition by the British of a set of

Emergency Regulations to combat guerrilla militancy. The Emergency Regulations were promulgated into law in June 1948, and the ensuing period of armed insurrection became known, euphemistically, as the "Emergency." Two salient features emerge as basic to any study of this period: first, the armed struggle was instigated and led by the MCP, and second, the MCP guerrillas were almost entirely Chinese in ethnic origin and derived the bulk of their support from the Chinese sector of the population, only small numbers of Indians and Malays participating in the guerrilla movement. The MCP's inability to organize across ethnic boundaries can be ascribed in large part to Malay antipathy toward an ethnic group they considered to be alien and to pose a threat to their privileged position in the peninsula—or at least to its potentiality. Most Malays saw the outbreak of guerrilla Communism not simply as an attack upon British colonialism, but ultimately as an assault upon the homeland of the Malays, an attempt to transform Malaya into a province of China. Although British and Commonwealth forces were heavily committed to the suppression of the revolt, and British civil servants, police officials, and military officers directed the fight, victory over the MCP guerrillas could never have been achieved without the wholehearted cooperation of the Malay community.

At the end of World War II, the MCP found itself in a strong military and political position. It was in the latter arena, however, that the party was most active from 1945 to 1948, a period that might be called the constitutional phase of its operations. By various means the party came to dominate almost three-quarters of the labor force through the machinery of the Pan-Malayan Federation of Trade Unions,[6] and strike after strike was successfully implemented; in 1947, for example, three hundred major strikes resulted in the loss of seven hundred thousand working days.[7] Despite these initial tactical successes, internal and external factors disrupted and eventually destroyed this "moderate" stage of the MCP's program—"moderate" in the sense that conditions were

6. The British legally recognized the MCP at this time. See Anthony Short, "Communism and the Emergency," in Wang Gungwu, ed., *Malaysia: A Survey* (New York: Praeger, 1964), chap. 10.

7. Harry Miller, *The Communist Menace in Malaya* (London: Harrap, 1954), p. 76.

deemed not to favor armed struggle at that time.[8] The party was riven by internal dissent. Lai Tek (or Loi Tak), the secretary-general of the party and always a shadowy *eminence grise*, disappeared in March 1947, carrying much of the party coffers with him amid rumors that he had been a Japanese as well as a British double agent. His disappearance provoked fierce discussion within the party, he was replaced as secretary-general by Ch'in Peng, and the moderate national united front policy he had advocated was superseded by one of armed struggle. Severe measures taken by the British against the MCP-controlled trade unions, coupled with an improvement in the country's economy, also contributed heavily to the MCP's change of direction.

The origins of the MCP's armed revolt are still in dispute. One school of thought, to which most British officials and some scholars subscribe, is that it was ordered by Moscow via the Cominform in consonance with an integrated revolutionary strategy throughout Southeast Asia. Other commentators suggest that the need for armed struggle was dictated by worsening conditions in Malaya and dissent within the party. Reality may fall somewhere in between, but a central question in any analysis of the MCP's autonomy is whether the party has a life of its own and an ability to control its own affairs or whether it is merely an adjunct of outside Communist forces, especially the Chinese Communist Party. There is powerful evidence for both premises;[9] my own analysis inclines toward a middle ground that admits the relevance of local factors, yet acknowledges the MCP's obligations in 1947–1948 to international Communist ideology. It is impossible to marshal all the evidence, pro and con, in these few pages—a definitive study is yet to be published—yet one impression, accrued from personal experience, persists. *Both the British and the MCP guerrillas were militarily unprepared for the outbreak of armed revolt.* The late Ian Morrison of

8. See G. Z. Hanrahan, *The Communist Struggle in Malaya* (New York: Institute of Pacific Relations, 1954), chap. 4, "The Period of Indecision and the Policy of Moderation."

9. See the British Government's *The Fight against Communist Terrorism in Malaya* (London: Central Office of Information, 1962). Ruth T. McVey, *The Calcutta Conference and the Southeast Asian Uprisings* (Ithaca, N.Y.: Cornell Modern Indonesia Project, Interim Reports Series, 1958) and Stenson, *Industrial Conflict in Malaya*, offer expositions of the opposing viewpoint.

the *London Times* commented upon the MCP's position as follows: "An incontestable conviction is being developed that the Malayan Communists were compelled to launch military operations earlier than they were prepared for them, i.e., it seems though they were drawn into the revolution."[10] Such unpreparedness accounts for the comparative lack of meaningful success against the British, who were equally disarrayed.[11] A better equipped and more properly planned guerrilla campaign could have brought the Malayan economy to the brink of disaster.

There is little doubt that friction within the MCP and its declining political influence on the Malayan scene, together with repressive antiparty measures instituted by the British, led MCP leaders to embark upon a major reappraisal of their policy and thence to armed struggle. But this radical change of policy also coincided neatly with Zhdanov's speech to the Cominform in Warsaw in September 1947, in which he divided the world into two hostile camps, characterized by "the crisis of the colonial system" and thus necessitating "a powerful movement for national liberation in the colonies and dependencies."[12] The Communist revolt in Malaya, then, though probably inevitable in any case, may have been accelerated by Cominform plans for national liberation revolutions throughout Asia.

In addition to these political and organizational factors, societal ingredients underpinned the development of the revolt. Victor Purcell, a former British colonial official in Malaya, has written about the circumstances of the Chinese "squatters," from whose numbers the MCP drew the bulk of its support and recruits.[13] In 1948 the Chinese squatter population was estimated at almost half a million, occupying land either without any official title or by virtue of a "temporary occupation license"—a flimsy document the

10. Ian Morrison, *Far Eastern Survey*, no. 24, December 22, 1948.

11. As a young innocent in 1948, I was sent casually into the jungle with makeshift equipment more befitting a formal parade ground than guerrilla warfare.

12. A. Zhdanov, "For a Lasting Peace, for a People's Democracy," *Cominform Journal*, No. 1, November 10, 1947.

13. Victor Purcell, *The Chinese in Southeast Asia*, 2d ed. (London: Oxford University Press, 1965), pp. 334–337, and, by the same author, *Malaya: Communist or Free?* (Stanford: Stanford University Press, 1955), chapter 6, "The Chinese Squatter," pp. 73–83.

government could abrogate at any time. Much of the land occupied by the squatters in 1948 had been acquired "illegally" during the exigencies of the Japanese interregnum in Malay Land Reservation areas—a fact that was not lost upon the squatters and that added to their disquiet. Most of the squatter territory, too, was situated in the no-man's-land of the jungle fringe between the natural habitat of the guerrillas and the more populated areas. Once the guerrilla war had reached its full intensity, it was obvious that the Chinese squatters, many of whom were naturally sympathetic to the MCP because of wartime and other experiences, were providing a logistic sea in which guerrilla fish could swim. Police and military search operations in squatter areas often turned into destroy operations, as peasant huts were burned down, crops destroyed, and, in some instances, unarmed squatters shot.

Before 1948, squatter contact with the government had been minimal and negative. Very few government services were provided to the squatters; schools were built and operated by the squatters themselves, communications were bad, electricity was rarely if ever supplied, and health services focused on hospitals in the towns and cities, often far away. Chinese squatters had little opportunity to obtain alternative land with real title because of opposition from the Malay community. Few non-Chinese government officials spoke the Chinese language and those who did were considered eccentric, if not freakish; only in the mid-1950s, when the government established a Government Officers' Chinese Language School, was this situation remedied. Thus the majority of squatters had no great reason to invest their loyalty in the Malayan government.

As the Emergency got under way with a vengeance, British officials had to find some way of bringing the squatters under their control and "protection." In 1950 the Director of Operations, General Sir Harold Briggs, instituted the so-called Briggs Plan,[14] a

---

14. The plan was slow in getting started, and cynical critics soon began to call it the "Briggs Perlahan-perlahan" ("*perlahan-perlahan*" is Malay for "slow"). Implementation of the plan was considerably aided by the excellent state of the Malayan economy. The rubber boom, brought about by the Korean war, had resulted in vast economic profits. This happenstance, of course, also helped to keep the Malayan population as a whole reasonably contented.

system of "New Villages" that entailed the forced resettlement of half a million squatters behind barbed-wire and police checkpoints. Some benefits to the squatters did accrue—electricity, better school buildings, Red Cross clinics, community centers—but in the main the massive disruption of lives and the ensuing hardship only served to heighten the squatters' alienation from the government.[15] Militarily, however, the resettlement program was extraordinarily successful, in the long run effectively separating the Malayan Races Liberation Army (MRLA) in the jungle from its main source of recruitment and supplies.

Another potent source of Chinese social unrest was the vexed question of Chinese education. Prior to the outbreak of the Emergency the majority of Chinese students attended Chinese vernacular schools,[16] many of which were operated and paid for by the Chinese community. The quality of education was adequate, except that it was in the Chinese language and therefore fitted students emerging from the primary and middle (or secondary) schools with few of the tools necessary to climb the ladder of social mobility, an ascent generally predicated upon a knowledge of the English language. As a result, a vast pool of intelligent and well-educated (albeit in the Chinese language) Chinese youths grew in the towns and cities and in the countryside, finding employment only at the most menial levels as shop assistants, coffee-shop waiters, and the like. Finding their life chances inconsistent with their abilities and aspirations, it is small wonder that many of them turned to the MCP as a conduit for their frustrated energies. Above all, the insular and parochial nature of the Chinese-language school system, allowed by British authorities to remain segregated from the other language streams of education, meant that Chinese vernacular-school students were deprived of the opportunity to intermingle with non-Chinese students, especially Malays, and perhaps to gain an insight into the workings of other cultures in Malaya. Except for those chosen few who were able to attend

15. See Han Su-yin's perceptive novel *And the Rain My Drink* (London: Jonathan Cape, 1956) for a description of life in a New Village.
16. In 1951, 206,000 Chinese students attended Chinese-language schools, whereas only 56,000 Chinese students attended English-language schools. Figures quoted in Purcell, *Malaya*, p. 153.

English-language schools, the educational system fostered ethnic segregation and, for the Chinese-language student, prevented the emergence of any truly "Malayan" consciousness.

MCP strategy in the early days of the Emergency was for the guerrillas who were to become the MRLA to establish "liberated areas" and for the party to construct a widely based united front, including the petty and national bourgeoisie.[17] After some initial successes, the fortunes of the MRLA declined dramatically. The guerrillas made little headway in allying themselves with non-Chinese elements of the population, and they were thereby excluded from large areas of the countryside where they might have established liberated areas. The deep jungle, whither they eventually were forced to flee, was mostly uninhabited except for small groups of aborigines, so the MRLA had no sea of population in which to swim. In populated areas, use of indiscriminate terror tactics against Chinese and Malays alike alienated them from much of the population. Both militarily (the establishment of liberated areas) and politically (the shaping of a united front) the MCP strategy failed dismally.

In 1951 the MCP leadership admitted the lack of success of this first phase of the party's policies.[18] New tactics that emerged following this recognition of failure resulted only in a limited and temporary improvement in the guerrilla situation, and the party admitted that it had "aimed too high"[19] and thus had alienated the masses. From the end of 1952 onward, MCP policy tried to reestablish communication with the masses in order to renew support and sympathy within the confines of a new version of the united front. By now, however, the Malayan and British police and military had gained the initiative in the jungle war, the police Special Branch had achieved remarkable success in penetrating the ranks of the party and the MRLA, and the guerrillas were forced to retreat into

17. MCP strategy, outlined in a party document entitled "Strategic Problems of the Malayan Revolution" (see Hanrahan, *Communist Struggle*, p. 64), closely followed that prescribed in Mao Tse-tung's work "Strategic Problems of China's Revolutionary Wars" (Mao Tse-tung, *Selected Military Writings* [Peking: Foreign Language Press, 1963], pp. 75–150).

18. Hanrahan, *Communist Struggle*, pp. 117–130.

19. Editorial in the MCP publication *Freedom News*, August 15, 1952, quoted in *NYT*, November 1, 1952.

the innermost recesses of the rain forest, whence they were generally unable to maintain effective lines of communication with the
outside world. At the end of 1954 the MRLA hard line of armed
struggle had become, in any meaningful sense, moribund. The
party looked for more appropriate strategy.

The virtual end of the insurrection in the mid-1950s can be
attributed to a number of factors, indigenous and external: (a) by
1954 it had become clear that the armed revolt had no chance of
immediate success; (b) in 1954 legal Malay and Chinese political
parties joined together to demand independence from the British,
eventually promised for 1957,[20] a promise that deprived the MCP
of a major opportunity to construct its own movement for independence from colonial rule; and (c) from late 1951 onward, the
foreign policy of the People's Republic of China (PRC) changed to
emphasize "united front" tactics based on "peaceful coexistence"
between Asian states,[21] a policy that culminated in the endorsing of
the Five Principles of Peaceful Coexistence at the Bandung Conference of April 1955.

The first general elections were held in Malaya in 1955, and
shortly thereafter Tunku Abdul Rahman was elected chief minister. One of his first acts was to declare an amnesty for all MRLA
guerrillas, and in November 1955 Ch'in Peng offered to negotiate
terms with the Tunku and with David Marshall, the chief minister
of Singapore. The talks were held in Baling in December 1955, but
they failed when the Malayan government negotiators refused to
agree to Ch'in Peng's proposals that the MCP be legalized. The
mere fact that the talks were held at all, at the behest of the MCP, is
highly significant. As John Brimmell says, "for some considerable
time the MCP leaders must have been aware of the fact that their
position was out of step with the international communist line of
peaceful coexistence, and that they had lost the political initiative in
Malaya."[22] Immediately preceding the Baling talks the MCP issued

20. See Victor Purcell, *The Revolution in Southeast Asia* (London: Thames &
Hudson, 1962), pp. 101–103.
21. David Mozingo, "The Maoist Imprint on China's Foreign Policy," in *China
Briefing*, (Chicago: Center for Policy Studies, University of Chicago, 1968), p. 31.
22. J. H. Brimmell, *Communism in Southeast Asia* (London: Oxford University
Press, 1959), p. 332.

a directive containing both organizational and programmatic changes.[23] Malay and Indian party members were appointed to the positions of chairman and vice-chairman, respectively, of the Central Committee and it was clear that the new program was designed to exploit the new political situation, to attract a wider nationalistic line embracing all ethnic groups. The MCP's demands were extremely moderate and directed in particular toward Malays. Even the Malay sultans were to be afforded their full rights and privileges. The program stressed the application of the Five Principles of Coexistence and concluded by saying that the new line conformed "to the actual conditions in Malaya today." Clearly, conditions inside Malaya (primarily the military failure of previous strategy) together with the evolution of a more moderate PRC foreign policy had combined to change strategy from a rigidly exclusive revolutionary united front to one embracing much wider categories. Finally, even though the Baling talks failed, Ch'in Peng announced that the MCP would refrain from armed revolt when Malaya achieved genuine independence; but to all intents and purposes, the armed struggle—or at least this phase of it—was over.

Guerrilla activity did not completely fade away, for the Emergency dragged slowly along for another five years, well after the declaration of independence in 1957. Gradually, however, British and Malayan armed forces were able to lift the Emergency Regulations in more and more areas up and down the country by proclaiming "white areas" (the opposite side of a coin called "liberated areas"!) as they cleared the guerrillas out of each successive district. Almost three thousand guerrillas surrendered to the government, and the remnants of the MRLA moved northward across the international border into sanctuaries in southern Thailand, where they have remained to the present as a nucleus for any future recrudescence of the armed struggle in Malaya. The Emergency was ended officially by the Malayan government in 1960. (A new stage of the armed struggle appeared in the early 1970s and is described in Chapter 5.)

At the height of the Emergency, the guerrillas and their active

23. Published by the *NCNA* (Peking), January 6, 1956.

supporters never numbered more than fourteen thousand men and women, but they were able to tie up as many as one hundred thousand Malayan police and British and Commonwealth troops. Casualty figures for the Emergency are listed in Table 2.

Table 2. Casualties during the Emergency

	Killed	Wounded	Captured or missing	Surrendered
Guerrillas	6,711	Not known	1,289	2,704
Security forces	1,865	2,560	—	—
Civilians	2,473	1,385	810	—

SOURCE: Short, Malaysia, Table 12, p. 160.

But the implications and consequences of the Emergency go far beyond casualty figures, as tragic as these were to those concerned. On the one side, thousands of Chinese guerrillas and their sympathizers were killed and wounded and otherwise made to suffer, while on the other a similar fate was visited upon many hundreds of Malay police, troops, and civilians. Even though a substantial number of Malayan Chinese opposed the guerrilla insurrection, many of them fighting as part of British, Commonwealth, and Malayan armed forces, the MRLA guerrillas themselves were largely Chinese. Often, too, Malay communities that had incurred death or wounding at the hands of the guerrillas vented their wrath on neighboring Chinese villagers notwithstanding the latter's lack of complicity.[24] The twelve violent years of the Emergency, a period that saw the hopeful birth of an independent Federation of Malaya, free for the first time of the strictures of direct colonial rule, also witnessed increased ethnic tensions, surely an ominous backdrop for the entrance of a new multiracial state.

The Road to Independence: Party Politics Are Established

As has been shown, the communal Malay UMNO was born out of a set of circumstances in which the position of the Malays as an ethnic community had come under assault. Then came the Emergency, the stringencies of which were felt most strongly by the

24. I witnessed the aftermath of several tragic and ugly incidents of this nature in Province Wellesley and southern Kedah in 1950–51.

Chinese, placing that group in a defensive position. It became difficult for the Chinese community, or at least the portion of it that wished to be identified as anti-Communist in support of the government, to organize itself politically because of this defensive posture and the British and Malay suspicions directed at it. Unwilling to mobilize as an overt political party to protect Chinese interests against militant Malay nationalism, leading Chinese public figures formed the Malayan Chinese Association in 1949 ostensibly to organize the Chinese population behind the government as an alternative to the MCP. The MCA's long-term goals, however, probably were designed to represent Chinese interests in relation to Malay political dominance. Unlike the UMNO, which clearly represented a genuine cross section of Malay society, the MCA was never representative of all Chinese in Malaya. Leadership positions within the MCA were based on economic power and social status in the Chinese commercial community. Contact with and influence on the Chinese working class was minimal, limited in the main to participation in artisan-employer guilds and in traditional Chinese district and class associations. The MCA management committee consisted of wealthy tin-mine owners, rubber-estate proprietors, merchants, compradores, and entrepreneurs, leading lights all in trade associations and chambers of commerce and inevitably conservative in character. As such they were able to wield much authority within their own restricted area of trade and commerce, but had little influence on the mass of Chinese squatters, tin-mine workers, rubber tappers, and other workers.

Later the MCA leadership was able to form a natural alliance with the UMNO elite. In its early days, however, the group functioned less as a political party in competition with others than as a pressure group, furthering Chinese interests, and as a social welfare association, distributing aid to needy Chinese in the towns and in the resettlement villages. Yet the MCA never lost sight of the future, and its leadership equated Chinese interests with long-term Chinese and Malay compatibility. The first president of the MCA, Tan Cheng-lock (later Sir Cheng-lock Tan), stressed this point in his inaugural address: "It is a matter of supreme significance and indusputable necessity that a basic purpose of this organization must be the attainment of inter-communal understanding and friendship, particularly between the Malays and Chinese. . . . Wake up and unite not only among yourselves, but also with the Malays and other communities, to make this land one country and one nation."[25]

Despite many appeals for unity among the races in Malaya, politics continued to be defined by ethnic boundaries. In September 1951, Dato Onn bin Jaafar, the former and first president of UMNO, who had failed to enlarge its membership to include non-Malays, resigned from the UMNO and established Malay's first attempt at a multiethnic political party, the Independence of Malaya Party (IMP). Dato Onn had received encouragement from the British, from Tan Cheng-lock, and from the Indian leader of the Trade Union Council with regard to the formation of this new concept in political parties, and, sensing the pitfalls ahead in a system of parties each confined in membership to one ethnic group, he felt convinced that Malaya was ready and willing for such a move. He was wrong. Support from neither of the main ethnic groups, Malays and Chinese, was forthcoming; Tunku Abdul Rahman, who had replaced Dato Onn as president of the UMNO, called the latter's move "destructive" and thereupon IMP members were expelled from the UMNO. Obviously the special position of the Malays and the political dominance that derived therefrom was of greater moment to that community than the construction of a pan-Malayan identity. (The IMP's proposal to decrease the authority and position of the sultans proved to be especially irksome to traditional and conservative Malays.) The MCA gave initial lip service to the IMP's aspirations, but had little faith in its potential; the only consistent support given to the party came from substantial numbers of Indian intellectuals. The IMP dissolved itself in 1953; from auspicious beginnings a noble experiment had failed.

Following the provisions of the Federation Agreement, which had proclaimed Britain's intentions of granting future independence, elections were held at local, municipal levels in 1951 and 1952. Of these the Kuala Lumpur municipal elections of February 1952 were the most significant inasmuch as they signaled the first

25. Quoted in K. J. Ratnam, *Communalism and the Political Process in Malaya* (Kuala Lumpur: University of Malaya Press, 1965), p. 154.

coming together of the UMNO and MCA, that is, the birth of an alliance, later expanded, that has ruled Malaya and Malaysia ever since independence in 1957. The UMNO and the MCA joined for several reasons to contest the 1952 Kuala Lumpur elections. First, the British government had made it plain that independence would not be granted until such time as the various ethnic groups in Malaya had proved that they could work together in harmony; the alliance to contest the Kuala Lumpur elections was an admirable opportunity to demonstrate this ability. Second, the UMNO and MCA wished to assert positively that they could provide an alternative to the multiethnic IMP, which was also contesting the elections. Third, the UMNO had been set back by its conflict with Dato Onn and the IMP; because its morale was shaken and its support decreased, an electoral alliance with the MCA would provide an ideal means to enhance the UMNO's popularity. Fourth, both the UMNO and MCA elites found they had interests in common: both were rational and pragmatic, both were essentially conservative, both were drawn mainly from the English-language schools and had many shared values and experiences, and both appreciated that direct electoral confrontation between unabashedly communal parties would be likely to lead to interethnic violence.

A tacit understanding was therefore reached to the effect that leaders in both parties would keep the more radical elements in their respective organizations in line. The Malay elite, furthermore, was willing to sacrifice a portion of its political power in return for Chinese financial assistance—and vice versa—although both elites recognized that, in the final analysis and in long-range terms, the Malays would retain their political dominance while the Chinese would continue to operate in the economic arena unimpeded by overly militant Malay demands. The UMNO-MCA alliance was successful in the Kuala Lumpur elections, winning nine to the IMP's two seats. Further local elections around the country were equally profitable for the UMNO-MCA ticket; the group gained a total of twenty-six out of thirty-seven seats contested. The stage was set for a more permanent form of alliance.

Now that an indigenous base for political organization had been established and the MCP guerrilla insurrection was virtually defeated, it was time to think in more urgent terms of *merdeka*—independence. The success of the UMNO-MCA merger, in what was clearly a strong show of unity between leaders of the two major ethnic communities, enabled local politicians to demand from the British an accounting of earlier promises. In August 1953, a UMNO-MCA convention was held, at which it was resolved, first, to demand that general elections be held to a Federal Legislative Council in 1954 and, second, to strive on that basis for complete independence, within the Commonwealth, on as early a date as possible. In April 1954, a UMNO-MCA delegation journeyed to London to try to persuade the British government out of its procrastination. The group met with little success and returned to Malaysia in some anger. Immediately UMNO-MCA members started a boycott of all government deliberations, forcing the British to agree to an elected Federal Legislative Council with a majority of unofficial (that is, not government-appointed) members.

The first country-wide federal elections were scheduled for July 1955. Fifty-two seats were to be contested out of a ninety-eight-member Federal Legislative Council, the remaining seats being reserved for appointed members. The Kuala Lumpur municipal elections in 1954 were to prove to the British that Malay and Chinese groups could work together in pursuit of a common goal; the 1955 federal elections were to demonstrate the strength of the Alliance throughout all areas of the peninsula. The Alliance, as it was now officially called, was overwhelmingly successful, winning fifty-one out of the fifty-two seats contested, representing a total of over eight hundred thousand votes out of an estimated one million cast.[26]

By this time a third leg had been added to the Alliance—the Malayan Indian Congress (MIC). Founded in 1946, the MIC at first was as concerned with politics in India as with representing Indian interests within Malaya; indeed it took its name from the Indian Congress Party. After a brief flirtation with left-wing politics

26. The dominance of the Malay component of the Alliance was evident: most of the registered electorate was Malay, and out of the fifty-two Alliance candidates who stood for election, thirty-five were Malays, fifteen Chinese, one Indian, and one Ceylonese.

inside the AMCJA, the MIC soon became a purely communal and conservative representative group.[27] The MIC has never fully represented the Indian community in Malaya; like the MCA, the MIC reflects only a small stratum of Indians, a small commercial and professional elite. The masses of Indian workers and rubber tappers have never found a home in the ranks of the MIC: their more natural affinity is either in the trade unions or in left-wing parties.

Merdeka and the New Federation of Malaya Constitution

The Alliance Party had now proved to the British the potency of its prescription for ethnic cooperation (albeit at an elite level) and, buoyant with the party's electoral successes, in January 1956 a delegation of Alliance leaders plus representatives from the rulers journeyed to London under the leadership of Tunku Abdul Rahman to discuss plans for independence. From the outset of the London talks, it was obvious that Britain had resigned herself to the inevitable; the opportunity was seized, in view of the winding down of the MCP insurrection, to arrange an orderly transition of power to a postindependence government with which a degree of compatibility could be achieved. Arrangements were made whereby immediate responsibility for internal affairs could be assumed by Alliance ministers, provision was made for the setting up of a Constitutional Commission, and August 31, 1957, was tentatively suggested as the date for the granting of complete independence.

The Constitutional Commission, consisting of five members selected from Commonwealth countries under the chairpersonship of Lord Reid, sat from June to October 1956, hearing representations from all interested individuals and groups. Its findings are of relevance to the course of future events in Malaya (and Malaysia) and can be summarized as follows:[28]

(a) *Citizenship.* The commission recommended, inter alia, that all persons born in Malaya after independence be granted automatic citizenship on the principle of *jus soli*. Noncitizens could obtain citizenship by fulfilling certain residential and other requirements.

---

27. Ratnam, *Communalism*, pp. 154–155.
28. See Great Britain (Colonial Office), *Report of the Federation of Malaya Constitutional Commission 1957* (London: H.M. Stationery Office, 1957).

(b) *National Language.* Malay was to be made the national language, English would remain an official language for at least ten years, and Chinese dialects and Indian (that is, Tamil) could be used in parliamentary proceedings at federal and state levels.

(c) *Malay Special Privileges.* The commission had been requested by Alliance leaders to reinforce the basic "given" that Malays alone were the true indigenes of Malaya and were therefore entitled to special privileges. Yet the commission had to reconcile this assumption with the concept of a common Malayan (as opposed to Malay) nationality, in which was implicit the notion of equal rights for all regardless of ethnic affiliations. A compromise was reached, specifying that existing preferences in favor of Malays (quotas for entrance into the public service, for business licenses, and for educational assistance, together with a system of Malay land reservation) be continued, but only as a temporary expedient. Islam was made the state religion, while freedom to worship other religions was guaranteed.

(d) *The Rulers.* The commission had to work out a method to reconcile the status of the Malay sultans with a federal system of parliamentary democracy. The obvious answer was some form of constitutionalized monarchy, and to this end a head of state, to be elected for a period of five years by the rulers themselves on the basis of seniority in office, was to be installed. This head of state, or paramount ruler, was constitutionally bound to accept the advice of the federal prime minister. In short, the position of the rulers was to be subordinated in every real sense to the authority of the elected representatives of the federal and state governments.

(e) *Legislative Bodies.* The commission recommended a two-chamber federal parliament: (1) an elected House of Representatives (initially to consist of one hundred members elected for five years from single-member districts) would exert primary legislative responsibility, supported by (2) an appointed Senate (thirty-three members, twenty-two of whom would be appointed by the state legislatures, the rest to be nominated by the paramount ruler under advisement). The functions of the Senate, like the British House of Lords, were restricted in scope; the chamber was empowered to act merely as a delay mechanism on the enactment of legislation, with the one real exception that any constitutional amendment could be passed only with the consent of two-thirds of the Senate. The Senate's purpose, like that of the United States Senate but without the latter's legislative primacy, was predicated upon the intention that it should personify the rights and opinions of the states vis-à-vis the federal elected representatives ensconced in the House. The Senate's ability to act in this regard, however, was to be severely circumscribed. The commission did recommend that the centralization of authority in Kuala Lumpur, provided for in the Federation Agreement, 1948, be diminished, and that certain powers, such as control over land, agriculture, and Malayo-Muslim religious and customary law, be vested in state governments.

Other constitutional articles recommended by Lord Reid's commission included liberal provisions on civil liberties, the incorporation of the former Straits Settlements of Penang and Malacca in the new federation as states in their own right, and the establishment of an independent judiciary on British lines. The commission's report did not please everyone. Both Malay and non-Malay groups attacked a number of its recommendations, and certain modifications were made before the new Constitution was promulgated. In general the most vociferous complaints stemmed from opponents of the Alliance Party, since the commission's report had accommodated so many of the latter's proposals. This opposition found its main support in the murky waters of ethnic antipathies, defined mainly by non-Malay unhappiness with the continued recognition of Malay special privileges, with the perceived stringency of citizenship qualifications, and with the failure to recognize Chinese as an official language.

The Malays themselves were dissatisfied with the lack of a specific article embodying Malay special privileges and rights as an intrinsic component upon which the Constitution would be built. A Working Committee consisting of equal representation from the Alliance and from the rulers, plus British colonial officials, was appointed to consider the commission's findings and revise them where necessary. It completed its task by May 1957, and the new Constitution was ratified in August of that year. The main modifications adopted by the Working Committee were concerned with Malay special privileges (the commission's recommendations as to their temporary nature were deleted, and they were enshrined as part of the Constitution), the use of the Malay language, the rulers (certain powers concerning constitutional amendments and the upholding of the Muslim religion were granted to them), and with the strengthening of states' rights in regard to the use of land. In sum, most of the modifications represented concessions to the political dominance of the Malays; the recognition of the principle of *jus soli* was the only blandishment offered to non-Malay sensitivities. The new Constitution did not contain any long-term formula for the resolution of ethnic cleavages, but it did represent a compromise of sorts and was therefore acceptable. But clearly the Malays were unwilling to vacate any of the safeguards concerning their privileged status and continued political hegemony; equally obviously, the liberalized citizenship requirements could in time result in the emergence of a substantial non-Malay electorate, dissatisfied with the inherent inequality contained in the Constitution, and able to mount a challenge in the democratic process to Malay dominance in the political arena. In any event, *Merdeka* Day was proclaimed on August 31, 1957, and a new independent state came into being.

The British Borneo Territories Prior to Malaysia
Sabah

The British North Borneo Chartered Company ceased its existence in 1946, and the Colony of North Borneo, administered directly by Britain, was constituted in its stead. The country had been ravaged by the Japanese war: all its major towns were flattened by Allied bombing. The immense task of reconstruction got slowly under way without any stimulus from local political activity—there was none. The British administered the territory by their usual formula: authority was centralized in the person of the governor, whence it emanated through a Secretariat down to Residents, and from them to the various district officers. The latter were virtually omnipotent within their little fiefdoms, although they were assisted by government-appointed native chiefs. Under the native chiefs was a system of village headmen and subheadmen, responsible to the district officer. Two legal systems prevailed in the colony: a juridical system based upon British law modified through the Indian experience and a native court system based upon local *adat* custom and religious law (the latter mainly in Muslim areas). An Advisory Council was provided for in the 1946 Constitution to "advise" the governor, but it was an appointed body and dominated by official members. No military force was raised or stationed in the colony; what few ripples there were on the surface of public tranquillity were smoothed by a small and benevolent police force. In 1950 the Advisory Council was replaced by an executive and a Legislative Council, whose deliberations were conducted in English, though brief speeches in Malay were "tolerated."[29]

No indigenous political movement was to emerge in North Borneo of its own accord. The postwar British government in London urged upon its colonies a movement for local government as a prelude for independence, and this pattern was followed in North Borneo. Various stages of local government—Town Boards, rural authorities, and the like—were instituted on the instructions of the governor, but difficulty was encountered in finding responsible and interested citizens for appointment thereto. One reason for this lack of political ambition stemmed from the nonexistence of an advanced educational system in the territory. Few local persons possessed a secondary education (under Chartered Company rule they had to leave the country to reach even this level) and practically none were able to attend a university. This factor, coupled with the obvious benignity of a colonial government whose policies (or lack of them) kept the various ethnic groups in a state of placid dormancy, held the level of politicization down to a minimum.

Almost out of desperation the governors (especially Sir Roland Turnbull in the mid-1950s) actively sought out enterprising local people from all ethnic and occupational backgrounds who might provide indigenous political leadership. These personages, of whom Donald Stephens (later Haji Mohammed Fuad) and Datu (now Tun) Mustapha were prominent,[30] were then groomed by the

29. M. H. Baker, *North Borneo: The First Ten Years* (Singapore: Malaya Publishing House, 1962), chap. 4.

30. Donald Stephens turned out to be a natural politician and leader, but he once told me that Governor Turnbull had persuaded him against his will (at the time) to enter politics. Turnbull was also protective of Datu Mustapha, once shielding him against possible legal action. Turnbull told me that it was better to have the Datu as a friend than as an enemy "with a host of piratical relatives in the southern Philip-

colonial administration to assume influential positions in the Legislative Council, on Town Boards, and the like. Some of them vanished into the mists of political oblivion, but many remained to play major roles in the evolution of domestic politics. Yet no political party emerged at this stage, although several Kadazan welfare and social associations were formed in the coastal plains around Jesselton; these were later to constitute the foundations for a Kadazan political party.

Political awareness underwent a quantum leap in February 1958, when Turnbull broadcast over Radio Sabah a proposal for some form of closer political association among North Borneo, Brunei, and Sarawak. The governor did not propose an immediate amalgamation of all three territories; rather, the emphasis of his address was on "closer association," starting with the unification of certain government bureaucracies. Public meetings were held throughout the country to discuss the proposals, and eventually a motion in favor of further examination of the concept was passed by the Legislative Council, not without misgivings on the part of some ethnic groups, each of which feared future dominance by another.[31] In fact, little headway was made in the implementation of Turnbull's suggestions because the sultan of Brunei evinced little support for them. Even in North Borneo (and in Sarawak) clearly there was no ground swell for closer association or for the ultimate independence from Britain that the proposals implied. Interest had been stimulated, but had not been transformed into a political movement.

On May 27, 1961, however, Tunku Abdul Rahman proposed in a speech in Singapore that a new Federation of Malaysia be formed, to include not only Singapore but also Sarawak, North Borneo, and Brunei in one single political system. Reaction in North Borneo was swift: local leaders at first wanted nothing to do with the idea; with prominent figures in the other Borneo ter-

---

pines"! The selection process was one in which the governor looked around for potential anticolonial "malcontents" and then circumscribed this potential by appointing them to responsible positions in governing bodies.

31. Baker, *North Borneo*, chap. 9. I myself embarked on a three-week walk of some 240 miles among the Murut longhouses of the Pensiangan district, trying to allay rumors that their land was being taken away from them.

ritories they formed a united front against Malaysia. But gradually pressure was exerted by the British and Malayan governments, including the organization of a number of "goodwill tours" to and from Malaya, and North Borneo opposition to merger diminished, if reluctantly at first. By the end of 1961 five political parties had been formed in North Borneo as a consequence of the Malaysian proposals.

The first to make an entrance was Donald Stephens' United National Kadazan Organization (UNKO), which found its main support among the Christianized Kadazans of the western coastal plain. The party's platform was pro-Malaysia, with specific safeguards built in for the retention of a measure of Bornean autonomy, especially regarding immigration, education, and freedom of religion and language. The UNKO was not the sole repository of Kadazan/Dusun[32] opinion, and the Dusuns, Kwijaus, Muruts, and others of the Interior Residency set up their own party, the United Pasok Momogun Organization (*pasok momogun* means "sons of the soil"). Pasok Momogun had reservations about Malaysia[33] and on the whole felt happy under continued British rule. Several years passed before the two Kadazan/Dusun groups were able to reconcile their differences, and in the meantime much animosity surfaced between them. The Muslims, too, led by Datu Mustapha and his brother, founded their own party (the United Sabah National Organization, or USNO) in 1961; it was to prove the most resilient, which is not surprising in view of its dedication to Malaysia and its close connections with brother and sister Muslim Malays in Kuala Lumpur. The USNO took a position similar to that of the UMNO in Malaya, stressing the primacy and special position of all indigenous Borneans, including non-Muslim indigenes.

The Chinese as usual found themselves in an unenviable position as perceived "outsiders," even though their relations with the native population had never been of an abrasive nature. Two

32. "Dusun" is a Malay word denoting a small farmer. Newly surfaced nationalists in North Borneo/Sabah rejected the word for the term "Kadazan," which was not at first acceptable to the conservative interior hill peoples.

33. I was often told by Pasok Momogun leaders of their deep-seated distrust of all Muslims and also of their suspicions regarding the better-educated, more sophisticated Kadazans of the plains. Hatred of Muslims seemed to be historically based on past interactions with the Brunei sultanate.

Chinese political parties were established in 1961, both representing Chinese communal interests. One, the United Party was based in Sandakan and supported by wealthy Chinese in that and other towns. The second, known as the Democratic Party, had its headquarters in Jesselton and derived some working-class support as well as that of more wealthy Chinese. Both these parties originally were opposed to Malaysia, believing that North Borneo should first obtain independence in its own right, but later they bowed to reality and to combined indigenous and British pressure. Thus the emergence of political parties in North Borneo, which by 1961 was being called Sabah, can be seen as the result of ethnic organization, for even though many of the parties called themselves "multiracial," their foundations were built on the need to protect communal interests.

The colonial government, under some urgency to promote popular participation in politics, held the first elections in Sabah in December 1962—not a general election but to Town Boards and district councils. The Sabah Alliance, patterned on its counterpart in Malaysia, had been formed by this time, but despite the merger (of the USNO and UNKO at first, followed later by the inclusion of the Sabah National Party,[34] Pasok Momogun, and the inconsequential Sabah Indian Congress) intra-Alliance competition, strident at times, persisted, and a number of seats were contested by several Alliance constituent groups. The only organized opposition to the Alliance came from independent candidates who stood because of their opposition to Malaysia or because of sheer political naiveté and exuberance. The results were a foregone conclusion: everywhere the Alliance was successful, winning all but 6 out of 137 seats. An analysis of the election and of the parties contesting it[35] shows that—as in Malaya—political affiliations followed along ethnic lines, with cooperation between ethnic communities meaningful only at the elite level. The potential for ethnic conflict, although present, was not as sharply etched as in Malaya; political

34. A Chinese party formed from the old Democratic and United parties.
35. See K. J. Ratnam and R. S. Milne, *The Malayan Parliamentary Elections of 1964* (Singapore: University of Malaya Press, 1967), chap. 10, and J. P. Ongkili, *Modernization in East Malaysia, 1960–1970* (Kuala Lumpur: Oxford University Press, 1972), chaps. 4 and 5.

awareness was of recent origin, sophistication was lacking, economic configurations were different, and there was more non-competitive intermingling of ethnic groups.[36] There was also no left-wing organization capable of crystallizing anti-Malaysian sentiment.

Sarawak

The political situation in Sarawak after the establishment of a British Crown Colony there in 1946 in place of the Brooke regime was more volatile than that in neighboring Sabah. The second British governor, Duncan Stewart, was assassinated in Sibu in 1949 by a clandestine Malay group formed to protest the cession of the Brooke rajahdom to the British government, believing that their privileged status under the Brookes would be eroded under the less personal ministrations of direct British colonial rule. Feelings in the Malay community ran high for many years after this event, and the community was riven by those who were for and those who were against the cession. For a decade afterward Malay associations of any kind were viewed with suspicion by the British, an attitude obviously detrimental to the growth of a legitimate nationalist movement. Not until the late 1950s did another Malay political group reappear.

Sarawak nevertheless forged ahead of Sabah with constitutional development. Local government authorities were established in 1947; at first members of these bodies were nominated by the British; the intention was to change them later to elective appointments. A new constitution promulgated in 1957 provided for indirect elections to the Council Negri (the "State" Council, the equivalent of the Legislative Council in Sabah), by means of direct elections to the local councils, that is, those elected to the district councils would in turn elect a certain proportion of Council Negri members. Otherwise the administration of the colony under the governor was identical to that described for Sabah in the preceding section. The country was, and is, divided into four divisions, each under a Resident.

36. There was, for instance, a large Sino-Kadazan community brought about through intermarriage. Islam was not a factor here, of course.

Consequent upon the more rapid evolution of local government and elections thereto in Sarawak, political parties made their appearance at an earlier date than in Sabah, though not, of course, as early as in Malaya. Unlike Sabah, too, left-wing ideology found more fertile ground for its propagation, especially among the Chinese.[37] The first political party to be founded in Sarawak, the Sarawak United People's Party (SUPP), made its appearance in June 1959 as a multiracial party, although its leadership was mainly Chinese. From the beginning the SUPP was tilted distinctly toward the left, most of its militants being radical Chinese dissatisfied with colonial policy regarding their education. It also gained surprising support from small Chinese traders and shopkeepers, unhappy at increased taxation they felt was directed against their community, and from numbers of farmers and smallholders who felt they were being discriminated against in land allocations.[38] The SUPP at first attracted many non-Chinese supporters, although membership fell off when the colonial government expressed its stern disapproval of alleged pro-Communist elements inside the SUPP and when the Brunei rebellion led by Azahari broke out in 1962. Even so, a substantial core of non-Chinese support remained fast within the party. It is interesting to note the parallels between the formative years of the SUPP and those of the People's Action Party (PAP) in Singapore: both had solid multiracial support, both contained leftist and moderate components, and in both the moderates emerged victorious following selective arrests and detentions by the government in power at the time. In addition to opposing the government's

37. It is difficult to pinpoint the reason for this difference. Postwar Chinese leadership in Sabah had forged strong ties to the KMT regime in Taiwan and KMT adherents in Hong Kong, and this in turn generated a strong anti-Communist bias. Chinese in Sarawak, especially those in Sibu, had always been reputed to be more stubborn and individualistic than their counterparts in Sabah. Their trade contacts, too, tended to be with Singapore Chinese, where left-wing groups were much stronger. Another factor may have been the Brooke regime's suspicions of Chinese motivations, lacking in Sabah. Postwar colonial policies regarding education and land were also qualitatively different in the two territories. But these reasons are not fully explanatory; further research is needed.

38. Michael B. Leigh, *The Rising Moon: Political Change in Sarawak* (Sydney: Sydney University Press, 1974), chap. 1, contains an excellent account of the background to party formation on Sarawak. See also Ratnam and Milne, *Malayan Parliamentary Elections*, pp. 266–295, and Ongkili, *Modernization in East Malaysia*, pp. 43–50.

policies regarding Chinese education and landholdings, the SUPP from the outset took a firm stand against the Malaysian proposals, preferring that Sarawak achieve independence first in its own right, following which some form of closer association with the other British Borneo territories could be examined.

A second party strongly supporting Malaysia was established in April 1960 under the name of the Partai Negara Sarawak (PANAS, the Sarawak State Party). Like the SUPP, the PANAS claimed to be a multiracial party; its main membership was Malay but it also included Ibans, Land Dayaks, and other indigenous peoples. Only a handful of wealthy Chinese were affiliated with the Malay-dominated PANAS, which was formed in part as a reaction to the SUPP's platform and its perceived threat to the advantageous position the Malays had occupied under the Brookes. The SUPP had enjoyed a degree of success in the 1959 local government elections, and moderate and conservative groups in Sarawak, spurred on by an apprehensive colonial government, felt a sense of urgency in the need to organize a valid political counterweight to its early magnetism. The PANAS's unabashedly pronative stance meant that mass Chinese support could never be garnered because of the zero-sum ethnic competitive spirit to which most of the protagonists subscribed. The PANAS remained a "multiracial" party, but only if that term was defined by the exclusion of Chinese.

Several other political parties were formed in the eighteen months that followed. These were the Sarawak National Party (SNAP), the Barisan Ra'ayat Jati Sarawak (Sarawak Native People's Front, or BARJASA), the Sarawak Chinese Association (SCA), and the Partai Pesaka Anak Sarawak (Sons of Sarawak Party, or PESAKA). The SNAP's original membership was composed mainly of Ibans from one geographical location, the Second Division, and many of its leaders had worked for the Shell oil refinery in nearby Brunei. Its formation was a surprise to the government and to the other political parties, the more so since it was able to spread its influence to Ibans in other parts of the country. It existed solely for the promotion of the sectional interests of the Iban. (Its leader, Stephen Kalong Ningkan, later became the center of Sarawak's first real political crisis.) The SNAP, like the UNKO in Sabah, at first opposed Malaysia, but changed its mind in 1962.

The BARJASA was basically composed of Malays who were opposed to the PANAS and reflected the residues of the pro- and anti-cession rift in Malay society. As the remnants of the anti-cession movement, the BARJASA and its members represented an antiestablishment position; the PANAS generally was comprised of proestablishment figures (the term "establishment" here denotes both a pro-British and a pro-Malaysian position). There the differences ended for the BARJASA eventually adopted a pro-Malaysian stance, although it had demanded a greater emphasis on Sarawakian states' rights than had the PANAS. The BARJASA, too, was a failure as a multiracial party, especially since it explicitly failed to mention the Chinese as one of the races of Sarawak in its program.[39]

The SCA obviously was based on similar premises as the MCA in Malaya proper and indeed received advice from that association. Both its leadership and the majority of its membership were wealthy Chinese merchants and businessmen who were fearful of the left-wing potential of the SUPP. Essentially conservative in character, the SCA became an interest group striving "to establish itself as the party for the rich young aspiring Chinese executive."[40] Just as the two Malay PANAS and BARJASA parties reflected a split in Malay society, similarly the PESAKA was derivative of historical (and geographic) divisions among the Ibans. From its inception the PESAKA was in favor of Malaysia, sensing that if the Ibans were to have an adequate voice in the new federation they would need to organize politically. The PESAKA originated in the Third Division and drew Iban supporters away from other parties in the area, particularly the SUPP and PANAS. Membership in the PESAKA was limited to those of Iban stock, and its sole avowed raison d'être was to further Iban goals and rights. Its leader was Temenggong Jugah, the Iban paramount chief. It obviously was closer to the government's position than was the SNAP; in fact many of its

39. At the very beginning the BARJASA had a strong protoleftist, anticolonial orientation in its leadership, but this was destroyed by the failure of the Brunei rebellion. The moderates in the BARJASA were more attracted by the coming reality of independence through Malaysia than by the more uncertain, if romantic, future of a left-wing stand against that concept. See Leigh, *The Rising Moon*, pp. 128–129.
40. Ibid., p. 23.

middle-echelon leaders were government-appointed headmen.

The pattern of party formation in the early days of organized politics in Sarawak was thus unlike that of either Malaya or Sabah. Each ethnic community—Malays, non-Muslim natives, and Chinese—was represented by two parties, each with opposing viewpoints, although there was a great deal of overlapping of interests. It follows that since there was no intraethnic communal unity, multiethnic parties along ideological lines should have stood a good chance of being formed, as Michael Leigh has argued: "The very cleavages that militated against communal unity created a multiplicity of disagreements which in fact promoted conflict resolution through a process of flexible realignments. Rather than making racial blocks more rigid, as occurred elsewhere in Malaysia, this political division within racial communities provided a ready basis for compromise, forcing the factions to seek allies outside their community in the quest for political power."[41]

Proposals that led to the formation of Malaysia, however, shattered this tendency before it had time to crystallize. A tentative coalition between the BARJASA and SNAP (two parties with natural affinities because of their mutual antiestablishment views) was mooted in early 1962 but never materialized. In January 1963 the Sarawak Alliance was formed, on the advice of and under pressure from Alliance leaders in Kuala Lumpur, from all existing parties with the exception of the SUPP, which remained adamant in its opposition to Malaysia.

The pattern followed in the formation of the Sarawak Alliance was similar to that of the Malayan Alliance, that is, the overall political creature was composed of five communal, or ethnic, legs controlled by a multiethnic brain in which leaders of the five different legs, or parties, came together to bargain with each other, to resolve conflicts, to keep their respective legs in order, and, finally, to present a united front to the outside world. Unlike Malaya, however, no one ethnic group was dominant inside the Alliance brain. The original body of the Sarawak Alliance did not last for long, as one of the legs, the PANAS, broke away in April 1963 because of political rivalry and personal jealousy, not because of any

41. Ibid., p. 39.

ideological differences. (The PANAS rejoined the Alliance two years later, after a brief and barren flirtation with the SUPP in 1963.)

General elections were held under the provisions of a law promulgated in 1962 that instituted a "tier" system of voting similar to previous local government elections whereby membership in the Council Negri was determined indirectly by the result of elections to municipal and district councils. In other words, the elected local authorities decided who was to be represented in the state government—the antithesis of the one-person-one-vote method of electoral participation. Liberal voting requirements were allowed: the franchise was extended to those over twenty-one years of age who had been resident in Sarawak for seven of the preceding ten years, and candidates for office had to be above the age of twenty-five years.[42] The elections were held between April and June 1963 (bad communications were the reason for this extended voting period), and a high turnout of 73 percent of registered voters was recorded. The elections turned into a three-way contest between the Alliance, PANAS, and SUPP, and in some respects could be considered to be a referendum on entry into Malaysia, each party having made its preference clear. The SUPP claimed afterward that the elections were not free, that several key SUPP figures had been arrested and detained prior to the polling dates, and that government officials (local and expatriate) conducted a quiet campaign against the SUPP as the repository of pro-Communist sentiment.[43]

The results of the elections gave 21.4 percent of the vote to the SUPP, 14.3 percent to the PANAS, 34.2 percent to the Alliance, and 30.2 percent to independents of various political hues and ethnic backgrounds. Leigh characterizes the elections as follows: generally speaking the Chinese favored SUPP, Malays supported PANAS, Melanaus (mainly Muslims) went for BARJASA, Ibans SNAP and PESAKA, Land Dayaks distributed their votes widely but mainly to PANAS and SUPP, while voting for independents also followed along the lines of local ethnic communities. In certain areas, too, the

42. This provision excluded many young Chinese SUPP militants from standing as candidates, which pleased some of the moderates in the party (and certainly the government). See Ratnam and Milne, *Malaysian Parliamentary Elections*, p. 274.

43. Former colleagues of mine in the Sarawak government have confirmed this latter accusation.

SUPP was able to garner significant Iban support.[44] If one considers that the great majority of the independent vote was pro-Malaysia, however, the majority of votes cast were in favor of that concept. In the ensuing elections by the victorious local government representatives to the Council Negri, under the tier system, an anomaly becomes immediately obvious: regardless of their strength at the polls (21.4 percent), the SUPP could translate this percentage into only five out of thirty-six seats in the Council Negri—only 13 percent of the total. The Alliance won twenty-three seats, PANAS five, and independents three.[45] With the Alliance now firmly in control of the Sarawak state government, the arena had been cleared for the final conflict over entrance to Malaysia.

The Formation of Malaysia

The concept of Malaysia was first given a public airing by the prime minister of Malaya, Tunku Abdul Rahman, on May 27, 1961, during an exploratory speech, significantly, in Singapore. Stressing the need for a closer association between Malaya, Singapore, and the British Borneo territories, the Tunku made it clear that he considered ethnic conflict to be the chief danger facing the new federation, should it be implemented: "[We should] think of a plan whereby these territories can be brought together in political and economic cooperation. This will not be possible if the Chinese start to think and talk of everything Chinese. The Malays will be made to think nervous, if they do, of their presence as Chinese and not as Malaysians. The Chinese are a practical people and as such must think clearly ahead. Above all Malaysia must be the sole object of their loyalty."[46]

This speech made it appear that the impetus for Malaysia came from the Malaysians themselves, but my impression, based on conversations with senior British officials at the time, suggests that it

44. Leigh, *The Rising Moon*, p. 61. The large number of independent candidates reflects the lack of party organization in certain areas. Many victorious independents quickly joined various parties, the great majority going to the Alliance.

45. Ibid., pp. 72–80. Here Leigh describes the complicated series of events that led to this apportionment—mainly the sudden rush of elected independents to join the Alliance bandwagon.

46. See Federation of Malaya, *Malaysia in Brief* (Kuala Lumpur: Department of Information, 1963).

is more probable that the British government persuaded the Tunku to promote the idea of Malaysia, first because of the possibility of a takeover in Singapore by the allegedly pro-Communist Barisan Sosialis, and second because of British desires to withdraw, gracefully as ever, from direct colonial rule in Southeast Asia.[47] Even so, the Malayan government could not be sanguine over the eventuality of a Communist-controlled Singapore in so close and so strategic a position, but would probably not have been willing to absorb Singapore unless the British Borneo territories were included to counterbalance the heavily preponderant Chinese population of that island city. It matters not, then from whom the original stimulus for Malaysia came—whether from Britain or Malaya—since both protagonists had valid motives for its creation.[48]

British Borneo

As already suggested, most local leaders in Sabah and Sarawak reacted strongly and adversely to the Tunku's first pronouncement ("Why should we," one leading Sabahan told me, "be forced to exchange one form of colonialism for another?"), but following a series of visits by Malayans to Borneo and vice versa, most were won over to the Malaysian cause; only the SUPP remained adamantly opposed. (There is no way of knowing whether the payoffs to Borneo leaders were psychological or material.) The next problem was to persuade the Borneo peoples themselves to embrace the proposals, and to this end a joint commission, appointed by the British and Malayan governments, was formed under the chairpersonship of Lord Cobbold, governor of the Bank of England.[49] The

47. A North Borneo government paper in January 1962 pointed to "two stark political facts which must be faced, namely the very real threat that Communism is presenting to Southeast Asia, and the turbulent and predatory nature of the world into which North Borneo, its independence accelerated as a consequence of the mounting strength of world opinion against Colonialism, would be plunged" (quoted in a speech by the British chief secretary in North Borneo to the Legislative Council, September 12, 1962).

48. Obviously, for political reasons, the Malayan government had to make the first public proposals.

49. Consultations regarding the terms for entrance to Malaysia had previously been held under the auspices of the Malaysian Solidarity Consultative Committee, comprised of representatives from the five governments concerned under the chairpersonship of Donald Stephens. There is some evidence to indicate that he was considerably influenced by Lee Kuan-yew, a firm proponent of Malaysia at this time.

Cobbold Commission traveled throughout Sabah and Sarawak in early 1962, endeavoring to ascertain the wishes of the inhabitants. Despite its "joint" nature, the commission was, as I personally became aware, a British contrivance, activated and organized by British officials. Prior to (and indeed following) the visit of the commission the population of Sabah and Sarawak was subjected to sustained pressure by British colonial officials (many of whom were able, through the strengths of their relationships with the local people, to exert a deal of moral suasion) to accept merger with Malaysia. British officials of all government departments were instructed to leave their offices, eschew paper work, and tour their respective areas of responsibility, "selling," as it were, Malaysia to the peoples therein.[50]

The Cobbold Commission issued its report in July 1962;[51] it stated that a majority of the inhabitants of British Borneo favored Malaysia. The commission assessed the evidence it collected as follows (the remarks in parentheses are based on my own analysis and experiences): (a) about one-third of the population in each territory (almost entirely Muslims) strongly favored early realization of Malaysia without too much concern about terms and conditions: (b) another third (mainly educated non-Muslims and Chinese), many of them favorable to the Malaysia project, asked, with varying degrees of emphasis, for conditions and safeguards; (c) the remaining third was divided between those who wanted independence first (mainly nonestablishment Chinese, such as those in the SUPP) and those who wanted British rule to continue for some years (mainly the less "sophisticated" interior non-Muslim hill peoples).[52]

Shortly afterward, because of repercussions from Indonesia and the Philippines (the former protesting a neocolonialist plot, the latter claiming the territory of North Borneo for herself), the

50. The simplistic argument I used with the hillpeople living in the Residency in which I was then stationed was that Sabah was an island of peace and stability in a sea of crocodiles (that is, Indonesia and the Philippines); only by merging with Malaya, Singapore, and Sarawak to form a new Federation of Malaysia could their future prosperity and security be assured.

51. Federation of Malaya, *Report of the Commission of Enquiry, North Borneo and Sarawak* (Kuala Lumpur: Government Printer, 1962).

52. Ibid., p. 30.

Malayan government asked the United Nations to send a commission to Sabah and Sarawak to confirm or disprove the accuracy of the Cobbold Commission's survey. This new commission visited Borneo in August and September 1963 and reported to U Thant, UN secretary-general, on September 14—with unseemly haste, it may be thought. U Thant consequently proclaimed that "there is no doubt about the wishes of a sizeable majority of the peoples of these territories to join in the Federation of Malaysia."[53] Unlike the Cobbold Commission, which had been a creature of the British, the UN commission's visit was engineered almost entirely by local politicians; so as to denude the visit of any semblance of colonial manipulation, British colonial officials were told to keep their distance, and they did. Wherever the UN commission traveled it was met by thousands of cheering, pro-Malaysia crowds (except in one or two SUPP-organized instances in Sarawak) whose members had been effectively mustered by the local political parties.

When the terms upon which Sabah and Sarawak would join Malaysia were announced, they were greatly favorable to those two territories. Sarawak was allocated twenty-four seats in the federal parliament and Sabah sixteen; special safeguards and guarantees granted a higher degree of latitude and individual autonomy than that enjoyed by other state components in the federation (apart from Singapore). Special privileges, identical to those extended to Malays in Malaya, were to be offered to all the indigenous peoples of Sabah and Sarawak, including non-Muslims.[54]

Brunei

The original Malaysian concept had included the British-protected sultanate of Brunei as an integral part of the federation. The sultan acquiesced, if in a lukewarm fashion, in the first proposals, but later refused to agree to the terms of entrance despite British and Malayan pressure. The reasons are twofold. First, sitting on top of a large, lucrative oil field and sheltered beneath the British strategic umbrella, the sultan felt no immediate imperative to enter

53. U Thant, in *United Nations Review*, 10 (October 1963), 15.
54. Events in Singapore that led up to the formation of Malaysia are described separately, insofar as they relate to Singapore's domestic politics as well as to relations with Kuala Lumpur.

Malaysia. Indeed the state had much to lose financially. Second, political events inside Brunei forced the autocratic sultan to take a closer look at the future of his sultanate. In 1956 a mercurial Malay-Arab living in Brunei, A. M. Azahari, formed a left-wing Malay party, the Partai Rakyat (People's Party) to further Azahari's romantic and grandiose vision of enlarging the Brunei sultanate to include all of its former territory in Sarawak and Sabah. A dynamic orator and organizer, Azahari soon gathered round him a group of young Malay militants dissatisfied with the painfully slow social progress allowed by the sultan, for although the revenues accrued by the state from oil made the sultanate extraordinarily wealthy, the conservative (and frequently corrupt) state government was not eager to see this money used to free the largely Malay population from its traditional restraints. The Partai Rakyat gained in strength and in 1962 succeeded in capturing all of the sixteen elected seats in the newly formed Legislative Council.

Unhappy with slow constitutional developments within the state, which remained mired in conservatism despite the Partai Rakyat's electoral successes, and alarmed at the threat posed by Brunei's possible entrance into Malaysia, Azahari and his associates started quiet but well-organized efforts to build a revolutionary base in order to overthrow the sultan and his government. Their endeavors spilled over into some neighboring areas of Sabah and Sarawak, where the residents had lived for years in isolation, totally neglected by the governments concerned. Azahari had also forged links with leftists in the SUPP and in Singapore, Malaya, and Indonesia and with one faction in the Philippines, but his main hopes were invested in Indonesia. In December 1962, Azahari and his followers erupted in open revolt, calling themselves the Tentera Nasional Kalimantan Utara (Northern Borneo National Army). Part of Azahari's forces were trained secretly in a base in Indonesian Borneo, and undoubtedly Azahari believed (or had been led to believe) that his revolt would receive Indonesian support and material reinforcements. These were not forthcoming, and after a brief initial period of success and confusion the revolt was extinguished by police from Sabah and British troops from Singapore. The casualties were minimal, but the political consequences severe. Arrests of hundreds of leftist supporters were carried out throughout British Borneo (especially in Brunei and Sarawak), Singapore, and Malaya, the Partai Rakyat was proscribed, and a prosultan Alliance Party organized in its stead. Azahari, safe in Manila when the revolt broke out, fled to Jakarta in February 1963. But the greatest consequence of the Brunei revolt was the refusal of the sultan to participate in Malaysia. The overt reasons for this demurral were reportedly the dispositions of oil revenues and the sultan's own precedence in relation to other sultans in the federation, but undoubtedly the shock of the revolt, engendered in part by the Malaysian proposals, was the key factor in his decision.

Indonesian Opposition to Malaysia: "*Konfrontasi*"

When the formation of Malaysia was announced, Indonesia (part of the so-called Peking-Jakarta axis at the time) vehemently opposed the concept as a neocolonialist plot, claiming that the new state was designed to inhibit the growth of a genuine nationalism in the region and to separate Indonesia geographically from her ally, the People's Republic of China. A policy of "*konfrontasi*" ("Confrontation") was pursued by Sukarno, verbally at first, moving into a military stage later. Attempts were made by the British and Malayan governments (plus a visit by Robert Kennedy on behalf of the U.S.) to assuage Indonesian anxieties, and at one stage, following the report of the United Nations mission, it was thought that Sukarno might accept Malaysia.

But the precipitate haste with which the official inauguration of Malaysia was announced (there was some confusion as to the actual date—for reasons of his own, Lee Kuan-yew in Singapore announced an earlier date than Kuala Lumpur had intended), coupled with some clumsy blundering by the British and Malayan governments in their inability to understand Sukarno's motives,[55] resulted in a resurgence of *konfrontasi*, this time in a more militant form—"*infiltrasi*"—infiltration of Malaysian territory by groups of armed Indonesians. Mass rallies were held in Jakarta and elsewhere in Indonesia, the Tunku was villified as a colonial *boneka* (puppet), and then burned in effigy. Armed marauders penetrated into Sabah

---

55. These were informed more by Indonesian nationalism than by any alleged international Communist plot.

and Sarawak and conducted guerrilla activities, terrorist bomb attacks were carried out in crowded areas in Singapore, and parachutists dropped into peninsular Malaya. In many instances— in Sarawak, Singapore, and Malaya, but not in Sabah—the Indonesian incursionists received assistance from local leftist groups, mainly Chinese but including some Malays, but this was not enough to ensure the success of the *"Ganjang Malaysia"* ("Crush Malaysia") campaign. If the British and Malayan governments had sadly underestimated the vehemence of Indonesian reaction to the establishment of Malaysia, the Indonesian government had failed to assess the attitudes of the population generally throughout Malaysia. Indonesian parachutists who landed in Malaya fully expected that the Malay peasantry would rise up in joint opposition to the British-inspired Malaysian plot. In fact the reverse happened. The Tunku was seen as the benevolent and successful father figure of *"Bapa Malaysia"* (that is, "the Father of Malaysia"), and far from inspiring mass opposition to Malaysia, the Indonesian adventure actually helped to cement pro-Malaysian solidarity. This was particularly true in British Borneo, many of whose inhabitants had firsthand knowledge of the economic and social havoc obtaining in Indonesia, and among the Chinese population generally, who were well aware of anti-Chinese repression in that country. Indonesian confrontation came to an end when Sukarno was toppled from power in the coup of September–October 1965, and thereafter relations with Malaysia followed a different course.

The Philippine Claim to North Borneo: Reaction to Malaysia

The basis for the Philippines' claim to the former British colony of North Borneo is to be found in the convoluted domestic politics in that country and need not be examined here. The claim was first given a trial run in 1962; it had not surfaced in any official form during the previous decades of British administration, although private attempts to further the claim had been made as early as the 1930s. Whatever the merits of the claim (and they do exist, notwithstanding the almost flippant circumstances that gave birth to the demands), their articulation led to an embitterment of previously amicable relations between Kuala Lumpur and Manila. Normal diplomatic intercourse was severed for a period, regional cooperation came to a temporary halt, and a residue of suspicion on both sides still remains.

The claim itself centers on a disputed document, made in 1878 between the sultan of Sulu and a representative of the British firm Dent Brothers, forerunners of the Chartered Company. This document nominally ceded title to Dent Brothers of a stretch of territory along the coast of North Borneo (it did not include the hinterland) in return for a small annual cash payment. The British, and subsequently the Malaysians, claimed that title to the land was ceded by the sultan and his heirs in perpetuity, while the Philippines held that the land was only leased on the basis of payment of an annual rental.[56] The dispute turns upon the translation of a Malay-Arabic work (*"pajak"*) in the native version of the 1878 document. The word is ambivalent inasmuch as it may be used to denote both "lease" and "cede" (the English-language document made at the time states categorically that the land was ceded "forever and until the end of time"), but the matter has never been placed before the World Court or any other judicial body and has thus never been resolved in a legal sense. Whatever the legal nuances involved in the claim, it was obvious that political leaders and the vast majority of the peoples of Sabah strenuously objected to the notion that they might be incorporated into that volatile political system known as the Philippines. Manila applied pressure on the infant state of Malaysia—some psychological, some more physical (Philippine air force planes flew over Sabah territory on several instances, for example)—but Kuala Lumpur stood firm, refusing to accede to Manila's demands.

Malaysia formally came into being on September 16, 1963, when a series of ceremonies were held throughout Malaya, Singapore, Sarawak, and Sabah. Indonesia and the Philippines immediately broke off diplomatic relations, and the former instituted a serious military campaign against Malaysia—surely an ominous set of circumstances for the transition from political embryo to reality. The Malaysian government soon found, however, that partial disintegration was to stem from internal, rather than external, strains.

56. For fuller details of the dispute see B. K. Gordon, *The Dimensions of Conflict in Southeast Asia* (Englewood Cliffs: Prentice-Hall, 1966), chap. 1.

Less than two years later Singapore was summarily ejected from the Federation of Malaysia (see below for an account of this event) as the result of a series of differences too fundamental to overcome. Sabah and Sarawak had not been consulted over Singapore's abrupt departure, and many leaders in the Borneo territories were openly unhappy over the ouster, several calling for renewed negotiations regarding their position in Malaysia. Donald Stephens even resigned from office.[57] Despite all the alarums and excursions, the tumult and the shouting, that surrounded Singapore's abrupt demise as a partner in the Malaysian enterprise, the new, smaller federation proved strong enough to maintain its political integrity intact, even though a series of shocks were yet to come.

57. There was some talk of a partitioned Malaysia, with Singapore, Sarawak, and Sabah, plus perhaps Malacca and Penang, forming their own federation. Intense pressure from Kuala Lumpur and from Britain and Australia quickly stifled any Bornean movement in this direction. (One Sabah informant told me that the Tunku had offered Stephens the post of ambassador to the Vatican as an inducement, Stephens being a devout Catholic at the time.) In 1971, I was told by a leading People's Action Party cabinet minister that Stephens had "let the PAP down" over Singapore's secession by refusing to participate more militantly in the Malaysian Solidarity Convention.

3 | The Contemporary Setting

The Economy

Malaysia is generally regarded as a successful case of economic development.[1] But insofar as the economic system helps define political configurations this statement needs to be qualified, for development (or the level of participation in the economy) means different things to each ethnic component, which in turn affects the way ethnic groups interact within the political system. Differentiated rates of economic participation of the Malays, the Chinese, and the Indians and of the towns and the countryside have had profound effects on political relationships, lending strength to ethnic passions and the violence that has followed.

One beneficial legacy of British rule was that the well-developed economic and administrative infrastructure was left in place. Road and rail communications are excellent (except in Sabah and Sarawak), among the best in Asia. Sound educational facilities are available to all those near urban areas, most towns and villages have electric power, and the telecommunications network is efficient. Prior to the arrival of the British, the economy of the Malay states was peasant-agrarian in nature: wet-rice and cash-crop farming and considerable fishing. The British rapidly changed the whole character of the economy by introducing commercial agriculture in the form of rubber and by taking over (with the assistance of the Chinese) and expanding a small native tin-mining industry. Malaya soon became the world's foremost exporter of natural rubber and tin, a position she holds to the present. Since independence in 1957

1. Wolfgang Kasper, *Malaysia: A Study in Successful Economic Development* (Washington, D.C.: American Enterprise Institute for Public Policy Research, 1974), p. 1.

(1963 for Sarawak and Sabah) a policy of diversification[2] and industrialization has been pursued, but rubber and tin remain the major products for the present, with petroleum and associated products looming in the background. Table 3 shows the value of products at the end of 1974.

Table 3. Malaysian economy, 1974

Product	Value in $M	Percentage
Rubber	2882	30
Timber	1272	13
Tin	1408	15
Palm oil	1022	11
Petroleum	940	10
Other	2056	21
	$M9580 million	100

SOURCE: *FEER*, January 10, 1975, p. 31.
Note: $M2.48 equals one U.S. dollar.

By the end of 1973, Malaysia's economy was sound in terms of overall GNP statistics, and foreign capital investment continued to flow into the country.[3] By the end of 1974 and the start of 1975, however, the international recession began to be felt, and imbalances in the economy started to manifest themselves in a political as well as in an economic sense. The reasons are clear. As demonstrated earlier, historically the Malays had been sheltered from the competitive ethos of the marketplace both by British colonial policy and their own traditional value system. By 1970, despite thirteen years of independence and Malay political power, Malays were still not sharing proportionally in the state's economy, as Table 4 indicates.

The preponderance of Malays in the agricultural and public (utilities, transport/communication, services) sectors contrasts strongly with the percentage of Chinese employed in mining, commerce, manufacturing, and construction. The figures are even more striking when one looks at Tables 5, 6, and 7.

2. Palm oil has now become a major primary product. Others, new or expanded, include timber, cocoa, pineapples, and pepper. Rice production has also expanded to the degree that Malaysia today is almost self-sufficient.

3. James Morgan, "Malaysia: Strong Dollar Brings in Capital Flow," *London Times* (International Supplement), September 24, 1973.

Table 4. Employment by race and sector in West Malaysia, 1970 (in percentages)

	Malays	Chinese	Indians	Others
Agriculture	67.6	21.4	10.1	0.9
Mining	24.8	66.0	7.1	0.8
Manufacturing	28.9	65.4	5.3	0.4
Construction	21.7	72.1	6.0	0.2
Utilities	48.5	18.0	32.3	1.4
Transport/Communications	42.6	39.6	17.1	0.7
Commerce	23.5	65.3	10.7	0.5
Services	48.5	35.7	14.0	1.8

SOURCE: Mid-term Review of Second Malaysia Plan, quoted in *FEER*, December 3, 1973.

Table 5. Distribution of households by income and race, Western Malaysia, 1970 (in percentages)

Income range per month	Malays	Chinese	Indians	Others	Total
$M1–99	22.9	2.6	1.3	0.2	27.1
100–199	19.1	7.8	4.4	0.1	31.4
200–399	10.4	11.9	3.5	0.1	25.9
400–699	3.0	5.3	1.2	0.1	9.6
700–1499	1.1	2.9	0.6	0.1	4.7
1500–2999	0.2	0.7	0.1	0.1	1.1
3000+	trace	0.1	0.1	0.1	0.3
Total	56.7	31.3	11.2	0.8	100.0

Table 6. Ownership of assets in modern agriculture and industry, Western Malaysia, 1970 (in percentages)

Ownership	Modern agriculture		Industry	
	Corporate sector	Noncorporate sector	Corporate sector	Noncorporate sector
All Malaysians:	29.2	94.1	42.8	97.4
Malay	0.3	47.1	0.9	2.3
Chinese	25.9	32.8	26.2	92.2
Indian	0.3	10.1	0.1	2.3
Others	2.7	1.8	14.3	0.1
Government	—	2.3	1.3	—
Non Malaysians	70.8	5.9	57.2	2.4

Table 7. Ownership of share capital of limited companies by race and sector, Western Malaysia, 1970 (in percentages)

	Malays	Chinese	Indians	Foreign
Agriculture, forestry, fishing 0.9	22.4	01.	75.3	
Mining	0.7	16.8	0.4	72.4
Manufacturing	2.5	22.0	0.7	59.6
Construction	2.2	52.8	0.8	24.1
Transport/Communications	13.3	43.4	2.3	12.0
Commerce	0.8	30.4	0.7	63.5
Banking/insurance	3.3	24.3	0.6	52.2
Other	2.3	37.8	2.3	31.4
Total	1.9	22.5	1.0	60.7

The balance of share capital is held by the federal and state governments.

Source of Tables 5, 6, and 7: H. Stockwin, "A Racial Balance Sheet," *FEER*, December 3, 1973.

Two salient facts emerge from the figures given in these tables: first, again, they show how little the majority population of Malays share in the more lucrative sectors of the economy and how badly they lag behind other communities in terms of income distribution, and second, although the Chinese share of the economic cake is many times larger than the Malay portion, the biggest slice of all goes to foreign investors.

The federal government has long been aware of these anomalies. The First Malaysia Plan, formulated in 1963, generated much economic development, but did little to correct inequities among ethnic groups apart from creating a handful of wealthy Malays. Most educated Malays were able to climb the ladder of socioeconomic success only in the public service. Yet politicization of Malays, including those resident in rural areas, proceeded steadily as the ruling Alliance (especially the UMNO segment) sought to expand its political base, a process that heightened economic expectations as well as increasing political consciousness. One observer in a recent study of politicization in a Malay village has commented:

Since independence, the villages have looked increasingly to the government to provide educational and job opportunities for Malays, the best-educated men wanting the government to ensure more Malay employment in business and commerce. However, there has been a growing gap between the Malays' economic desires and achievements. Since 1945 [even more so since independence] they have experienced mounting frustrations as a result of rising material aspirations, increasing competition with Chinese, and growing realization of the extent of Malay backwardness in comparison with the relative affluence of the immigrant communities. These developments have increased the salience of politics.[4]

These pressures created the interethnic violence that exploded in the bloody race riots in Kuala Lumpur in May 1969.[5] After a period of reflection and reappraisal, the government instituted the Second Malaysia Plan, designed to have a greater impact in shaping the Malaysian economy in the direction of ethnic equality.

The aims of the Second Malaysia Plan are ambitious and are political as well as economic: "National unity is the over-riding objective of the country. A stage has been reached in the nation's economic and social development where greater emphasis must be placed on social integration and more equitable distribution of income and opportunities for national unity and progress." The long-range goal is no less than the complete restructuring of Malaysian society in order to correct the ethnically defined economic disproportionment, at the same time eradicating poverty among all Malaysians regardless of ethnic origin. The former phrase clearly is directed at the Malay community, for it envisages a process involving "the modernization of rural life, a rapid and balanced growth of urban activities and the creation of a Malay commercial and industrial community in all categories and at all levels of operations, so that Malays and other indigenous people will become full partners in all aspects of the economic life of the nation."[6]

4. Marvin Rogers, "The Politicization of Malay Villagers," *Comparative Politics*, 7 (January 1975), 205–225.

5. Chinese-instigated riots had broken out in Penang in November 1967 as a result of financial losses suffered through the British devaluation of the pound. The Chinese reaction was further provoked by the Malayan government's refusal to absorb part of the losses so incurred, which exacerbated the effects of devaluation. The Malayan government thus passed its own losses on to the people, and the hardest hit inevitably were the Chinese. The riots evoked a Malay response; group violence in Malaysia often provokes interethnic conflict, no matter what the original issues are.

6. Government Malaysia, *Second Malaysia Plan 1971–1975* (Kuala Lumpur: Government Printer, 1971), p. 1.

The problem obviously is to raise the socioeconomic standards of Malays without interfering too much in a delicately honed economy and without depriving the Chinese community of any of its existing share of the economy; to this end "no particular group will experience any loss or feel any sense of deprivation." The plan implies a high degree of social engineering in addition to economic planning if Malays are to participate in all sectors of the economy; through increased educational opportunities and the modernization of rural life[7] Malays are to be persuaded to loosen old ties, to question traditional values, and "to search for new sources of meaning and understanding, particularly among the youth of the society." In view of the preponderance of Malays living in rural areas, the plan places a major emphasis on achieving a balance between the urban and rural sectors by providing amenities "of as good a quality in the rural areas as in the urban areas" and by utilizing modern techniques of agriculture and the financing thereof. Malaysia's future as an ethnically tolerant society perhaps rests on the success or failure of the Plan because it attempts to come to grips with the basic problems that for so long have bedeviled the body politic. If the plan is only partially successful in its objective of raising the position of the Malays in relation to other communities, then some of the ever-present ethnic tensions may be reduced to tolerable limits.[8]

Approximately one-half of planned investment generated through the Second Malaysia Plan (or the New Economic Policy as it is often called) is aimed at developing the rural sector of the economy—a decision obviously made on the basis of political imperatives, of the necessity of satisfying the urgency of Malay economic expectations, as much if not more than economic planning. But industrial-commercial development in the urban sector is also stressed as a major means through which Malaysia hopes to diversify an economy previously patterned along the lines of colonial dualism and concerned mainly with the exploitation of pri-

---

7. One problem here is the high rate of absentee landlordism in Malay wet-rice landholding patterns. See Government of Malaysia, *Second Malaysia Plan*, p. 39.

8. I do not believe that economic equality alone can resolve the problems of ethnicity; psychological considerations, too, stand in the way of the creation of a genuine Malaysian identity, if this is indeed ever to emerge.

mary products. Many new factories have sprung up in Western Malaysia, chiefly in the industrial estates and satellite towns around Kuala Lumpur.[9] The majority of the factories are not large; they function in the field of light manufacturing (the processing of local products, assembly plants, and the like) and represent subsidiaries of the multinational corporations. There has been, subsequently, a movement of rural residents, Malays more than non-Malays, to the cities, and this has brought about its own problems—primarily (but not only) those of underemployment and unemployment. As will be suggested below, there is a pronounced Malay predilection in favor of white-collar work and against blue-collar work. When one considers that the level of Malay education in urban areas has risen rapidly over the past decade or so, the problem of finding adequate white-collar employment for these educated Malays leaps quickly into focus. Under- and unemployment in the urban sector remains high among non-Malays as well as Malays, a potential flash point amid an already volatile situation.

The Society

There can be little doubt, as indicated on numerous occasions in this study, that the dimensions of the problems facing Malaysia are measured by the extent of ethnic diversity. Table 8 provides population figures at the end of 1968.

Ethnic diversity alone, needless to say, does not necessarily provoke intergroup conflict; but when ethnic value systems[10] are seen by the protagonists to be mutually incompatible within the same political system and when socioeconomic differences are demarcated by ethnic boundaries, diversity is sharpened to the fine edge of antipathy and often violence. All communities in Malaysia, to

9. The government had hoped to regionalize industry, bringing it into less-developed areas. These much-publicized schemes have not been too successful, inasmuch as foreign investors have been unwilling to move into the designated areas, some of them on the jungle fringe where labor is unreliable and electricity and communications inadequate for industrial purposes. See *NYT*, September 9, 1975.

10. By "value-system" is meant a set of referents that help to define an ethnic or cultural organism, that is, "in every society there is generally an agreed upon set of moral standards and value orientations that serve to guide choices and influence thought and behavior." (Philip Olson, *The Study of Modern Society: Perspectives from Classical Sociology* [New York: Random House, 1970], p. 55).

Table 8. Population by ethnic groups, Malaysia, 1968

	Malays	Chinese	Indians[a]	Others[b]	All ethnic groups
West Malaysia					
Perak	687,404	739,905	248,167	26,397	1,701,873
Selangor	443,875	698,492	286,607	48,561	1,477,535
Johore	675,450	544,720	100,638	31,697	1,352,505
Kedah	655,279	193,610	90,927	24,129	963,945
Penang	225,706	443,254	92,923	16,864	778.747
Kelantan	644,458	38,837	8,329	11,858	703,482
Negri Sembilan	225,724	211,892	80,216	12,950	530,782
Pahang	254,652	152,454	32,868	5,505	445,479
Malacca	216,616	168,201	34,677	8,650	428,144
Trengganu	365,004	23,545	4,832	1,290	394,671
Perlis	93,945	21,821	2,203	3,898	121,867
Total	4,488,113	3,236,731	982,387	191,799	8,899,030
East Malaysia					
Sabah[d]	[e]	135,710	[e]	486,770	622,480
Sarawak[d]	170,698	309,610	[e]	453,301	933,609
Total	[c]	445,320	[c]	940,071	1,556,089
Total state of Malaysia	[c]	3,682,051	[c]	1,131,870	10,455,119

[a] Includes those who originally came from Ceylon and what is now Pakistan.

[b] Mainly Eurasians, Europeans, Australians, New Zealanders, Americans, Arabs, Thais, etc.

[c] Not available.

[d] Estimated Population at Mid-1968 + Migration surplus + Excess of Births over Deaths.

[e] Included under "Others."

SOURCE: Malaysia, *Annual Bulletin of Statistics, Malaysia 1969* (Kuala Lumpur: Department of Statistics, 1970).

some degree, hold stereotypes of each other through which their perceptions and their behavior toward each other are filtered. As with most stereotypes, one or two meager grains of truth are transplanted into a seedbed of ignorance and hatred. Yet the existence of differences between ethnic groups in Malaysia cannot be denied, and an attempt at description must be made—one hopes not at the expense of maintaining stereotypes.[11]

11. A classic stereotype perpetuated by a British colonial police commissioner is reflected in Rene Onraet's statement that "generally speaking the Malays squat, the Indians labour, and the Chinese work." See his *Singapore—Police Background* (London: Crisp, 1947), p. 13.

The Malays

The British colonial stereotype of the Malays (an ethnic community for whom the British in fact felt much empathy and attraction) suggested that while Malays were "nature's gentlemen," they lacked responsibility, could never make decisions, were superstitious, had few ambitions, and were basically lazy.[12] It is not the intention here to dignify the myth of the "lazy native," which by now has been effectively dispelled, as it ought. For such an analysis is superficial in the extreme, yet it is subscribed to (perhaps even more condescendingly) by many Chinese. It fails to consider the social and economic history of the Malays and their reactions to an environment often beyond their control (certainly in the colonial days) and changing with sometimes bewildering rapidity.

Two pervasive cultural strains help shape the Malay value system and behavior: traditional custom, or *adat*, and Islam. Often the two are inextricably intertwined, so that *adat* is perceived to be a genuine part of Islam,[13] when this may not be the case. *Adat* tends to be more significant among poorly educated Malay villagers, giving rise to certain tensions and anomalies. Ritual practices, including propitiatory ceremonies directed toward a pantheon of spirits, observance of the Islamic lunar calendar, physical enervation due to the month-long Ramadan fast,[14] all are necessary to the integrity of rural Malay culture as it is presently constituted, but they inhibit the introduction of more sophisticated agricultural practices. Another well-documented Malay trait is profligacy in spending and inability to accumulate capital; one observer has noted that "the typical Malay peasant maintains a precarious balance between income and consumption" and suggests that one reason may lie in the absence of class differences among the bulk of the Malay population which has led to an intense concern with *malu*, or shame. Status is expressed through the possession of

12. See for instance J. Ruth Crandall, "Social Customs of Malays," in *Sociology and Social Research*, 12 (July-August 1928), 567–572. She states that "*tidapa* ('never mind') is the keyword to the Malay psychology. . . . If the Mexican lives in tomorrow, the Malay lives in *lusa*, the day after tomorrow."

13. See Mahathir Mohammed, "Interaction: Integration," in *Intisari*, 1 (1963), 38–44.

14. Lim Joo-hock, "Tradition and Peasant Agriculture in Malaya," *Malayan Journal of Tropical Geography*, 3 (October 1954), 44–47.

consumer goods which results in a vicious circle of keeping up with one's neighbors.[15]

Another aspect of this improvidence has been ascribed to *rezeki*, or fate. *Rezeki*, in its economic aspect, has been defined[16] as a divinely determined economic lot, a marked fatalism that induces both an inability to accept temporary setbacks and a lack of will to go on striving. God controls all destinies and determines all daily acts; there is no way of altering or fighting against fate. One Malay author describes this attitude in a novel: "Each person who comes into this world has his fate, his *rezeki*. God has predetermined this fate, the consequences of which will reach even unto a man's grandchildren. The means of seeking one's livelihood is in the hands of God. It is all the will of Almighty Allah."[17] Whatever the reasons, heavy spending—and the consequent indebtedness—to finance weddings, ritual *kenduris* or feasts, religious occasions, and other events is an accepted fact of Malay life against which Malay reformers have long fulminated. The president of the Religious Affairs Department in Kuala Lumpur in his *Hari Raya Puasa* (End of Ramadan celebration) message in 1960 made a strong appeal to Malays not to be too lavish in their spending so as not to go into debt. They should instead, he urged, save money, especially for their children's education. Islam preaches moderation, and festivals should not be "overcelebrated."[18]

There is no one reason for the present socioeconomic position of the Malays. The grinding mills of history and the atavistic pressures of a social value system rooted in a rural past contribute to present reality. One Malay scholar, Syed Hussein Alatas, has suggested that the *gemeinschaft* of the Malay peasantry inhibits self-confidence about "the mastery of nature, entrepreneurship, and invention";

15. M. G. Swift, "Economic Organization and Malay Peasantry," in Maurice Freeman, ed., *Social Organization* (London: 1967), pp. 241–269. A study by a Malay scholar supports Swift's contention regarding the pressures applied to conform to village tradition: A. Wahab Alwee, *Rembau: A Study in Integration and Conflict in a Village in Negri Sembilan, Malaya* (Perth: University of Western Australia, 1967).

16. M. G. Swift, *Malay Peasant Society in Jelebu* (London: Athlone, 1965), pp. 29–30.

17. Shahnon Ahmad, *Ranjau Sa-panjang Jalan* (*Pitfalls All Along the Way*) (Kuala Lumpur: Utusan Melayu Press, 1966), p. 5. Translation is my own.

18. *MM*, March 24, 1960.

reliance on magicoanimistic practices also exerts an adverse effect on the emergence of a scientific explanation regarding one's environment, as does a similar set of attitudes stemming from "passive resignation and self-reproach." Naturally the cumulative effects of these tendencies "converge to form an inhibition towards economic development."[19] In another article, the same writer traces the effects of Malay feudalism on the grading of occupational prestige among Malays and concludes that because of the value system promoted by the Malay aristocracy—and reinforced by the effects of British colonial policy—professional and business occupations are graded lower than employment in government service. The result has been that "the persistence of the traditional feudal outlook on occupational prestige has hampered the occupational diversification of the educated class of Malays." In Malay feudal society, the grading of occupational prestige was derived from association with the sultans and the aristocracy, resulting in an emphasis on "clean hands" in the type of occupation desired, and ipso facto, an aversion to manual labor (including blue-collar work), among other consequences[20] —hardly motivations compatible with the modernizing imperatives of the Second Malaysia Plan.

Insofar as Islam is concerned, there has long been a rift between conservatives (perhaps fundamentalists is a better word) and reformers, with the existing Malaysian government officially espousing and actively propagating the reformist view. The fundamentalist elements in Islam in Malaysia view the world in holistic terms; a knowledge of the teachings and jurisprudence of Islam is all that is required to lead its adherents through this life to the most important destination—the *akhirat*, or the life hereafter. Man is fated by God's will and grace to receive a predestined reward or punishment in the hereafter; nothing he does in this life, no material success that he is able to achieve, will bear upon his

19. Syed Hussein Alatas, "Collective Representations and Economic Development," *Kajian Ekonomi Malaysia* (*Malaysian Economic Research*), 2 (Kuala Lumpur, June 1965).

20. Syed Hussein Alatas, "The Grading of Occupational Prestige amongst Malays in Malaysia" *Journal of the Malayan Branch of the Royal Asiatic Society*, 41 (Kuala Lumpur, 1968).

ultimate lot unless it is God's will. Such an attitude stands in diametric contrast to the teachings of the reformers who reject the doctrine of predetermination; nothing in Islam, they claim, denies that a person's relationship to God can be affected by hard work (leading to material success) and selfdetermination—provided, of course that each Muslim fulfills his or her obligations of daily prayers, the *Haj* pilgrimage, and the payment of religious tithes. Alatas—an outspoken reformer—scathingly sums up the ills perpetrated on Malay society by the fundamentalist viewpoint:

Unfortunately the Islamic intellectual spirit . . . has to contend with formidable forces of psychological feudalism and obscurantism. Unless the younger generation, particularly the students, learn to imbibe the genuine Islamic spirit, the forces of reaction . . . will continue to distort the development of Islam in this region as they have done in the past, by devoting attention to the trivial, by reviving archaic mythologies characterized by total intellectual poverty, by association with magic and atavistic cults, by entrusting the affairs of Islam in the hands of those whose ignorance of Islam is matched by their ignorance of modern science.[21]

An example of what Alatas is talking about came to light in 1960, when a Malay journalist investigating teachings in a rural mosque found that faith in Islam was bolstered by a vision of magnificent palaces in the hereafter on one hand and a glimpse of the eternal fires of purgatory on the other. The essence of teaching by the uneducated village *imam* was that this world was one of transition and of no consequence to the good Muslim, meant only for the unbelievers.[22]

I do not wish to imply that Malay society is ossified by its past and unable to come to terms with its future. The Malay proverb *"biar mati anak, jangan mati adat"* ("better the death of one's child than the death of one's *adat*") is being strongly assailed by the government and by educated Malays. Within Malay society, both urban and rural, the pressures of social change are intense. Change appears to be taking place at different rates within the Malay community, but it is nevertheless occurring at all levels throughout Malay society. In rural areas the educational process in particular is causing a generation gap between young and old. For the older generation, swad-

21. Lecture to the University of Singapore Muslim Society, September 10, 1971.
22. *Sunday Mail*, August 28, 1960.

dled in the confines of *adat* custom and used to unquestioning obedience from the young, most of their behavior is controlled by tradition and they are reluctant to change. The better-educated younger generation, however, is beginning to question the old ways and is receiving new sets of value directions from the educational process[23] and from an effective government communications network.

Social change among Malays is more pronounced in urban areas, where the members of a steadily increasing middle class have accepted universalistic values concerned with the logic and science of modernity.[24] This urban Malay middle class is at once becoming an adapter (and introducer) of non-Malay ways as well as a role model for urban and rural lower-class Malays. Islam is far from being the inhibiting factor many casual observers impute it to be when given a modernist, or reformist, interpretation, for it can at once provide an impetus for change and prevent the erosion of social cohesion that often accompanies unordered change. Indeed, as one reformer has suggested, Islam has introduced "a highly intellectual and rationalistic religious spirit" into the receptive minds of a people previously immured in the superstition and obscurantism of animistic magic.[25] For its part, the government in Kuala Lumpur is steadfastly publicizing reformist policies, especially in the areas of birth control and the reconciliation of capitalism with certain contradictory Islamic beliefs. Whether all these cultural crosscurrents will result in the emergence of a Malay society able to participate fully in the modern sector of Malaysia's socioeconomic life is yet to be determined, but on this circumstance hinges the future of *bumiputera* attitudes toward Chinese, Indians, and others—and ultimately perhaps the very existence of Malaysia in its present form.

Yet at the same time one must ask what adverse effects, in long-range terms, will the government's efforts at social engineering and the well-nigh irresistible dynamism of external change in

23. See A. Wahab Alwee, *Rembau*, pp. 45–51.
24. S. Husin Ali, "A Note on Malay Society and Culture," in S. T. Alisjahbana, S. T. Nayagam, and Wang Gungwu, eds., *The Cultural Problems of Malaysia in the Context of Southeast Asia* (Kuala Lumpur: Malaysian Society of Orientalists, 1965), pp. 65–74.
25. S. Naguib Alatas, "The Islamic Cult in Malaysia," in ibid., pp. 123–130.

the Malaysian environment have on Malay culture? How will the advance of "modernity" (especially in its grossest materialistic sense) affect the more gentle and tolerant aspects of the Malay personality? Unless the value change sought by the government is of a positive nature (that is, the process of change retains certain traditions that make the Malays cohere as a cultural community) and is not too rapidly and too traumatically implemented from without, the resultant uncertainty may lead to some hideous, bastardized set of life styles embodying the worst of "modern" (or Western) culture, giving rise at best to apathy, at worst to downright alienation. The conversion of the Malays to the leadership's vision of modernity, if it is to be achieved, will not take place overnight; in the meantime the Malays may be left culturally rootless, with no compensatory values or justifications for the new existence they must endure.

The Chinese

I have dealt at length with Malay values because I believe that, in view of the political hegemony of the Malays and their control over the coercive forces of the state, their perceptions and behavior are the most important ingredients contributing to the success or otherwise of Malaysia. There is no such problem with the Chinese, at least as it relates to value change, for the community has made the transition from traditionalism to modernity with a minimum of social upheaval. Chinese problems lie in other areas, ambivalent political attitudes toward the Malaysian state being of the greatest saliency. For the Chinese are faced with this contradiction: how can they maintain their identity as Chinese (derived from a culture that is one of the richest and the proudest in the history of the world) with their political need to be considered as first-class Malaysian citizens, loyal to the state and essentially supportive of the government's policies? Already many Chinese, through the process of an English education, have lost an essential part of their Chinese heritage and, certainly before the savage race riots of May 1969, were prepared to look inward to Malaysia as their permanent home. The very fact of their "Chineseness," however, renders their avowed loyalty to Malaysia suspicious in the eyes of many Malays, and these political perceptions are reinforced by nonpolitical images.

The British, with a few "eccentric" exceptions, were often uncomfortable in their dealings with the Chinese, seeing in them a competitive ethos the equal of their own and a cultural history they could not understand. They saw the Chinese as unscrupulous merchants whose word was less than their bond—hardworking, yes; but potentially disloyal (to the Crown) and, for the most part, uncouth.[26] Malays generally share most of these stereotypes (adding some of their own), viewing Chinese as offensively unclean (an untrue image fostered entirely by the Chinese predilection for rearing pigs and eating pork—to most Muslims an emotional symbol of repugnance), as unreliable in interpersonal transactions, as exploiters of the Malay peasantry, as materialistic sybarites, and, significantly, as alien transients whose loyalty is directed outward toward a Communist China looming threateningly off stage.

The Chinese, of course, find these strictures unjustified. Arriving in the country as impoverished immigrants, inured by conditions in China to the famines and pestilences of natural disasters and the inequities of political chaos, they view life, in part, as a struggle for survival. Yet they sustain themselves by the richness of Chinese culture and secure their identity through a network of social obligations centering on family, clan, village, and dialect group, in that order. They consider that through the sweat of their collective brow the Chinese brought economic prosperity to an erstwhile backward country and for that reason alone they deserve a political stake in Malaysia. As Tan Siew-sin (former finance minister and leader of the MCA) once stated, "The greatest assets in our [Chinese] possession are our own qualities, our vigour, our resourcefulness, our capacity for hard work and our other qualities which make for progress and achievement."[27]

26. Some person once remarked that throughout the colonial empire, the British loved only those of their subjects who wore "fancy dress"! In other words, the British felt at ease with those who shared their own love of ritual and ceremony—like the Malays. Most Chinese who came to Malaya eschewed such fancy frills and trappings.

27. Speech on Chinese unity, Seremban, March 14, 1971, reported in the *ST*, March 15, 1971.

Chinese acceptance into Malaysian society, apart from the aforementioned Malay perceptions of them, has been hindered by two factors. First, for a variety of reasons, the British historically preferred that the Chinese govern themselves, almost as a nation inside a nation. Chinese communities appointed their own representatives (known as *Kapitan China*, or Chinese Captains), meted out their own sanctions, formed their own secret societies—still a pervasive menace on the Malaysian scene—and organized and financed their own Chinese-language schools. Second, the Chinese are by no means a monolithic community, but are riven by fissures along the lines of dialect groups (Hokkien, Teochew, Hakka, Cantonese, and Hainan) as well as political configurations. Many dialect and clan groups and the secret societies perpetuate the ethnocentricity of Chinese chauvinism[28] and inhibit the emergence of a Malaysian outlook—to say nothing of fostering an inability to speak with one voice when bargaining with Malays at a political level. These factors, however, are becoming less potent under the influence of the Malaysian educational system.

Far from all being wealthy capitalists and exploiters, many poor Chinese make up an urban proletariat and are rural farmers and smallholders. (Milton J. Esman has estimated, for example, that 50 percent of Chinese live outside the larger cities.) Many of the Chinese urban proletariat earn only about U.S. $30 per month when they can find work: "They are poor and often embittered, and from their ranks the secret society criminals and the Communists recruit their numbers."[29] In the countryside the situation is just as desperate for many Chinese, although without the urgency that accompanies urban alienation. Resettlement of scattered Chinese squatters and farmers during the Emergency resulted in new settlement patterns known as New Villages. By the end of 1954 over a half-million Chinese had been resettled in a total

28. As a Chinese-language student for two years in a school in Malaya, I learned a polite Chinese phrase that involved asking a new acquaintance, "Where is your ancestral village? [in China]" The majority of respondents knew exactly where this was, even though their family may have been resident in Malaya for several generations.

29. Milton J. Esman, *Administration and Development in Malaysia* (Ithaca, N.Y.: Cornell University Press, 1972), p. 48.

of 438 New Villages.[30] The majority of these settlements still exist, and the problems they face (and those of other Chinese rural inhabitants) are accentuated by an increasing lack of availability of land for non-Malays, especially as the population increases. The allocation of land is controlled by a Malay-dominated bureaucracy, and it remains an emotional issue with Malays and a frustrating obstacle to the basic needs of non-Malay (especially Chinese) farmers. No Malay bureaucrat today can allocate a piece of public land to a non-Malay without raising an outcry from local Malay politicians, who see all such land as the exclusive domain of the Malays. ("You control the economy," they imply to the Chinese, "allow us at least ownership of the land, the womb [*tanah tumpah darah*, the place where our blood issued forth] of our ancestors.") The resulting non-Malay dissatisfaction with an inability to acquire land can be readily understood.

The wealth and conspicuous consumption of a large and conservative Chinese elite and the middle class that feeds upon them, however, continues to exercise Malay sensitivities, along with the fear of loyalties extending to the MCP and outward toward China.[31] The statistics given in the previous section show definitively the imbalance in allocation of economic rewards between Malays and Chinese as groups; this inequality will persist in real and symbolic terms for a considerable period to come. Efforts by the government, no matter how well-intentioned, to rectify economic anomalies are bound to have an effect on Chinese youths, many of them well-educated but without a secure economic future. These youths, male and female, will not be content with the old trade-off of Chinese economic dominance at an elite level in return for Malay political power. Just as Malay youths are clamoring for more economic power, their Chinese counterparts are

30. See Anthony Short, *The Communist Insurrection in Malaya, 1948–1960* (New York: Crane Russak, 1975), p. 184n, and Ooi Jin-bee, *Land, People and Economy in Malaya* (London: Longmans, Green, 1963), pp. 167–169.

31. This impression was reinforced in 1971, when a visiting cultural troupe from the Peoples' Republic of China was mobbed by thousands of enthusiastic Malaysian Chinese wherever the troupe appeared. See Jackie Sam, "Appearance of Silver Star Troupe in K. L. is More Diversive than Unifying." *NN*, April 2, 1971.

becoming increasingly politicized and not disposed to suffer the status of less than first-class citizenship. (It should be remarked in parentheses, however, that there are many moderate Chinese spokespersons who publicly advocate that the Chinese community must be patient and less economically aggressive, so that the Malays might have a chance to catch up with them.)

The Indians

It is not the intention of this study to denigrate the important role of the Indian population in the political and economic development of Malaysia, but it is a plain fact that they are not such an inherent part of interethnic conflict as is Malay-Chinese hostility. The term "Indian," although accepted widely throughout Malaysia, is inaccurate, for it includes Tamils, Sikhs, Gujeratis, Pakistanis, Banglas from Bangladesh, and Ceylonese, among others.[32] Like the Chinese, Indians were brought to Malaysia chiefly as immigrant labor in the interests of colonial commercial exploitation and, like the Chinese, many of them have been able to break out of the manual labor mold to become lawyers, doctors, other professionals, journalists, and politicians. A substantial percentage, however, remain in the working-class sector of the population (in 1957 almost half the Indian working population was employed on rubber estates). Indian workers dominate also in government services, such as the railways and the public works department. In the cities a wealthy middle class—Muslim and Chettiar—control the textile and moneylending fields. As in India, those Indians who subscribe to the Hindu religion (the great majority of Malaysian Indians) remain embedded in a rigid caste system, and this in turn shapes employment patterns and stultifies ambitions. There is some evidence, however, that a better-educated younger generation is no longer so fettered by the confines of caste.

At an elite level the Indians, with their innate flair for political participation, are well represented in Malaysian politics; several

32. The Tamils form the majority of these subgroups. An estimated one million Indians lived in Malaysia at the end of 1967. Only a handful live in Eastern Malaysia, and in Western Malaysia most are concentrated on the west coast.

Indians from the MIC hold cabinet posts. But the MIC is representative only of a small wealthy class of Indians, and a substantial majority are believed to support left-wing parties—at least they have in the past in terms of electoral politics. Unlike the Chinese, the Indians do not seem to have a problem of double identity. While proud of their homelands and their cultural heritage, most Indians appreciate the conditions of poverty and lack of economic opportunity that obtain in their mother countries and are willing to make their permanent home, politically and culturally, in Malaysia. Although in the days prior to World War II many Indians attended Indian vernacular schools, using Indian-language textbooks replete with Indian cultural symbolism, this is no longer the case. Most Indians now attend state schools (or private English-language schools), and there is no movement comparable to the Chinese drive to retain their own stream of education.

Unrest among Indians is not as much political as it is economic, although the latter variable can be transformed rapidly into the former. For one thing, in 1967 some 160,000 nationals of India were resident in Malaysia, plus an additional 130,000 stateless Indians.[33] In August 1968 the government required these two groups (and other resident aliens) to register and obtain work permits—although the majority either had been resident for many years in Malaysia or Singapore or had been born in the peninsula. Many Indians were unable to obtain work permits, and much unemployment resulted. (A MIC leader in 1971 said in a speech that during the previous eighteen months 60,000 noncitizen Indian workers had lost their jobs, of whom 15,000 had returned to India.[34]) The presence of a substantial Indian unemployed proletariat, most of whom cannot go back to the country of their ethnic origin, will add to the existing tensions and instability, for they will tend to vote for and otherwise support anti-Alliance forces—a tendency aggravated by the riots of May 1969 in Kuala Lumpur, when Malay rioters suddenly (and to some observers inexplicably) turned on Indian areas, causing extensive damage and casualties.

33. Bob Reece, "Deepavali Blues," *FEER*, October 30, 1969.
34. *ST*, February 8, 1971. For many years Indians had remained indifferent to the pleas of their leaders to obtain Malaysian citizenship.

Eastern Malaysia

Ethnic conflict has never been as pernicious a problem in the two Borneo states as in peninsular Malaysia, although it does exist. There is a greater level of ethnic diversity (non-Muslim indigenes interposing themselves, in a sense, between Muslims and Chinese). The census figures in 1960 are given in Table 9.

Table 9. Ethnic composition of the population in Sarawak and Sabah

Ethnic group	Sarawak	
	Population	Percentage
Chinese	244,435	31.5
Sea Dayak (Iban)	241,544	31.1
Malay	136,232	17.5
Land Dayak	60,890	7.8
Melanau (mainly Moslems)	45,976	5.9
Other indigenous	39, 262	5.1
Other nonindigenous	6,914	0.9
European	1,737	0.2
Total	776,990	100.0

Ethnic group	Sabah	
	Population	Percentage
Dusun/Kadazan	145,229	32.0
Chinese	104,542	23.0
Other indigenous (mainly Moslems)	79,421	17.5
Bajau (Moslems)	59,710	13.1
Murut	22, 138	4.9
Europeans	1,896	0.4
Others (mainly Moslem, Indonesians, and Filipinos)	41,485	9.1
Total	454,421	100.0

Sources: Great Britain, *Sarawak: Report for the Year 1962* (London: H.M. Stationery Office, 1963); Great Britain, *North Borneo Annual Report 1962* (London: H.M. Stationery Office, 1963).

In Sarawak, as in Sabah but unlike Western Malaysia, no one ethnic group dominates numerically. The Chinese, like their brethren in the peninsula, are by no means homogenous, consisting of Hakka, Foochow, Hokkien, Teochiu, Cantonese, Hainanese, and other dialect groups. In the early days of Chinese migration these groups formed the basis for community control—including the establishment of separate dialect schools—with results similar to those in Western Malaysia. The Chinese rapidly came to control the world of commerce and what little industry existed, but compared to the peninsula proportionally more Chinese were and are engaged in agricultural pursuits than in other occupations—43 percent in 1960. The Chinese control the production of primary agricultural commodities, principally rubber, pepper, and timber. The youth cohort of the Chinese population is large, comprising over 50 percent, a factor that has led to under- and unemployment with a consequent rise in support for anti-government forces.[35] Once again a major contentious form of ethnic competition centers on the availability of land. The Brooke regime had limited the use of land by nonindigenes, and as a result only about 3 percent of suitable agricultural land came to be owned by the Chinese, whereas the Iban farmers practicing chiefly swidden, or shifting cultivation, were able to farm almost 20 percent of this available land. The Chinese argue for a more equable distribution of land, stressing that agricultural production cannot be improved without rezoning and redistributing. The Ibans and other natives claim that their livelihood and their cultural traditions are based on swidden farming, and they therefore require larger areas of land for this purpose.

The government tried in 1965 to introduce a new land bill that would have enabled Chinese to purchase land in so-called native zones. Native reaction was immediate. An alliance of native political groups was formed to contest the bill's provisions, and it was quickly able to force the withdrawal of the new legislation. (The bill was also used as an issue to restructure Sarawak party politics,[36] but this does not detract from the gravity of the land problem.) By 1969 several land development schemes had been implemented, "aimed at raising social and economic standards in rural areas, satisfying demands for land by Chinese agricultural communities and encouraging indigenous people to abandon the practice of shifting cultivation"[37]

35. Michael B. Leigh, *The Rising Moon: Political Change in Sarawak* (Sydney: Sydney University Press, 1974), p. 5.

36. Ibid., pp. 86–88.

37. Lee Yong-leng, "Land for All," *FEER*, March 6, 1969. The author is a senior lecturer in geography at the University of Singapore.

—a politically motivated policy designed to decrease ethnic frustrations, although it does not seem to have stilled Chinese demands. A pessimistic assessment suggests that the new land development policies have increased rather than decreased ethnic animosities because they have neglected Chinese interests at the expense of promoting the socioeconomic welfare of the *bumiputera* population:

The single most important limiting factor in Sarawak [is] the different socioeconomic environment of the cultivators (the Chinese smallholder) and the noncultivators (the indigenous hunter-subsistence farmer). It underlines what is considered to be the worst of all dangers throughout the whole of Malaysia, the latent racial hostility between the rural Malays and the urban Chinese. Native land rights have always been a sore point in Sarawak, even with the rubber and timber companies. This is dramatically drawn by the existence of a hostile and politically oriented group of fairly advanced Chinese farmers. They see their own expertise and economic value sown to the wind by development schemes designed primarily to assist an unwilling native cultivator who would often seem far happier practising shifting cultivation in the traditional way of his ancestors. Today the Chinese see native land rights as a means of containing their own rural expansion. Conversely, indigenous groups see the Chinese as the shopkeeper or the hateful creditor whose economic role far outweighs his numbers and importance in the State.[38]

The Ibans, or Sea-Dayaks as they were improperly called, have acquired over the years a reputation for their aggressiveness, bravery, and lateral mobility. They are now dispersed in the Second, Third, and Fourth Divisions of Sarawak, live mainly in longhouses in a virtually classless society where the Iban "freedom of ego . . . powerfully developed sense of individuality and personal advancement"[39] can flourish—characteristics that have contributed to the fragmented nature of their political affiliations. They cultivate smallholdings of rubber in addition to their swidden pursuits. Other indigenous non-Muslim peoples tend also to live inland, on rivers and in longhouses, and to exist by shifting cultivation. The Malays and other Muslims live mainly along the coast and in the towns, areas where they long have wielded influence. These Malays are not

38. Kieran Broadbent, "Smallholders vs. Efficiency," ibid. Broadbent is with the Commonwealth Bureau of Agricultural Economics, Oxford University.
39. Tom Harrisson, *The Borneans* (Singapore: Straits Times Press, no date, pamphlet/manual for British Security Forces).

migrants from elsewhere in Southeast Asia—they are not immigrant Malays from the Malay Peninsula or Indonesia—but are indigenous peoples. The emergence of the Malay population was not wrought from the arrival of external peoples, rather it was "much more a matter of ideas, of words, and of a new and definite code [Islam] impacting forcibly."[40] The prime historical determinant in the formation of Sarawak Malays was Islam; that is, the Malays appeared as such only in comparatively recent times, as the result of the proselytizing activities of Islamic missionaries. Perhaps the numbers of Islamic adherents will increase in the future (the Ibans apart!), as non-Muslim indigenes are persuaded to forswear their old religious traditions. In Sarawak today stricter Islamic observances are being imposed (and each and every devout Muslim is expected to act as a proselytizer) under the impact of entrance into Malaysia; Islam is the "national" religion of Malaysia and a purification/reformist campaign has been conducted for some years from the Muslim Religious Council in Kuala Lumpur. By and large, Malaysia has come to Sarawak without any discernible rise in the previously minimal level of interethnic violence. What Malaysia has done—and this was inevitable given the extension of the special privileges concept to all the indigenous peoples of Sarawak and Sabah—has been to weld the various native ethnic groups, Muslim and non-Muslim, into an artificially and politically created *bumiputera* in an obvious competitive juxtaposition with the Chinese, a development that has caused much concern among the latter.

In the population figures for Sabah the Dusuns/Kadazans predominate, a statistic that was and is not always expressed politically, as will be shown below. Previously known as Dusun (a nonpejorative Malay word connoting a small-time farmer), the group—in fact a whole range of linguistic subgroups—now prefers to be known as Kadazan, a name considered to be more suitable than one given by outsiders. Kadazans are resident in the western coastal plain areas and in the interior plains of Keningau, Tambunan, and Ranau. They are primarily growers of wet rice (and recently of rubber), but substantial numbers of the coastal Kadazans acquired an English

40. Tom Harrisson, *The Malays of South-West Sarawak before Malaysia* (London: Macmillan, 1970), pp. 154–225.

education from Roman Catholic mission schools (as well as the religion itself) and entered into the lower echelons of the government service as clerks and the like.[41] As already stated, there has been considerable intermarriage with the Chinese. The Muruts, inhabiting the deep and rain-forested mountains of the Interior Residency, were neglected by the colonial regime (in part because of their inaccessibility),[42] and received little in the way of educational and health services, except for the few who either joined the police or worked seasonally on rubber estates. Muruts are swidden farmers and hunters of considerable prowess. The various groups—Bajau, Brunei, Bisaya, Kedayan, Javanese, Tidong, and others—that make up the Muslim population live in coastal areas on both the west and east coasts and on the Kota Belud plain. They grow wet rice, are fishermen and seamen, and a few, on the Kota Belud plain, have taken to the horse to become colorful Oriental cowboys riding herd on native cattle. A large nonindigenous, non-Chinese population from Indonesia and the Philippines—Timorese, Butong, Bugis, Suluk, Ubian, and others—live chiefly on the east coast and work as laborers on the rubber, coconut, and abaca plantations and in timber camps. They are substantially Muslim, albeit with a small but influential number of Christian Filipinos occupying positions of responsibility in government service and in commerce. Most wish to stay in Sabah and have acquired or are seeking citizenship. The Muslims identify with the local Muslims, with whom they are easily assimilable.

The Chinese in Sabah play a role similar to that elsewhere in Malaysia, dominating, with foreign interests, commerce and other important parts of the private sector, and engaging in agriculture, including the production of rubber, palm oil, and coconuts. The bulk of the Chinese in Sabah are Hakka (especially those in agricul-

41. These were considered suspect, in a strange way, by some British colonial administrators (especially those from the Chartered Company) for possessing that dangerous thing represented by a little knowledge of English. They were, for instance, only reluctantly accepted into the police force, whose senior officers preferred the less sophisticated natives of the interior, who could be shaped into the right mold.

42. I was the first European police officer ever to visit the Murut center of Pensiangan on the Indonesian border, a trip that entailed a 216-mile walk, there and back.

ture) with a large pocket of Cantonese in Sandakan and some Hokkien and Teochiu residing in the smaller seaport towns. Because of their superior level of education (what English schools existed under the British were as usual situated in the towns) the Chinese have also filled most of the middle-level positions (clerical and skilled artisan) in the public and private sectors of the economy.[43] In brief, although the Chinese have attained a position of economic dominance and in the past have coexisted with the indigenous peoples with little overt hostility, they look to the future with some trepidation. The underpopulation of Sabah has meant that there has been no intense competition for land such as exists in Sarawak, but the pro-*bumiputera* economic policies of the present state government, coupled with the autocratic and mercurial personal rule of the previous chief minister (see below), offer little hope either to the many thousands of Chinese have-nots or to the well-educated Chinese younger generation as they enter the economic sector. The only cause for optimism in this respect lies in the further development of the state's rich natural resources—particularly oil, timber, copper, and other minerals—that will then demand continued Chinese participation, offering employment and other economic opportunities.

Apart from the construction of a long-needed communications infrastructure (roads, harbor extension, airfield extension, and the like) the state's Second Five-Year Plan is allocating the highest percentage of its budgetary resources to the development of agriculture, especially land settlement schemes designed to wean the rural population away from swidden farming.[44] As in Malaysia the aim is to improve the socioeconomic status of the rural *bumiputera* and thereby "to limit and reduce economic and social inequalities."[45] It is

43. In 1971 the Chinese constituted 85 percent of the enrollment of the top secondary school levels. See Paul Sack, "Politics and Economics in Sabah" (mimeo, December 1971).

44. Six thousand Muruts are being resettled away from their hill retreats to more accessible areas, a revolutionary change with political undertones. An educated Murut, head of the Murut section of the local radio station, was quoted in 1970 as saying that the Muruts "have to keep abreast of the changing times and share the fruits of *Merdeka*. The education of the younger generation is especially important." Quoted in "New Era of Beer and Filter Cigarettes," *Sunday Mail*, November 22, 1970.

45. Quoted in Sack, "Politics and Economics in Sabah," p. 45.

unlikely that many Chinese will share in the land development schemes—indeed the state government has been trying to recruit agricultural workers (Malays) from Western Malaysia to bolster land settlement and other agricultural schemes.[46]

Sabah until recently was a difficult state about which to collect reliable information and analyze events. The mass media, public and private, were either the private fiefdom of the then chief minister, Tun Mustapha, or were thoroughly cowed by him. Foreign journalists were banned from the state unless they were seen as "sympathetic," as were academic researchers from the social sciences, whether from foreign institutions or from other parts of Malaysia. The reasons for this state of affairs focus on the personality of Tun Mustapha and the strange policies espoused by him. Of Suluk ancestry, Mustapha was born in Kudat, the son of a native chief. He received the minimum of formal education, starting his working life at the age of twelve as a houseboy to a British official. He has come a long way. His drive, charismatic leadership, immense personal charm, and obvious ambitions brought him to the attention of the British and, as stated earlier, under the tutelage of Governor Turnbull he rose to prominence. (Turnbull sent him for a year to England to study local government and learn the English language.) After the formation of Malaysia he was appointed to the ceremonial office of head of state, but by various manipulations succeeded in having himself appointed as chief minister, the leading executive position in the state, as head of his USNO party. He held this position until April 1976, and from it he dominated all life in Sabah. He is a far shrewder politician with a greater base of local support than his opponents initially (to their cost) believed. His political machinations will be described below.

His efforts at constructing a unified state in Sabah are of the utmost interest. Never himself a devout Muslim (certainly in my own considerable personal knowledge of him),[47] the Tun and his

46. Ten thousand workers and their families had arrived in Sabah by the middle of 1971. *NN*, October 29, 1971.

47. The Tun leads a life of sybaritic pleasure previously hidden from his constituents by his total control over the media. He reputedly has a number of European mistresses ensconced in various houses around the world, taking care not to bring his chickens home to roost. For example, in Australia he built a A$1,000,000

associates have consciously adopted a policy of mass conversion to Islam of the state's non-Muslims, including the Chinese, as a means of creating a single "national" identity. The process of becoming a Malay has always been known as *"masok Melayu,"* or "entering Malayhood" (it is now called *"masok Islam,"* or "entering Islam" by the newly sensitive government leaders), and it goes further than a simple religious exercise. To become a Muslim implies also the assumption of Malay cultural attributes (the Chinese are the exception here), and in Sabah the process goes one political step further: to convert to Islam is also to become a Sabahan and a Malaysian, in a real political sense, symbolizing acceptance not only of a new religion but also of a new political order. Tun Mustapha believed that political—and cultural—homogeneity could be accomplished by mass conversion to a single religion, and so all non-Muslims, Christians included, were constantly exhorted by various means (some not so subtle) to swear allegiance to the Crescent of Islam. Indeed the haste, the numbers of persons involved, and the methods of persuasion exerted gave pause to many devout Muslims, who believe that to become a Muslim is an intense individual and spiritual act, not to be lightly undertaken for the furtherance of mundane pursuits. The result cannot as yet be predicted.

Many Christians in particular have been incensed by the high-handed proselytizing activities of the Tun and his men. Although the Constitution of Malaysia states that religions other than Islam will be allowed to pursue their faiths without hindrance, in Sabah a campaign was instituted in 1970 and 1971 that actively discriminated against Christian sects. Many foreign priests, nuns,[48] and missionaries were expelled from the state on the grounds that they were spies for foreign powers, that they had refused to train local people to replace them in their functions (there is some truth in this latter assertion), or that they had become involved in local politics.

"palace" for a young Australian "shopgirl," then bought two small factories where the latter's father and brother worked in low-prestige jobs and installed them in each as director/manager. See D. Brunton, "Shopgirl Finds Love—And Riches," Melbourne *Herald,* June 22, 1974.

48. One nun, over eighty years of age, who had been resident in Sabah for more than forty years, was suddenly ordered to leave on a moment's notice on the grounds that she was a security risk. She was carried onto the airplane on a stretcher.

A number of bishops and churches throughout Malaysia com-
plained bitterly to the prime minister in Kuala Lumpur, but were
informed that Kuala Lumpur could not interfere because Sabah
had autonomy over immigration and educational matters.[49] A few
anti-USIA (United Sabah Islamic Association, the chief proselytizing agency) pamphlets were scattered around the capital, Kota
Kinabalu,[50] but Christian complaints were muted in their infancy.
First, Donald Stephens, the leading Sabah lay Catholic in political
life, and his family converted to Islam in January 1971. Stephens
henceforward wished to be known as Mohammad Fuad and stated
that his decision to convert "was another step in his effort to bring
about greater *Bumiputera* unity."[51] Second, Peter Mojuntin, an
erstwhile young Kadazan anti-USNO militant, who had toyed with
the idea of forming a Kadazan political party to oppose the Tun's
policies, was persuaded to withdraw his proposals, either through
threats or material inducements. Other Kadazan and Chinese
leaders who showed qualms at converting to Islam were removed
from their jobs, refused promotion, refused renewal of timber
licenses, and generally received other offers that were difficult to
refuse, so that the rate of conversion at an elite level has been
high—including numbers of Europeans.[52] Thousands of conver-
sions at lower levels have also taken place, four thousand Muruts
embracing the faith at a single ceremony on one occasion.[53] By
1974 one reporter who was allowed entry into the state estimated
that seventy-five thousand persons had converted since 1971.[54] In
recent months, important political events (see the following chap-
ters), including the rise of a new political party, have considerably
eroded Tun Mustapha's ability to manipulate the course of political
affairs according to his own often bizarre wishes, and it is difficult to

49. *SH*, December 12, 15, 18, 1970. The retiring Roman Catholic bishop of Sabah
claimed that Sabah was a police state. The Swiss Embassy in Kuala Lumpur also
lodged complaints.
50. *ST*, December 22, 1970.
51. *SH*, January 12, 1971.
52. James Morgan, "Porkboys Complaint" and "Meccanization," *FEER*, January
2, 1971.
53. *ST*, April 14, and *SH*, April 30, 1971.
54. Edward Fiske, "Islam Growing Fastest in a Malaysian State: Charges of
Pressure to Convert are Heard," *NYT*, September 18, 1974.

predict what the future holds. Certainly, until the present, all the resources of the state, economic and political, have been brought to bear on this exercise in state building.[55] One must ask the question: what will happen to indigenous non-Malay culture (including the folklore that stems from it) under the impact of all these policies and processes and what will be the long-term political consequences?[56] Will Islam become more eclectic, retaining—as in Western malaysia—certain pre-Islamic beliefs and customs to create a new indigenous culture, a true Sabah identity as it were? These questions can be only asked, and not answered, at this stage.

55. Equally important is the question of Chinese conversion to Islam. Will those Chinese who become Muslims also become Malay—or at least Malaysians? Or will they remain discernibly ethnic Chinese with Malay names? Experiences in Indonesia suggest the latter, but in view of the long history of Chinese intermarriage with indigenous non-Muslim natives in Sabah and Sarawak a greater level of integration may be achieved, although one doubts it.

56. In March 1974 the government-operated Radio Sabah abolished all Chinese, Kadazan, and other local language programs, retaining only the use of Malay and English.

4 | The Political Process

Malaysia today is a democratic country in the sense that the term "democracy" is defined in the West. Because of long connections with Britain, the pre-Malaysian *merdeka* Constitution has many correspondences (as well as differences) with the systems of government both of that country and of India, whose political process was felt to be more adaptable to the Malayan environment. Specifically, the 1957 Constitution establishes a federal system consisting of an elected central government in Kuala Lumpur and elected state governments. A constitutional monarch (known as the Yang di-Pertuan Agong, or supreme head of state) is elected for a period of five years from a Conference of Rulers, which body is empowered to advise and consent on certain matters of government, chiefly those concerned with Malay custom, Islam, and states' rights. The monarch, on the advice of the prime minister, acts to dissolve parliament, but otherwise his duties remain ceremonial. Two houses form the legislature: (a) a directly elected parliament (Dewan Ra'ayat or the House of the People) of 104 members, elected from single-member districts for a term of five years and possessing primary legislative responsibility, and (b) a Senate (Dewan Negara, or House of the States) consisting of 38 members, 22 elected by state legislatures and 16 appointed by the monarch. Senate members hold office for six years, and their appointments are made as rewards for distinguished public service and to representatives of minority groups. Legislation may be originated in both houses, with the exception of financial matters, which must be resolved in the parliament. In real terms the Senate has done little of consequence during the years of its existence, acting mainly as a forum for seldom-heeded debate and as a rubber stamp for the parliament. The federal cabinet, organized along ministerial lines adapted from the British system, is led by the prime minister. All cabinet ministers are also members of parliament and are responsible, in the political sense, to that body.

The *merdeka* Constitution acknowledges and guarantees the existence of individual state constitutions and provides for their government structures. (Pre-Malaysian Malaya had eleven states—the nine former Malay states plus Penang and Malacca—each headed by a sultan as a constitutional head of state and by an appointed [ceremonial] governor in the case of the two former Straits Settlements.) Each state has a state assembly headed by a chief minister, elected by popular vote and supported by an executive council appointed by the sultan (or governor) on the advice of the chief minister. The federal system in Malaya has no basis for its existence (such as divergent populations, accidents of geography, and other idiosyncrasies) apart from political distinctions bounded by the historical role of the Malay sultans and their states, and the tensions between the center and the states have never been satisfactorily resolved, although the 1957 Constitution did its best to impose a definitive solution. Federal and state lists are contained in the Constitution in which various legislative and executive powers are assigned to the central and state governments respectively, with by far the greatest authority vested in the center in Kuala Lumpur. To the federal government is reserved, among other powers, authority over defense, internal affairs (including control over a federationwide police force), civil and criminal law, citizenship, state and federal elections, all financial matters, education, health, labor affairs, and communications—all the important implements, in fact, of a strong government. The states are allocated control over land laws, Muslim and Malay customary laws, and agriculture—and even in the latter area they are required to accept the advice of federal officers. Other subjects, such as social welfare, local and municipal government, and drainage and irrigation, are to be shared between the states and the center. When the elected state governments have been of the same political party and ideological persuasion as the elected government in Kuala Lumpur, tensions naturally are kept to a minimum, but when a state government is controlled by an opposition party, conflict is bound to occur, as happened in Kelantan and Trengganu when these two northeastern and largely Malay states were administered by the fundamentalist Pan-Malayan Islamic Party (PMIP), now simply known as Partai Islam (PI), the Islamic Party.

The judiciary, adapted from British and Indian legal institutions, is an independent body, consisting of a chief justice, a Supreme Court, and other courts provided for by legislative instrument. There are no courts established by the state governments, although "native courts," catering to religious and customary usages, are established under the laws of various states. The Supreme Court is empowered to interpret both federal and state constitutions and can act as arbiter in disputes between Kuala Lumpur and state governments. The Malayan Supreme Court, however, differs from that of the United States, inasmuch as the Constitution does not grant to the court the power to abrogate any piece of legislation on the grounds that it runs contrary to constitutional principles as they relate to civil liberties, the safeguards of which are left to the collective conscience of the federal legislature. Even though fundamental and liberal civil rights are guaranteed by the Constitution, under the provisions of the Emergency Regulations, the central government has been granted unbridled authority to abridge (or even to abolish) them under certain conditions of emergency defined by the central government.

The Malaysian Constitution, which was promulgated in 1963, changed few of the provisions of the 1957 Constitution except to add certain articles pertaining to Sarawak and Sabah. The federal and state lists were amended to afford the Eastern Malaysian territories a greater measure of autonomy, principally in the fields of revenue collection, immigration (including immigration from other states within Malaysia), and retention of the English language for an unspecified period. The federal parliament was enlarged from 104 to 144 members (24 from Sarawak, 16 from Sabah) to accommodate Bornean representation, and the Senate was increased by 16—2 elected and 6 appointed from each Borneo state.

Such were the appurtenances of the Malaysian democratic system until the events of May 1969 that were to exercise a profound effect on the course of future events in Malaysia.

The May 1969 Kuala Lumpur Riots and the National Operations Council (NOC)

Western Malaysia held its quintennial parliamentary elections on May 10, 1969.[1] In previous elections ethnic issues, although always present, had been muted, but in 1969 they were articulated in such a way as to stimulate ethnic passions to an intolerable level. Events in Malaysia since the last general elections in 1964 aggravated matters and laid the foundation for the 1969 campaign: these were the separation of Singapore (seen by most Malaysians as an ethnic issue), the Penang communal riots of 1967, the national language furore, and the emergence of certain non-Malay opposition parties as the repository of Chinese chauvinism. The PMIP had become increasingly strident in its role as the protector of Malay and Muslim rights and traditions (claiming that the UMNO had sold out Malaysia to the non-Malays), a position that forced the UMNO into a more conservative "Malay First" stance than its moderate leadership desired. The UMNO's strategy in the 1969 elections was to address itself to the Malay population in order to counteract the blandishments of the PMIP; consequently it paid scant attention to the need to campaign for non-Malay support, leaving this aspect of the elections to its Alliance partners, the MCA and MIC. They were to prove unworthy of the task.

The Alliance attacked the non-Malay opposition, comprised principally of the Democratic Action Party (DAP, the residue of the Singapore People's Action Party's [PAP] abortive sorties into Malaysian politics), the Gerakan Rakyat Malaysia (GRM, the People's Movement of Malaysia), and the People's Progressive Party (PPP),[2] as anti-Malay communal parties, reserving its main assaults for the DAP (apart from the UMNO's internecine struggle

---

1. See R. K. Vasil, *The Malaysian General Elections of 1969* (Kuala Lumpur: Oxford University Press, 1972), chap. 3.
2. The Socialist Front and the Labour Party boycotted the elections in 1969.

with the PMIP). The DAP campaigned for a multiracial Malaysia,[3] calling for the abolition of Malay special privileges and for an open, merit-oriented society even as it promised the highest priority to the eradication of Malay poverty. The DAP also pressed for cultural autonomy on ethnic lines, including retention of Chinese, Indian, and English (as well as Malay) as official languages. The DAP's program was seen as strongly supportive of the non-Malay sectors of the population, and it was not received kindly by Malays. The PPP's campaign platform was similar to that of the DAP. The GRM endeavored to present a more moderate facade of noncommunalism and did not specifically call for the abolition of Malay special privileges, but with one or two notable exceptions its leadership was non-Malay, as was its base of support.

A five-week electoral campaign was officially instituted on April 5. In most constituencies, the competing parties stood candidates of the same ethnic origins as the majority of the electorate concerned, and campaigns were conducted in this light. The DAP, PPP, and GRM arrived at a tacit agreement not to compete with each other in the same constituencies, which would have split the opposition vote; finally, these three parties even contrived an arrangement with the PMIP whereby the PMIP would divide the Malay vote in constituencies with Chinese majorities in return for an opposition split of the vote in Malay majority areas. The campaign increased steadily in acrimony—mostly expressed, if sometimes obliquely, in ethnic terms. The elections were held on May 10, and on the following day it became obvious that the Alliance's erstwhile mammoth base of support had been eroded. In Western Malaysia, the Alliance share of the total electoral vote fell from a majority of 58.5 percent in 1964 to 49.1 percent. Translated into parliamentary strength, the Alliance still retained 66 out of a total of 104 seats—down from 89 in 1964. Most of the losses were sustained by the MCA, although the PMIP gained 3 seats at the expense of the UMNO. (DAP, GRM, and PPP won 13, 8, and 4 seats respectively.) Disturbingly for the Alliance, the urban vote went

3. See Democratic Action Party *Who Lives If Malaysia Dies?* (Kuala Lumpur: DAP, April 1969).

two to one for non-Malay opposition parties, and only the electoral apportionment system, which gave heavy weight to rural representation, saved the Alliance from an even more severe setback. At a state level—and this point is significant in igniting the riots that ensued inasmuch as one of the major reasons for Malay concern was the potential loss of the Selangor state government to the opposition[4] —the PMIP retained control over Kelantan, Penang was won by the GRM, in Perak the combined opposition triumphed narrowly, and in Selangor there was an electoral dead heat.

A bitter debate immediately broke out between UMNO and MCA leaders, Malays being especially incensed at the MCA's inability to attract the Chinese vote. Malays generally saw the election results as the culmination of years of liberal citizenship requirements extended to non-Malays (in return for which Malays had not accrued any appreciable economic power), a process that had adversely affected the Malay political hegemony they had come to expect as an inalienable right. In Kuala Lumpur rowdy opposition party celebrants, reportedly hurling racialist epithets at Malays, contributed to a mounting atmosphere of fear and hatred. On the evening of May 13, 1969, serious interethnic rioting broke out in Kuala Lumpur, started by Malays under circumstances, they claim, of extreme provocation.[5] For two weeks thereafter Malays fought Chinese and Indians with an unprecedented ferocity, countless people were killed and injured, and thousands of homes and other buildings were destroyed by fire. The Chinese, with the Indians, bore the greatest toll of suffering, and the final casualty list will never be known. (The official figures of 196 dead and 439 injured are but a pale reflection of bloody reality; actual figures were far higher.)

---

4. The Malay rioters actually forgathered at the home of the Malay chief minister of Selangor.

5. For contrasting views of the riots, their causes, and consequences, see J. Slimming, *Malaysia: Death of a Democracy* (London: J. Murray, 1969); Goh Cheng-teik, *The May 13th Incident and Democracy in Malaysia* (Kuala Lumpur: Oxford University Press, 1971); Felix Gagliano, *Communal Violence in Malaysia 1969: The Political Aftermath* (Athens, O.: Ohio University Southeast Asia Program, 1970); the official Malaysian version, *The May 13th Tragedy* (Kuala Lumpur: National Operations Council, October 9, 1969); and Tunku Abdul Rahman's own account, *May 13th—Before and After* (Kuala Lumpur: Utusan Melayu Press, 1969).

Several reliable observers reported at the time that Malay troops, called in to assist the hard-pressed (and reasonably impartial) police in quelling the riots, acted in a brutal manner toward non-Malays, causing many casualties by indiscriminate and ill-disciplined acts of violence. The only thing that gave some relief to the government was that the riots were confined to Kuala Lumpur. For a number of reasons (chiefly because Malays in other states did not see their political power threatened at a state level) disturbances did not occur elsewhere in Malaysia.

A crisis of major proportions arose in all sectors of the non-Malay population, caused by the erosion of their confidence in the government (particularly the "security" forces) and its ability to maintain impartial public order. The government itself at first blamed the MCP, Chinese secret societies, and the racialist campaigns waged by opposition parties for exciting the Malays to mass violence, and this was further seen by non-Malays as an attempt to evade a true apportionment of the blame. The government suspended parliament for an indefinite period (at the same time postponing elections in Sarawak and Sabah) and ruled thereafter by decree through a National Operations Council consisting of Tun Razak (then deputy prime minister) as chairman, plus eight other members—senior Malay Alliance leaders, Malay bureaucrats, police, and military officers. The heads of the MIC and MCA were given representation on the NOC, but the running of the country at an elite level was now clearly and solely in Malay hands. The naming of Tun Razak as head of the NOC signaled the impending exit from the Malaysian political scene of Tunku Abdul Rahman, *Bapa Merdeka*, prime exemplar of moderation and racial tolerance. The Tunku came under savage attack from militants within the UMNO itself, and although he generated sufficient loyalty at the top levels of the party to stay on as prime minister for a short period, his dominance of Malaysian politics clearly was approaching its end. The Tunku long had been the right man in the right place, had led his country into independence, and had achieved a measure of understanding between ethnic elites that had led to a generation of tranquillity, but henceforward a new order would be required, able to mount a more determined attack on the root causes of the ills that had convulsed the Malaysian political system in 1969.

The NOC concentrated its early efforts on returning the country to normality, that is, to the state of affairs that existed prior to the riots. In tandem with the Emergency Cabinet with which it worked, the NOC adopted a moderate stance, setting up a series of "Goodwill Committees" at federal and state levels and repulsing the UMNO 'young Turks' who advocated more radical measures to reinforce Malay political dominance and ameliorate the Malay economic position. Slowly the NOC moved to generate new policies. A Department of National Unity was established in July 1969 with a mandate to draw up a new state ideology, to be known as the "*Rukunegara*" ("the articles of faith of the state"). These articles, published in mid-1970, consisted of five "beliefs" (a united nation, and a democratic, just, liberal, and progressive society) and five "principles" (belief in God, loyalty to the supreme ruler [now often known as "the king"] and to the country, support of the Constitution, good behavior, and morality). A National Consultative Council was formed in January 1970, consisting of Alliance leaders, members of the legal profession, economic experts, other professionals, and some opposition party representatives; the SNAP of Sarawak and the GRM, for example, agreed to participate, but the DAP refused.

There were two main results of all these activities: first, the Second Malaysia Plan was formulated and then put into effect, and second, preconditions were laid down for the reconvening of parliament and a return to constitutional democracy. The NOC interregnum, which many observers had thought to signal the end of democracy in Malaysia, undoubtedly served a useful purpose. It allowed ethnic passions to subside, at least to a superficial normality, and, from the government's viewpoint, it effectively quenched the militancy (and in some cases severely damaged the organization) of the non-Malay opposition parties, many of whose leaders had been arrested and detained as left-wing subversives. The NOC period demonstrated to the Malay populace that political power was once again firmly in the hands of a Malay leadership—a leadership that was at the same time avowedly determined to take concrete steps to improve the Malay economic status. Toward non-Malays the leadership adopted a moderate stance, promising Chinese and Indians that their rights would not be abridged in Malaysia's New Economic Policy, although adjustments would have to be made. The effects of the riots, of course, could not be so easily dismissed; the rift between Malays and non-Malays had widened to a perilous distance, bridged over by the usual, if by now shaky, agreement between English-educated elites. At a grass-roots level ethnic animosities still seethed; the Malays were confident that they had taught the non-Malays a much-needed lesson, while the non-Malays, especially the middle and lower classes, felt that they had been unjustly accused and assaulted and that their government had proved unable to protect them from these communally inspired attacks.

The Reconvening of Parliament

The government's decision to reconvene the legislature was predicated upon a number of factors and events. The Malay leadership had concluded that one of the basic causes of the May 1969 riots had been the unrestrained nature of the electoral campaign and that the Malays had been unnecessarily provoked because of what they perceived as an all-out, overt attack on their "sacred" special privileges and political prerogatives. Only if these campaign excesses and similar types of political activity could be curbed by constitutional means, the Alliance leaders thought, could conditions be fulfilled for a return to parliamentary democracy. A two-thirds majority vote in parliament was required under the terms of the Constitution to amend that document, and the Alliance wanted new provisions enshrined therein to ensure that public discussion of sensitive ethnic issues would be proscribed under the primary legal instrument of the land. The May elections had left the Alliance short of that majority, and its immediate goal was now to arrive at that figure.

It proved not too difficult for the Alliance to obtain the requisite majority. A number of opposition party members crossed the floor to join the Alliance, and then, surprisingly, five SUPP members from Sarawak (elected during the 1970 elections) announced that they would enter into coalition with the Alliance Party—presumably for reasons of expediency. The government had announced that the suspended elections in Eastern Malaysia would be held in June and July 1970. Forty federal parliamentary seats were at stake, and the Alliance needed a minimum of thirty of these to be certain of its two-thirds majority. Sabah, where the opposition was flailed by the heavy political bludgeon of Tun Mustapha, presented no problems. Elections were held in only five out of sixteen constituencies, all other seats returning Alliance candidates unopposed. There was no organized opposition; the only non-Alliance candidates were those "independent [and] foolhardy enough to contest the remaining seats."[6] The Sabah Alliance swept the polls with a majority of over 71 percent thereby presenting all sixteen seats to the Alliance party in Kuala Lumpur.

In Sarawak the elections turned out differently, the Alliance winning only nine (this included two PESAKA seats) constituencies out of a total of twenty-four. When the five SUPP members decided shortly afterward to join the Alliance as coalition members, however, the total Alliance vote in the federal parliament was sufficient to constitute a two-thirds majority. The government, under the new prime minister, Tun Razak, promptly declared an end to the state of emergency imposed following the 1969 riots, and parliament was reconvened to sit on February 20, 1971. The decrees promulgated by the NOC concerning the various measures with which it was hoped to remove ethnic issues from public debate were then introduced as constitutional amendments and passed with no difficulty—only thirteen DAP and four PPP members voted against the bill, while the GRM and PMIP supported it. The two amendments made it an offense (even in the federal and state legislatures) to question sensitive issues "which might arouse racial emotions in respect of the National Language [that is, Malay], the special position of the Malays and other natives [the *bumiputera*], citizenship rights and the sovereignty of the Malay rulers."[7] The amendments also provided for the redressing of racial imbalances by reserving a quota of places in institutions of higher learning for *bumiputeras*. In the words of Tun Razak, who moved the bills in parliament, their objectives were

firstly ... to remove certain sensitive issues from the realm of public discussion to ensure the smooth and continuing functioning of parliamentary democracy; secondly, to correct racial imbalance in certain sectors of the nation's life. . . .
There are no simple solutions, no text-book solutions, to our problems—in-

6. Vasil, *The Malaysian General Elections*, p. 52.
7. *SH*, February 24, 1971.

deed there are no solutions which do not take into account the historical, political and economic realities of Malaysia. We are what we are—a multiracial nation still imperfectly united.[8]

The constitutional amendments clearly were directed at improving the position of the Malay-*bumiputera* sector of the population, but they did contain one notable provision aimed at the susceptibilities of non-Malays—that is, citizenship rights were not to be questioned.

Political Parties: New Configurations

Having satisfactorily rearranged the arena within which political forces could maneuvre, Tun Razak's next series of actions were designed to redefine those forces so as to reduce the potential for ethnic strife even further. All political parties and the ethnic communities they variously represented had been staggered in one way or another by the May 1969 riots, and the Alliance found itself in a position to profit from this political trauma. A new spirit of cooperation seemed to arise, and the Chinese and Indians reacted to the apparently moderate policies of the Malay leadership by diminishing their demands on the political system.

The MCA underwent something of a renaissance, winning at the polls in one crucial by-election even as its leadership was wracked by dissent; the party seemed to attract a wider base of support, almost despite itself, from a Chinese population fearful for its lives and property should there be further bloody outbreaks of communal violence, and at the same time pragmatic enough, in view of the Chinese lack of any real armed strength outside of the MCP, to recognize the futility of political militancy at this stage in time.[9] The final retirement (in September 1970) of Tunku Abdul Rahman from the political leadership of the UMNO and of Malaysia gave his successor, Tun Razak, more space in which to pursue his policies; the new prime minister could and did introduce fresh faces into the UMNO's ranks, bringing a new vitality to the party. Gradually the

8. Ibid.
9. An attempt by young Chinese MCA members to forge a so-called "Chinese Unity" movement was not successful in the long run since it elicited adverse comment from the UMNO leadership. Not long after a number of these young Chinese activists were purged from the MCA, although one or two were brought into the MCA's higher ranks to give the appearance of a new image.

older Malay figures, products of the colonial era in more ways than one, were replaced by younger personalities—many of them educated in the West and otherwise "Westernized," but more militant, more willing to strike for the political jugular, than their predecessors. The Malay- and Arabic-educated wing of the UMNO has more in common with these new "Westernized" Malays than with the previous leadership; new educational policies, giving far greater emphasis to the use of the Malay language as the principal medium of instruction, have imbued them with an increased feeling of self-confidence in their ability to come to terms with the modern world and therefore to achieve a closer unity with English-educated Malays.[10]

Tun Razak assessed the situation in 1972, moved to create a series of "mixed governments" in several of the states, and finally formed a "National Front" (NF) in Kuala Lumpur. In January 1972 the GRM[11] in Penang united with the Alliance as a partner in a new experiment in joint state government, and in April 1972 the PPP in Perak, like other parties bowing to the inevitable, was persuaded to enter into a ruling coalition with the Alliance—retaining, however, its independence in the federal parliament. In September, Tun Razak administered his ultimate coup d'éclat, announcing that the former PMIP (now known simply as the Partai Islam, or PI) had agreed to join the Alliance as of January 1973, and as a quid pro quo Dato Haji Asri, head of the PI and chief minister of Kelantan, had accepted a cabinet position as minister of land development and special functions.

Thus by January of 1973 the National Front consisted of the UMNO, MCA, MIC, SUPP, GRM, and PI (plus the PPP in the Perak state government)—a coalition of sometimes strange companions that, according to the prime minister, now represented 80 percent of the electorate, or 122 out of the 144-seat federal parlia-

10. See, for instance, Wang Gungwu, "Malaysia: Contending Elites," *Current Affairs Bulletin* (University of Sydney) 47 (December 1970), 35–48.
11. The GRM had by this time split into two, the party's Penang faction retaining formal title and a splinter faction in Kuala Lumpur launching out on its own to found the Social Justice Party (Partai Keadilan Masharakat, or PEKEMAS) under the leadership of Syed Hussein Alatas. Essentially a party of noncommunal intellectuals, PEKEMAS acts as a moral gadfly, pointing out the debilitating aspects of corruption and other acts of misrule.

ment. The coalition was admittedly fragile (one PI official stated that the PI's controversial decision to participate was based on the "lowest agreeable denominator"),[12] cemented together by a judicious admixture of expediency and trade-offs, but it has proved to be surprisingly durable. Above all, from Tun Razak's moderate standpoint, it lowered pressures by reducing the capacity of the political system to indulge in overt interethnic bellicosity. Moreover, it increased the degree of cooperation between state governments and Kuala Lumpur (thereby enhancing economic development), for now the National Front had either full or partial control over all state governments throughout Malaysia. There is, of course, an inherent weakness in the National Front as presently constituted, for by the very process of subsuming most of what previously had been opposition parties within the ambit of the NF, an insurmountable barrier has been placed in the path of legitimate dissent and opposition. The result may well be that those persons or groups with genuine grievances toward the policies of the government will have nowhere to turn except to extralegal parties and leaders.

The opposition has indeed fallen into open disarray, right and left. On the right a number of Chinese guild and trade associations, plus alumni associations from Chinese-language schools and unhappy MCA members, tried to combine with leftist but non-Communist Chinese to revive the Chinese unity movement, which had lapsed into disrepair.[13] The new movement proved to be equally unsuccessful and short-lived. The DAP retained much of its support among left-wing (or antigovernment) Chinese and Indians in the urban and semiurban centers in the states of Perak, Selangor, Negri Sembilan, and Malacca, but the party was badly affected by arrests of party leaders, by a number of defections of some DAP figures to the MCA, and by an inability to establish an effective organization in the grass roots. The defections were caused by a moderate versus radical schism inside the party leadership: the radicals, led by Lim Kit-siang—who had been released from detention in October 1970—were able to rid the party of those who wished to seek accommodation with the government. These moderates, headed by Goh Hock-

12. M. G. G. Pillai, "Consensus Time," *FEER*, January 15, 1973.
13. M. G. G. Pillai, "National Front," *FEER*, September 16, 1972.

guan, claimed that beneath its multiracial symbolism the DAP was becoming simply a voice of Chinese chauvinism and dissent, too dependent on one single ethnic community.

For the opposition parties the problem was to voice their demands in a manner that would not be construed as an attack on the Malays (and therefore seditious), a difficult maneuvre to perform in a country where most issues focus around the question of ethnicity. In parliament a coalition opposition bloc was able to come together, if in a tenuous way. The coalition was led by Lim Kit-siang and consisted of the DAP, SNAP, PEKEMAS, and a new party, not represented in parliament, the Partai Marhaen. (The Partai Marhaen—best translated as the "peasants' party"—was formed by dissident Malay intellectuals, was vaguely leftist in orientation, and had some minimal support on university campuses.) As a coalition it suffered from the major defect of having to cater to too many conflicting personalities and ideologies. Such was the position in parliament when it was announced that the next Malaysian general elections would be held in August 1974, new electoral boundaries having been drawn in the meantime (to the undoubted advantage of the National Front) which added a further 10 to the existing 104 seats in Western Malaysia.

Many observers expected the National Front to be swamped by competing demands for parliamentary candidacies from the various parties within it, thus raising the possibility that the grand alliance might end up contesting itself, as it were, in many constituencies. But Tun Razak carefully controlled the pre-electoral bargaining and the electoral campaign itself, apportioning candidates according to the NF's best-perceived interests and differentiating between "government" candidates and those of a potential opposition. The expected jealousies inside the NF did not erupt into public conflict. Discontent within the PI, felt to be the most volatile element in the NF, was contained by its leadership. The MCA had benefited by the departure of its long-standing leader Tan Siew-sin, which had opened the way (as had Tunku Abdul Rahman's exit from the UMNO) for the introduction of new and younger blood. As far as the Chinese were concerned, Tun Razak's foreign policy of constructing closer relations with Peking undoubtedly gave off reflected light onto the MCA's fortunes, which had begun to wane with mass defections of MCA members and branches to the GRM.

The August 1974 elections resulted in almost total triumph for the NF. The dissident Malay parties failed to win a single seat.[14] The PEKEMAS gained but one seat; only the DAP fared reasonably well. Although losing five of its 1969 seats it gained others elsewhere; overall its parliamentary strength was reduced from thirteen to nine. Its electoral support, again, was drawn from the urban areas of Kuala Lumpur, Ipoh, Seremban, Malacca, and Alor Star. The NF's constituent components did much as expected, the only surprise being the MCA's success in extending the number of its seats from thirteen to nineteen. This success can be attributed in part to the discipline of the UMNO and its ability to turn out the Malay vote for MCA candidates. The PPP, on the other hand, fared badly because of its inability to attract the non-Malay urban vote, losing much support to the DAP through its identification with the NF. The following figures indicate the balance of seats for Western Malaysia in the present federal parliament:

UMNO	62	
PI	13	
MCA	19	
GRM	5	NF 104 seats
MIC	4	
PPP	1	
DAP	9	
PEKEMAS	1	Opposition 10 seats
Total	114 seats	

The National Front was shaken by the untimely death of Tun Razak in January 1976. His loss will be keenly felt, for as well as being an able administrator, Tun Razak carried on the tradition of Tunku Abdul Rahman as conciliator of competing demands, both within his own UMNO party and also between Malays and non-Malays. Tun Razak was succeeded by Dato Hussein Onn, son of the late Dato Onn Jaafar. Hussein has proven his competency as a government

14. These were the old Partai Rakyat and the newly formed (and short-lived) Kesatuan Insaf Tanah Air (KITA, the Union for National Justice). Dissatisfied Malay independents, unhappy at the PI participation in the front but unwilling to work with the Malay left, were successful in garnering 6 percent of the vote, but did not gain any parliamentary seat.

executive, but he may lack the fervent and personal base of support within the Malay community that Tun Razak enjoyed. The immediate problem for Hussein Onn is to reconcile the opposing wings of the UMNO: the ultranationalists pressing hard (with the PI) for Malay rights and the moderates, who are willing to negotiate and compromise with non-Malays. The appointment of Mahathir Mohammed (author of the powerful and controversial book *The Malay Dilemma*, which definitively sets out the case for Malay rights and special privileges) as deputy prime minister is an indicator of the tensions inherent inside the large and unwieldy National Front, even if there are also some signs that Mahathir is not as much a Malay chauvinist as his detractors would have the public believe. This schism inside the UMNO was compounded in early 1976 by Hussein's determination to press the charges of corruption laid against Dato Harun. Harun was found guilty of the first series of charges in May 1976 and sentenced to a substantial prison term. Consequently he was expelled from the UMNO—not only because of his conviction but also because he embarked on a campaign among the UMNO and UMNO Youth groups around the country to drum up support for his cause—and ousted from his position as chief minister of Selangor. But Harun is more than an individual leader: he is symbolic of the ultranationalist position and as such he is viewed by many Malays as a persecuted martyr. In the UMNO annual meetings held in July 1976, two pro-Harun candidates were overwhelmingly elected to leadership positions in the UMNO Youth—one, Syed Jaafar Albar, (since deceased), was elected to succeed Harun as chairman of the Youth division—over candidates who represented the UMNO establishment. In addition, the UMNO Youth passed a resolution demanding the reinstatement of Harun as a member of the UMNO. In the face of these pressures Hussein compromised: he asked the UMNO disciplinary committee to study the matter. It has yet to be resolved, although Harun has been allowed to rejoin the UMNO, and the case of Dato Harun and what he represents is an ominous manifestation of current and long-term UMNO weaknesses.

In Sarawak party configurations changed appreciably in the years prior to the 1974 elections. The SNAP was in the ascendancy in 1966, with its leader, Datuk Stephen Kalong Ningkan filling the role of chief minister of the state. In mid-1966, however, a crisis arose within the Sarawak Alliance because of Kuala Lumpur's insistence on the introduction of Malay as the national language of Sarawak by 1967, which meant a proportional decrease in the significance and use of English. The SNAP and most of the Iban community hotly resisted this change in the Malaysian agreement, and relations between the SNAP and Kuala Lumpur deteriorated rapidly.[15] Twenty PESAKA and BARJASA members (plus one from the PANAS) in the Council Negri signed a petition of lack of confidence in Ningkan's administration, calling for his departure from office. Using somewhat doubtful constitutional devices, the Kuala Lumpur leadership prevailed upon the Sarawak governor (titular head of state) to have Ningkan removed from office in June 1966. (A sub-sequent and protracted court case supported the government's action.) The SNAP immediately withdrew from the Alliance; it tried to persuade other members of that coalition to do likewise, but was unsuccessful.[16]

In November 1966 the BARJASA and PANAS at long last decided to merge in order to unite all Sarawakian Islamic groups under one political banner; the new party would henceforward be known as the Partai Bumiputera. The new Alliance now consisted of the latter party as the coalition's major voice, plus the PESAKA and SCA. The continued identification of the PESAKA (the other Iban party) with the Alliance, coupled with a general Iban uneasiness with the state and federal governments, meant that the SNAP was able to consolidate and even to increase its strength, though it remained in parliamentary isolation. The SNAP was able to campaign in the 1970 elections on the slogan of "Sarawak for the Sarawakians," and it was no surprise that the SNAP emerged with the greatest number of federal seats (nine) of any single party in Sarawak; it was, of course, overshadowed by the totality of Alliance-PESAKA-SUPP seats.[17]

Nevertheless, the flimsy Alliance coalition in Sarawak (now part of

15. Other factors were involved, including the SNAP's allegedly close ties with the remaining British expatriate officials and conflict over educational policies.
16. See Michael B. Leigh, *The Rising Moon: Political Change in Sarawak* (Sydney: Sydney University Press, 1974), chap. 3, for details of these events.
17. In the elections for the state assembly (the Council Negri), the SNAP won twelve seats out of forty-eight, amassing 23.5 percent of the total votes cast.

the greater NF) had held together for three and a half years despite its amalgam of strange ingredients. By 1974 the ruling Alliance in Sarawak had changed somewhat in nomenclature, if remaining essentially the same. It consisted of the SUPP, SCA, and the Partai Pesaka Bumiputera Bersatu (PBB, the offspring of a 1973 merger between the Partai Bumiputera and PESAKA), the whole being led by Dato Rahman Yaakub as chief minister. The SNAP remained adamantly in opposition after having failed to form a united opposition (and potentially ruling) bloc in 1970 with the SUPP and PESAKA.[18] In the 1974 elections the SNAP demonstrated the continuing strength of its electoral support by retaining its nine seats in the federal parliament and increasing the number of SNAP representatives in the state legislature from twelve to eighteen. (The SNAP did suffer two setbacks: Ningkan was personally defeated in the elections, and Datuk James Wong, its deputy president, was arrested and detained by the state government on the vague grounds that he had conspired with an unspecified but "anti-Malaysian" foreign state.)

Party politics in Sarawak have changed in pattern since the early days, when, as has been demonstrated above, conflict between ethnic groups could be satisfactorily resolved because of political disagreements within each ethnic group. But by 1974 the shape of Sarawak's politics more closely paralleled the Malaysian pattern; that is, a multiethnic alliance ruled the state through a coalition dominated by the *bumiputera* component (PBB) and supported by other ethnically based parties representing the Chinese (SUPP and SCA). With the exception of the Malayo-Muslim sector, the parties in the coalition cannot be said to reflect the sentiments and aspirations of every level of the ethnic community they purportedly represent. Certainly many Chinese and Ibans totally reject the policies of the Sarawak Alliance government, and whereas the Ibans

18. The negotiations fell through after the Malaysian prime minister told SUPP leaders that Kuala Lumpur would not lift the emergency in Sarawak should the proposed SNAP-SUPP-PESAKA coalition gain power, which would have meant that Sarawak would remain under the control of the NOC and not participate in the return to parliamentary democracy. The SNAP was bitter at the SUPP's withdrawal from the negotiations, feeling that it had been double-crossed and that the SUPP had sold out to Kuala Lumpur in exchange for the appointment of a SUPP leader to a post in the federal cabinet. See *FEER*, July 16, 1970.

have their own channels of articulation through the offices of the SNAP, Chinese who disagree both with the SUPP and SCA find themselves without a political conduit for their grievances. There are a few signs that they may turn to the SNAP, thereby creating a genuine multiethnic opposition, but this tendency cannot as yet be confirmed.[19]

Little can be said about party politics in Sabah between 1967 and 1975, for the process was not allowed to exist outside of Tun Mustapha's own Sabah Alliance. Until 1967 a measure of interparty competition between the United Pasok Kadazan Organization (a merger between UNKO and Pasok Momogun), UPKO, USNO, and SCA was permitted. Donald Stephens, the only Sabahan with the personality and support to vie with the Tun, had been cleverly ousted from his position of chief minister in 1964 by a combination of Chinese and USNO pressure, and until 1975 Stephens was unwilling to assert himself politically as an opponent of Tun Mustapha (Stephens was ceremonial head of state up to 1975):[20] indeed, he did everything in his power to persuade his followers first to join and then to support the USNO-led coalition. Following the anti-Christian discriminatory campaign and the Muslim missionary crusade of the early 1970s, Peter Mojuntin, a young Roman Catholic Kadazan politician, announced in March 1971 that he would seek permission to register a new political party in Sabah, to be called the Partai Kesatuan Ra'ayat Sabah (USAP, the Union of Sabah People's Party), in opposition to the Alliance. Mojuntin bitterly attacked the USIA for its arrogance and crudity in seeking converts to Islam. As well as exerting pressure on educated non-Muslims, Mojuntin claimed that the USIA's paid canvassers had penetrated into the remote jungle areas of the hill peoples, where they had become even more reckless; as a result less sophisticated Sabahans, "the under-nourished illiterate peasants, were intimidated to the point of

19. In 1977 the SNAP finally entered the NF, thereby relieving some of the tensions. The underlying issues, however, of Iban versus Muslim dominance will not disappear so easily over the long haul.

20. I am at a loss to understand this lack of assertiveness. Donald Stephens had always been an individual of ambition and personal magnetism, well able to compete with Mustapha if he so chose. Reliable informants told me that he entered into a series of dubious financial transactions at the time he was Chief Minister, which had played into the hands of the Tun; others said that ill health had slowed him down.

actually being in fear of being sent to jail just like the innocent 40 political prisoners [political opponents of the Tun arrested and detained for no other apparent reason than their opposition]— nearly all Chinese and Kadazan—who for the past two years have been held in the Kepayan jail at Kota Kinabalu."[21] Mojuntin's object, apparently, was to establish his opposition party in Sabah and then to work in cooperation with the SNAP in Sarawak and the GRM in Western Malaysia.[22] Mojuntin's independence and militancy did not last long. Subjected to unknown but undoubtedly intense pressures (a mixture, informants have said, of psychological threats and material inducements), Mojuntin quietly withdrew his application to register the proposed new party, a few short weeks after the initial announcement, stating simply that "some people will be disappointed and some will be relieved with this decision."[23] Overt political opposition in an organized form in Sabah then lay dormant until mid-1975. In the 1974 elections the Sabah Alliance (by now simply the USNO and the SCA) won as usual all sixteen seats in the federal parliament. Fifteen of the seats were uncontested because of Tun Mustapha's actions in preventing, by arrest or other means of persuasion, the submission of nomination papers by opposition candidates.[24] The tragic contradiction of this democratic farce in Sabah is that the opposition was not, and never has been, expressed in "antinational" terms (as that phrase is commonly used), for Communism in Sabah has never been a potent force as it has in Sarawak and Western Malaysia. Between 1967 and 1975, any form of democratic party opposition in Sabah had to remain latent.

In this period the Tun's control over the state was rigid, carried out by several organizations. His USNO, by now an immensely wealthy party, employed a large number of full-time salaried po-

21. Quoted in *FEER*, March 27, 1971.
22. Mojuntin announced formation of the new party in Kuala Lumpur, in the presence of several SNAP members of parliament, among other supporters. *ST* and *SH*, February 28, 1971.
23. *SH*, May 4, 1971.
24. The procedure was for the police to mount raids on the opposition candidates' residences immediately prior to nomination day, detain the candidates for a few days until it was too late to file papers, and then release them—so that the seat concerned would go to the Alliance uncontested. For an example of this in a Sabah by-election, see *FEER*, October 15, 1973.

litical officers who were able to construct an effective statewide apparatus and who succeeded in dominating an erstwhile independent state bureaucracy. Another weapon was the Sabah National Youth Association (SANYA), which in 1970 claimed 550 branches and 60,000 members. Headed by a leading Muslim civil servant, the SANYA became a quasi-political organization used to exert control over government servants (many of whom had to become members) and to influence the youth of the land.[25] Similar groups included the so-called Sabah Foundation (an USNO-controlled organization that got its funding from state timber revenues and provided welfare amenities, including grants for education, to Sabah residents— normally *bumiputera*, of course) and the USIA, both of which acted as socialization and coercive agencies. The mass media, including the government-operated radio station, all either had been bought out by the Tun and his associates or had been otherwise browbeaten into total submission. The police force in Sabah is under federal control, but the Tun had at his command a local defense force and a vigilante corps. In short, the Tun had become firmly ensconced in command of all political resources in Sabah. Equally possessed of vast financial resources, the Tun also became somewhat of a hero to many young Malay militants in Western Malaysia because of his proselytizing activities on behalf of Islam. Government leaders in Kuala Lumpur began to look askance at many of his activities, regarding him as "the wild man of Borneo,"[26] and tried to induce him to leave Sabah for a senior cabinet post in Kuala Lumpur, but at that time he found the perquisites of office as chief minister of Sabah far too compelling.

A major event, however, took place in Sabah politics in 1975, the most significant occurrence in the state for many years. Jealousies (and well-founded complaints) within the USNO by the Kadazan membership and others dissatisfied with Mustapha's corrupt and dictatorial rule led to the formation in July 1975 of a new political party, a breakaway group from the USNO. The new party was called BERJAYA, a Malay word meaning "victory" and also an acronym representing the Malay phrase *Bersatu Rakyat Jelata Sabah*, or the United Peoples of Sabah. At first led by Datuk Harris Salleh and

25. Bob Reece, "A One-man Democracy," *FEER*, April 2, 1970.
26. Conversation with a senior Malay government official, December 1970.

Peter Mojuntin, BERJAYA was joined two weeks later by Tun Haji Mohammed Fuad (Tun Fuad, the former Donald Stephens), who resigned his position as ceremonial head of state in order to participate once again in active party politics. BERJAYA announced that the raison d'être for its foundation stemmed from the mismanagement, corruption, and dictatorship of Tun Mustapha. Clearly some initial support for the new party was forthcoming from Kuala Lumpur; Tun Razak for one reportedly had long been desirous of ousting Mustapha as Sabah's chief minister. The Malaysian prime minister was particularly incensed at Mustapha's alleged ambition to have Sabah secede from Malaysia, whereupon a new state would be founded comprising Sabah, Mindanao, Palawan, and Sulu[27] (the three latter areas are in the Philippines).

Tun Mustapha immediately returned to Sabah (stopping en route in Penang to visit Tunku Abdul Rahman in an attempt to gain his support) and at first appeared to have removed the fuse from the political time bomb. (On August 11, for instance, the Sabah State Assembly passed a motion of confidence in Mustapha by a large majority.) Gradually, however, Mustapha's authority was eroded in the face of opposition from the central Malaysian government, no matter how tacit this was. The chief of police and the head of the armed forces in Sabah were both replaced by officers of a high caliber and of proven loyalty to Kuala Lumpur; BERJAYA was accepted as a new member of the National Front to the exclusion of the USNO, and on October 31, Mustapha resigned as chief minister. Yet his influence at first remained considerable if muted, for his deputy and staunch adherent was appointed to succeed him and, since the State Assembly had not been dissolved, his USNO party stayed in power. Following the death of Tun Razak in January 1976, Mustapha's position as the *eminence grise* behind the doors of influence in Sabah seemed more assured, especially since the USNO won two important by-elections against strong BERJAYA candidates in late 1975. Mustapha's continued status now became predicated upon the results of general elections to the Sabah State Assembly, which were to be held in

27. R. S. Milne, "Malaysia and Singapore 1975," *Asian Survey* (February 1976), 186–192.

April 1976. In the meantime Sabah became a more open society with the cessation of arbitrary arrests and the reintroduction of a measure of freedom for the press. Pro-and anti-Mustapha elements in Sabah's newspapers embarked upon a vitriolic and strident political campaign, Mustapha's faction seeking to brand BERJAYA as a band of treacherous has-beens, BERJAYA exposing the extent of Mustapha's corrupt political and economic machinations. Police were placed on stand-by alert, and special units were flown in from Western Malaysia to forestall interethnic violence. The elections were held without serious incident. The surprising (to many) result was that BERJAYA emerged victorious over its USNO-Sabah Alliance opposition. BERJAYA won twenty-eight out of the forty-eight seats in the State Assembly, the other twenty going to the USNO. The Sabah Chinese Alliance, running on the same ticket as the USNO, lost all of the eight seats it contended.

Undoubtedly the central government was elated at the election results, for according to one observer Mustapha was attempting to use his vast private fortune, milked out of Sabah's natural resources, "to forge political links on a national, and even international, level"[28] and could have posed problems in Western Malaysia. The new chief minister of Sabah, Tun Fuad, and other BERJAYA leaders are cast more in the mold of the moderate, pragmatic bargaining style of the current National Front top leadership and may be expected to pursue rational policies of development in line with those of the central authority; Sabah may be more closely linked with the rest of Malaysia as a consequence. The new BERJAYA state government has announced a rigorous policy of curbing the excessive spending on grandiose projects (such as the Sabah Air airline) and of rooting out the widespread corruption. Tun Fuad also announced new policies concerned with the conservation of natural resources, with a reduction in nepotism and inefficiency in the state's bureaucracy, and with measures to decrease the cripplingly high cost of living. Tun Fuad initially ruled

---

28. Ibid., p. 189. The "international" reference is no doubt to Mustapha's connections with the so-called "strong man" of Libya, Colonel Qaddafi, who reportedly supplied Mustapha with arms and material for onward transmission to Muslim rebels in the southern Philippines.

out the possibility of a coalition between BERJAYA and the USNO, despite indications that National Front leaders in Kuala Lumpur would prefer some sort of merger between the two groups.[29] The latter eventuality may come about with the passage of time, when animosities aroused by the election campaign have subsided and it is seen that Mustapha's influence has been effectively diminished once and for all.

A few short weeks after taking office, Tun Fuad and many leading members of his state cabinet, including Peter Mojuntin, perished in an airplane crash on a flight from Labuan to Kota Kinabalu. In one disastrous stroke much of the young talent, upon which the BERJAYA's hopes had been placed to perform the awesome task of cleaning out the stench of Sabah's corruption and inefficiency, was decimated. The new chief minister is Datuk Harris Salleh, an able man but lacking the popular following enjoyed by both Tun Fuad and Mojuntin. He has been able to recruit some new blood to replace those who died in the crash, in particular James Ongkili, a political scientist from Sabah with excellent academic credentials. Nevertheless a leadership hiatus in the BERJAYA will persist for some time, and in the meantime the USNO's fortunes have improved—although the party has not been able to pose an immediate threat to the BERJAYA's rule. The USNO and BERJAYA are now officially part of the National Front, yet they continue to feud bitterly at a local level. Tun Mustapha was reelected president of the USNO in May 1977, and it remains to be seen whether this move represents his return to the political arena proper. The power struggle in Sabah, like that in Sarawak, is far from over.

The Bureaucracy

Under the British the civil service was a highly centralized, authoritarian decision-making organization, from the chief secretary at the top to the workhorse district officer below.[30] It was a

---

29. *ST*, April 16, 18, 1976.
30. For detailed works on the Malaysian bureaucracy see Milton S. Esman, *Administration and Development in Malaysia* (Ithaca, N.Y.: Cornell University Press); R. O. Tilman, *Bureaucratic Transition in Malaya* (Durham, N.C.: Duke University Press, 1964); Gayl Ness, *Bureaucracy and Rural Development in Malaysia* (Berkeley: Univer-

prestigious group that afforded high social status to its appointees. The district officer in particular considered himself (and was perceived by others) to be the praetorian embodiment of government, outside of and free from local political interference (if it ever existed) and responsible for his actions only to his superior in the civil service. Those Asians who were recruited into the civil service became imbued with a similar set of values and elite images and shared with British colonial officials the view that the administration, in the absence of meaningful popular political participation, *was* the government, responsible for the formulation and the implementation of all public policy. The various services and divisions within the bureaucracy were hierarchically (and fairly rigidly) stratified, so that "the services tended to be inbred and to resist external communication and programmatic coordination."[31] Operating alongside the federal bureaucracy were officials from the state governments, but for the most part the central officials exercised the major influence. In ethnic makeup, Malays predominated in the administrative services (Malay entrance thereto was and is ensured by an advantageous quota system), the police, prisons, forestry, and customs departments, while non-Malays were more numerous in the professional and technical departments such as public works, health, agriculture, drainage and irrigation, and telecommunications—a pattern that exists today.

The structure of the bureaucracy in the postindependence years still retains many of the colonial characteristics and problems. The government has needed to make the bureaucracy less aloof from the public it serves and more responsive to political or lateral imperatives such as ethnic conflict resolution without becoming unduly politicized, and in this it has been only partially successful. At an elite level senior civil servants and leading politicians tend to have much in common, inasmuch as many of the latter were recruited from the ranks of the civil service, and consequently administrative versus political conflict (that is "the experts versus the ideologues" classic controversy) has been kept to a minimum.

sity of California Press, 1967); and J. C. Scott, *Political Ideology in Malaysia* (New Haven: Yale University Press, 1968).

31. Esman, *Administration and Development*, p. 72.

Elite values in both groups have tended to coincide, especially since the leadership on both sides has been and is Malay. The prime minister, himself a former bureaucrat, for example, has tried in recent years to keep politics out of the administration by appointing senior civil servants to manage statutory government bodies such as the Federal Land Development Authority and Majlis Amanah Ra'ayat (MARA, the People's Trust Council, a body responsible for rural Malay development and improved social services). At a local level civil service attitudes have come into conflict with a younger generation of local politicians not so impressed with the prestige of the administrators or with their self-identification as the government. Attempts by these politicians to influence decision making by district administrators have increased, as Milton Esman has demonstrated, resulting in clashes that

force a painful and reluctant accommodation for junior administrators taught to believe that politicians should not interfere with administrative decisions and local politicians determined to demonstrate their power to influence local allocations of land, licenses, and other government benefits. . . . Administration will be more politicized, especially in dealing with particularistic claims for small public services and concessions sponsored by politicians, but not to the point that the administrative style of the polity or the important political role of senior administrators will be seriously impaired.[32]

On the whole, however, despite a significant increase in the level of corruption, the bureaucracy remains a moderate and therefore a stabilizing influence on the political process in Malaysia, particularly that pertaining to the domesticization of interethnic strife.

The Police and the Military

These primary coercive forces of the Malaysian state are kept determinedly under Malay control so that non-Malays in Western Malaysia and non-*bumiputera* in Eastern Malaysia possess no source of armed strength of their own with which to support their interests—other than extralegal groups like the MCP and the Chinese secret societies. Since the time of the British, the sale of arms in Malaysia has been carefully controlled and licensed, and there is no large pool of privately owned firearms that could be

32. Ibid., p. 65.

used by nongovernment forces. The exception is in Sarawak, where the indigenous peoples have been able to purchase large numbers of shotguns for hunting purposes.

The Malaysian military forces are based on the Malay Regiment (formed by the British in 1933), which is an infantry group with a strength in 1968 of ten battalions of Malay soldiers—twenty-eight thousand troops out of a total army of thirty-five thousand.[33] There is a multiethnic army group, known as the Malaysian Reconnaissance Corps, but it is far smaller than the Malay Regiment, and most command positions are filled by Malays. A navy and an air force both have a multiethnic officer corps, but they can in no way be considered as countervailing forces to the far larger Malaysian army. Since the establishment of Malaysia, non-Malay *bumiputeras* from Sarawak and Sabah have been recruited in some numbers into the armed services. The Sarawak Rangers, a renowned fighting force composed mainly of Ibans, was also incorporated into the Malaysian army and still exists as a unit. There have never been any real tensions, as far as can be perceived, between the armed forces and the political leadership,[34] chiefly because the top leaders in the military and in the world of politics are all Malays, and like the bureaucracy most have been educated in the English language, with a resulting pronounced convergence of world views and values. Tun Razak, the former prime minister, was also minister of defense, and he ensured that there was a steady increase in the federal budget as it related to defense spending.[35] Finally, Malay military leaders have forged strong links with their counterparts in Indonesia. (Combined operations against Communist guerrillas have been mounted for several years, for instance, with Indonesian forces on both sides of the Sarawak-Kalimantan border.) Whether this cooperation will ever extend

33. Quoted in Cynthia Enloe, "Civilian Control of the Military; Implications in the Plural Societies of Guyana and Malaysia," paper presented at the Interuniversity Seminar on Armed Forces and Society, SUNY-Buffalo, October 18–19, 1974.

34. Some foreign observers made much of the possibility of a military takeover during the riots of 1969, but I give little credence to this eventuality, then or in the foreseeable future.

35. In 1974, M$887 million was allocated to the military and police forces, amounting to 25 percent (and the largest share) of the total public expenditures. Enloe, "Civilian Control," p. 21.

into the political sphere cannot be predicted, but if MCP guerrillas in Malaysia ever obtain outside help in quantity and pose a serious military threat to the Malaysian government, several interesting scenarios can be constructed against a backdrop of joint Malaysian-Indonesian military cooperation.

Until 1969 the officer corps of the Royal Malaysian Police Force (RMPF) had never been as rigidly a Malay preserve as had the military,[36] although the rank and file of the force has always been preponderantly Malay. (The Chinese have traditionally been reluctant to enter either the police or the military on a voluntary basis, considering both occupations to be inferior.) Since 1969 there has been a major, if unpublicized, effort to reverse the ratio of Malays versus non-Malays in the officer corps, and non-Malays have been quietly transferred out of positions of command responsibility. The police force in Malaysia is a federal organization (there are no local police forces), accountable under the Constitution not to parliament but to the monarch, through an inspector general of police and a Police Service Commission. The inspector general of police is accountable to the minister of home affairs and the prime minister. As in the case of the military, there is a convergence of interests between the topmost ranks (all Malay) of the police leadership and the regime.[37] The RMPF is organized vertically, from the inspector general in Kuala Lumpur down through commissioners of police in Western Malaysia, Sabah, and Sarawak, through chief police officers in each state in Western Malaysia, to officers-in-charge of police districts at a district level—so that police divisions of responsibility correspond to the political boundaries of state and administrative districts. Horizontal pressures from local administrators and politicians are often exerted on police commanders on

36. In 1968 the ethnic composition of senior police officers (Division 1) in the RMPF was 45.1 percent Malay, 32 percent Chinese, and 22.9 percent Indian—a majority of non-Malays. The very top ranks, however, are exclusively Malay. See D. S. Gibbons and Zakaria Haji Ahmad, "Politics and Selection for the High Civil Service in New States: The Malaysian Example," *Journal of Comparative Administration*, 3 (November 1971), 341.

37. Zakaria H. Ahmad has given a thorough description of the RMPF in an unpublished paper, "Police Forces and Their Political Roles in Southeast Asia: A Preliminary Assessment and Overview," mimeo, Department of Political Science, M.I.T., 1975.

the ground, but such undue interference as has occurred has been of a parochial nature and within the bounds of an overall policy framework set at the top. The potential for conflict, however, would be increased should a state government be elected that stands in diametric opposition to the policies of the federal government—the more so in the case of an opposition state government representative of non-Malay communal parties.

The RMPF has a paramilitary aspect embodied by a number of police field forces and mobile reserve units stationed at strategic centers throughout the country to fulfill the RMPF's constitutional function concerned with the maintenance of internal security, in which the military are technically assigned a secondary, supportive role.[38] As such the police field forces and the specially trained police riot squads are responsible for counterinsurgency operations and for the suppression of other forms of domestic unrest respectively. Both of these roles impinge upon the domestic political scene, and the degree to which the police (and, of course, the military) perform their duties in an impartial manner—that is, not weighted in favor of or against any particular ethnic community—continues to have a significant impact on the political process as it relates to non-*bumiputera* confidence in the government. From the regime's viewpoint, for the present its position of supremacy has been ratified by the results of the 1974 parliamentary elections. On the surface the country is stable and relatively prosperous. Should conditions deteriorate, however, and violence erupt so as to constitute a serious threat to the status quo of Malay hegemony, both the military and the police may be called upon to center stage.

Other Pressure Groups

The Malaysian trade-union movement has never had affiliations with any particular party, except in the immediate postwar years when several unions were linked organizationally with the MCP. These contacts were severed in 1948, whereupon the British gov-

38. In reality the military, because of its superior strength and weaponry, generally acts as senior partner, subsuming the police field forces under its command during joint counterinsurgency operations, as was the case under the British during the Emergency.

ernment dispatched a trade union advisor to Malaya to reorganize the labor movement on socialist (British-style), anti-Communist lines. Stringent regulations were imposed thereafter to ensure that trade unions would be free from political control, moves that obviously inhibited labor from organizing itself in a political sense. This pattern has continued, with few changes, ever since, so that trade unions have never been able to wield any political leverage as they did in Singapore. Malaysian unions have been concerned mainly with improving the lot of their affiliated workers. A Malaysian Trades Union Council (MTUC) does exist, dominated by Indian labor leaders, but its effectiveness is blunted by the problem of organizing the working class of Malaysia across ethnic lines for reasons of class solidarity in a country where economic issues are defined more by ethnicity than by class. The government's attitude toward the MTUC is one of toleration mixed with firm control. New labor laws were enacted in 1971, purportedly "to encourage the growth of sound and responsible trade unions and to prevent them from being used for undesirable purposes,"[39] but in fact the laws imposed stringent curbs on the unions' effectiveness by preventing strikes, picketing, and other work action under certain conditions. The MTUC protested these new restrictions, but was politely ignored. The organized labor movement in Malaysia remains politically passive, although there were signs in 1977 that low-level government employees were beginning to become more militant.

A new and growing political pressure group—a negative one from the government's aspect—is the Malay student movement at the universities and colleges in Kuala Lumpur. This group, whose ideology in political terms is still inchoate, is a potent force in the movement to hasten the process of improving the Malay socioeconomic position. Malay students have strongly opposed the government on several social political issues (particularly in support of the November 1974 peasant demonstrations in Kedah), and as a result their freedom to act has been severely curtailed. In early 1975 the government amended the Universities and University Colleges Act of 1971 to ensure greater control over student

39. Speech by the Malaysian minister of labor, quoted in *NN*, February 19, 1971.

activities: among other things students are now prohibited from becoming members of, or otherwise supporting, political parties and trade unions without the prior approval of university authorities. Several well-known student leaders and faculty members have been arrested and detained indefinitely under the Emergency Regulations. As more and more Malay students are brought into the universities from rural areas, the student movement likely will constitute a strong link between intellectuals and the peasantry; should the latter become more disaffected than it is already, the Malay student movement could become an even more virile force for social change.

Other interest or pressure groups in Malaysia consist of a number of associations based on common interests that are to be found within each community. The most prevalent types are educational (Chinese school management committees, associations of former pupils, Malay and Chinese schoolteachers' associations), religious (Christian church groups, Islamic associations, Hindu groups, and the like), cultural (clan associations, literature societies, musical groups, and the like), and occupational (craft guilds, employers' groups, manufacturing associations, and the important Chinese, Indian, Malay, and European Chambers of Commerce). The effectiveness of these groups varies from issue to issue. Most of them are organized on ethnic lines, and their influence is exerted not directly on the government, but through the political party that represents them as a community.

5 | Major Problems

State Integration

Malaysia is, by most standards, a more "open" society than Singapore in the sense that access to the government is available in a number of ways through a variety of groups. Yet the problems in Malaysia are more acute, first because all competing groups inject their demands into the system along the arteries of ethnic particularities, and second because of the different nature of Malaysian society, in which ethnic groups are numerically more evenly balanced, each with its own peculiar strengths and weaknesses. The major problems of Malaysia thus center primarily on ethnic competitiveness, through which cut issues of education and culture, economic imbalance, and revolutionary threats from the MCP.

The vexed question of integrating the various components of the state into a coherent whole exercises the policy makers in Malaysia and will continue to do so for many decades to come. Conventional integrative theory[1] cannot be applied here, for the rigidity of ethnic boundaries does not admit to the probability that they will wither away and disappear beneath the benign influence of an efficient and modernizing government, as the theorists would have it. The official (or "national") ideology of Malaysia, the *Rukunegara*, contains a sense of ambivalence in this respect that continues to haunt the would-be makers of a modern, unified state. On the one hand, the *Rukunegara* states, Malaysia is dedicated "to achieving a greater unity of all her peoples" and "to ensuring a liberal approach to

---

1. The literature concerning "political integration" is substantial and cannot be analyzed here. For a compelling criticism of the fallacies that inform modern integrative theory, see Walker Connor, "Nation-building or Nation-destroying?" *World Politics*, 24 (April 1972), 319–355.

[Malaysia's] rich and diverse cultural traditions"; to this end "no citizen should question the loyalty of another citizen on the ground that he belongs to a particular community." On the other hand, it is intended that "the wealth of the nation shall be equitably shared" and that "a progressive society oriented to modern science and technology" shall be built.[2] The contradictions and tensions are apparent; ethnicity is recognized as a major element on the Malaysian stage, and somehow or other it has to be reconciled with an equitable distribution of political and economic resources, all within a determinedly modern society.

Despite an official ideology that implies that the goal is to construct, eventually, a unidimensional state identity in which all inhabitants of Malaysia, regardless of ethnic affiliation, will subscribe to a common set of values, the actual policies of the government continue to be nonideological and pragmatic in all but the symbolic sense. Attempts are made, through the use of Malay as the national language and the educational system generally, to forge a common Malaysian image (mainly by the use of symbols derived from the Malay community), but considerable accommodation to non-Malay sensitivities is practiced. And so it must, if the state is to survive in its present form. The problem for Malaysia is that it needs to balance Malay interests with the genuine aspirations of the non-Malays. Yet the dilemma thereby arises that these interests and aspirations are no longer confined to one mutually exclusive area of activity, such as the political and economic arenas respectively. The remainder of this chapter will give an indication of the magnitude of the task, together with some idea of how the Malaysian government is trying to grapple with it.

Educational Problems

The Malaysian government is attempting to reconcile two education requirements at the present stage of its state-building endeavors. First, in accordance with the Second Malaysia Plan (and with the *Rukunegara*), it has to enable Malays, through the educational process, to participate in a modern, innovative competitive

2. Government of Malaysia, *Rukunegara* (Kuala Lumpur: Government Printer, 1970).

and technological society. Second, the government wishes to ensure, through a revised educational system, that in future new generations of "Malaysians" will emerge instead of disparate groupings of Malays, Chinese, Indians, Kadazans, Ibans, and so on, although, to be sure, this new image is designed to be primarily Malay in orientation. The dimensions of the first problem are immense, for the government has to bring high-quality secondary education to the rural Malay community and at the same time to penetrate the traditional Malay value system, which, bolstered by British educational policy, has instilled attitudes in both parent and pupil that are incompatible with the government's ambitious program of raising the Malay socioeconomic status. Malays must be persuaded, for example, to enter more exacting disciplines in the tertiary educational tier than they have in the past—fields such as the natural and physical sciences, mathematics, engineering, and medicine have previously been avoided in favor of liberal arts degrees.[3] The causes of this predilection are partly cultural, partly historical in origin, and are not easily remedied. Lack of an adequate education in English—and most university education in the past has been given in English—has been a barrier to the rural Malay population, and educational policy is now gradually to introduce Malay as the principal medium of instruction at all educational levels, including the universities.

The motivations behind the government's policy of changing from English to Malay are political as well as educational, and there have been predictable political reactions from the non-Malay populace. The government's aim is to use the classroom as a forum for "planting the seeds of national unity" to further the ultimate objective of "a single united people derived from the country's various races, cultures and religions."[4] The National Language Bill of 1967 affirmed that Malay would become the only official language, although English would continue to be used, liberally where

3. In 1970, 858 of 1,217 students admitted to the University of Malaysia Arts Faculty were Malay, but only 5 Malays out of 131 went into the Engineering Faculty, and 53 out of 474 went into the Science Faculty. In the same year, only 4 Malay medical doctors graduated, only 1 received a degree in Engineering out of 71 graduates; for Science the figure was 21 out of 481 graduates (*ST*, November 16, 1970).

4. Speech by the minister of education, reported in *NN*, April 29, 1971.

necessary, in the legislature, in certain government departments, in the courts, and in higher education. The bill was assailed both by Chinese and others interested in preserving their culture and by radical Malays who thought it too moderate, but its provisions are slowly being enforced. By 1980 it is intended that all secondary education will be taught in Malay as far as standard five and that there will be a more gradual switch to Malay in the universities. This move has already resulted in some discrimination against non-Malays. In 1971, for example, a furore arose over the excessively high rate of failures among non-Malays in the Malaysian certificate of education examination—the equivalent of completion of high school requirements. The failure arose because of non-Malay inability to pass the Malay-language part of the examination, resulting from lack of opportunity and of trained teachers. Most of the loud and legitimate cries of protest went unheeded.

Obviously any government vitally concerned with the construction of a stable, unified state cannot tolerate educational and language policies that perpetuate cultural divisions and reinforce economic inequities. The haphazard educational system of apathetic coexistence allowed to evolve during the colonial period must be changed to one that is conducive to social cohesiveness. The problem for the Malaysian government is to reconcile this requirement with the cultural demands of non-Malays, including the non-Malay *bumiputera* of Sarawak and Sabah, who view the enforced move to the almost total use of Malay for official and educational purposes as an assault on their own traditions and ultimately on their self-identity. The government's rhetoric concerning the eventual emergence of a single "Malaysian" culture through the process of "integration" is, I believe, patently invalid. The persistence of ethnic diversity and its attributes cannot be confidently disregarded if Malaysia is to retain an acceptable level of stability as an ethnically tolerant state. The government must continue with an approach that stresses cultural accommodation rather than unilateral decisions beneficial to one community alone and discriminating against others, however inadvertently. Yet how is this process to be maintained without offending the susceptibilities of volatile Malay nationalists? To say that it is not an easy task is an understatement.

The Malayan Communist Party

In the period of quiescence that followed the ending of the Emergency in 1960, the MCP[5] quietly reorganized itself into what the Malaysian government calls the Communist Terrorist Organization, consisting of "small, viable units to provide a hard-core for future expansionism."[6] In 1963, however, the MCP reportedly embarked on, or at least prepared the ground for, another period of armed struggle; in 1965 the Malayan National Liberation League (MNLL) was formed in Jakarta and the MRLA became the Malayan National Liberation Army (MNLA). The MNLL leadership consisted at first of three Malays and one Chinese; its offices in Jakarta were closed down following Sukarno's ouster and its leaders imprisoned, but it opened again in January 1966, this time in Peking under the leadership of P. V. Sharma, an Indian. The Malaysian government assumes that both the MNLA and the MNLL are fronts for the MCP, the former being responsible for the armed struggle and the latter for the constitutional phase. The linkage between the MCP and the MNLA is obvious: they operate alongside each other in the same territory. But the function of the MNLL is more ambivalent; most probably it is the MCP's liaison office outside of Malaysian territory designed to further cooperation between fraternal parties. The Malaysian government alleges that the MCP is simply an adjunct of the Chinese Communist Party in Peking,[7] but there is some doubt that such control exists today, if it ever did. Unquestionably, the MCP's official sympathies lie with Peking and not with Moscow, and many of the party's published policies are explicitly modeled on Maoist doctrine; there is, however, no hard published data to prove that the MCP has no autonomy of its own and that it unswervingly marches to Peking's drumbeat. On the contrary, some evidence exists that a split has developed within the MCP concerning the contradictions posed by what might be called the rightward tendencies of current Peking

5. The MCP has always refused to recognize Malaysia; hence it remains the CP of Malaya, not Malaysia.

6. Government of Malaysia, *The Militant Communist Threat to West Malaysia* (Kuala Lumpur: Government Printer, 1966), p. 2.

7. Government of Malaysia, *The Path of Violence to Absolute Power* (Kuala Lumpur: Government Printer, 1968), p. 2.

foreign policy and the demands imposed upon MCP leaders by local reality. (Rightward, that is, in the sense that China wishes to enter into state-to-state relations with other foreign countries, regardless of their political orientation. This policy necessarily has entailed some diminution of China's support for revolutionary movements within those countries.)

In 1971 some discontent was reported within the MCP concerning the primacy of military over political struggle.[8] First, when an intensified military campaign was implemented in 1971 and 1972, MCP leaders still were making a specific appeal to develop other forms of revolutionary activity—primarily the piecing together of a multiethnic united front—in coordination with the new, increased military program.[9] (For example, one later report suggested that the ranking Malay in the MCP, Rashid Maidin, may have replaced Ch'in Peng as the party's secretary-general, although this has not been substantiated.[10]) The importance of attracting non-Chinese (that is, Malays) into the MCP's ranks was given major emphasis in the early 1970s in an attempt to widen the base of the united front, following the MCP's limited successes in enlisting dissident Thai Malays from the irredentist movement in southern Thailand—a new development that has caused concern to the Malaysian government.[11] Perhaps for this reason the MCP did not make a major effort to recruit potentially large numbers of angry and bitter Chinese youths after the 1969 riots, not wishing to alienate Malays who might otherwise be drawn into the MCP's camp. Instead, in a new policy announced in December 1975 by the Central Committee of the MCP, a direct call was made for the construction of broadly based front movements consisting of "ag-

8. *NN*, February 15, 1971.
9. Article by M. Pillai, *FEER*, December 24, 1973.
10. News items by M. Pillai, ibid., January 14 and January 21, 1974.
11. Thai Malay irredentism is a complex problem, described in Astri Suhrke's "The Thai-Muslim Border Provinces: Some National Security Aspects," in Robert Ho and E. C. Chapman, eds., *Studies of Contemporary Thailand* (Canberra: Australian National University, 1972). Briefly, the large Thai Malay population long has chafed under the oppression of Thai Buddhist rule, and in the past few years there has emerged, among other irredentist groups, the Patani Liberation Front, which has forged strong contacts with the MCP in southern Thailand. It is an all-Malay group, with links to some Malays living in the border states of northern Malaysia. See also "Rebels Are Active in Southern Thailand," *NYT*, November 2, 1975.

ricultural workers, peasants, and other laboring masses in the rural villages." This new policy envisages a sweeping program of land reform, turning over to the poor rural inhabitants the holdings of the "big landlords, big bureaucrats, big plantation owners and the foreign-monopoly capitalists who own large plantations." There seems little doubt that the new directive is designed to attract Malay peasants to the MCP in the border states (and possibly elsewhere), where tenant farming under gruelling conditions long has been endemic. The directive explicitly guarantees, for instance, that the holding of land by religious groups will be safeguarded, a promise that can be aimed only at the Malay-Muslim community.[12]

In the meantime, in October 1974 the split in the MCP leadership became overt with the appearance in several parts of the peninsula of pamphlets, banners, and flags announcing the formation of the "Marxist-Leninist" (M-L) faction of the MCP, with its own guerrilla arm to be known thenceforward as the Malayan People's Liberation Army. Another apparent breakaway group is the so-called Revolutionary Faction (RF) of the MCP.[13] Little information is available to explain in detail the ideological orientation and policies of these various MCP groups, although information released by a police spokesperson in Kuala Lumpur claims that the MCP split is a manifestation of the Sino-Soviet struggle for hegemony over Southeast Asian revolutionary forces—which if true would be a dramatic and far-reaching development.[14] In any event, both the MCP(M-L) and the MCP(RF) seem determined to pursue the path of revolutionary violence and armed struggle, while the official MCP is concerning itself with expanding the united front and working with legal "front" groups in the political

12. United Press International report from Kuala Lumpur, February 6, 1976, based on a broadcast from Suara Revolusi, the MCP's "Voice of the Malayan Revolution," on December 29, 1975.

13. One press report suggested that the MCP(M–L) strength was about three hundred and that of the MCP(RF) about one hundred. The MCP(M–L) group allegedly fought several battles with the "official" MCP forces in southern Thailand in January 1976 for control of territory. ST, April 21, 1976, and Bangkok Post, March 2, 1976.

14. News item by Denzil Peiris, FEER, January 23, 1976. The article claims that the official MCP is still pro-Peking in its sympathies, whereas the MCP(M–L) faction supports and is supported by the Soviet Union. I do not believe the latter orientation to be true.

arena, at the same time engaging in sporadic military activity in rural areas. No doubt the MCP's breakaway groups wish to take advantage of local and external realities that seem to prevail at present: by such means they may be able to resuscitate the guerrilla phase of the revolution to a more violent level. These realities are massive Chinese discontent following the May 1969 riots, the increasing militancy of the Thai Malay irredentists, the implications of the Third Malaysia Plan (which if unsuccessful will undoubtedly result in dissatisfaction among both Malays and Chinese), and (to a degree that is difficult to measure) the defeat of the United States in Indochina and the psychological impetus this may have given to revolutionary forces in Malaysia.

The end of the U.S. presence in Indochina and its effects on Malaysia require further adumbration. Some observers[15] believe that a new revolutionary struggle will be initiated, with the Socialist Republic of Vietnam (SRV) providing logistical and propaganda support. I do not believe that this will happen. The SRV, to be sure, has stated her support of certain insurgencies in Southeast Asia (specifically in those countries whose governments are not representative of the people and that permit a foreign military presence[16]), but during the visits of the SRV deputy foreign minister, Phan Hien, to various Southeast Asian countries in mid-1976, it was made clear that the SRV desired above all the normalization of state-to-state relations—which is not to say, of course, that the Lao Dong party in the SRV will not continue to broadcast fraternal greetings and verbal encouragement to other Communist parties in the region. But for the foreseeable future, the SRV will be too occupied with the task of national reconstruction to devote attention to the spread of revolution elsewhere. Furthermore, the SRV is too aware of the implications of the Sino-Soviet split, desiring above all to maintain a delicate balance between the need for Soviet material assistance and the proximity of a vast Chinese neighbor to the north, to embark upon uncertain adventures such as giving aid to Maoist, pro-PRC insurgencies of which the MCP's armed struggle is an example.

At any rate the Malaysian government undoubtedly is pleased at

15. An example is an article by Joseph Alsop, "Showdown over Southeast Asia?" *Readers' Digest* (December 1975), 137–142.
16. *NYT*, March 1, 1976.

the fragmentation that has occurred within the MCP, the sole revolutionary movement in Western Malaysia, although the full significance of the rift has yet to be made manifest.[17] The military threat facing the government has two faces: first, the sporadic guerrilla activity mounted by the "official" MCP (known as the MCP-CC or MCP-Central Committee) operating out of southern Thailand, and second, guerrilla operations conducted by the MCP(M-L) and possibly by the MCP(RF) in urban areas. In the first instance, the ability of the MCP to win over a segment of the rural Malay population in areas immediately south of the border with Thailand is worrisome to the regime. By the late 1960s the MCP's Department of Malay Work (DMW) had become well established in southern Thailand, and its activities soon spread southward into Malaysia where it set up "ostensibly Malay-inspired facade organizations" with the intention of championing the cause of Malay nationalism; according to the government, the DMW, cleverly using the teachings of Islam and giving concrete assistance to Malay villagers, had been effective: "This distortion by the MCP of the teachings of Islam to suit Communist ends has unfortunately found credence among Malays in one of the border states of West Malaysia [Kelantan]."[18] By 1971 the situation had deteriorated sufficiently that Kuala Lumpur issued yet another White Paper (entitled *The Resurgence of Armed Communism in West Malaysia*) in which it admitted that guerrilla operations had borne some results, even though the main threat had been contained. For the past several years the guerrillas had concentrated on carrying out ambushes, acts of sabotage, and assassinations of police officials, attacking Malaysian (and Thai) armed forces in the rural areas and this time making certain not to alienate the civilian population through gratuitous acts of violence. The Malaysian government believed that the official wing of the MCP had as its guerrilla strength not more than two thousand armed and uniformed personnel (many recruited from Thai Chinese and Thai Malays) plus several thousand other supporters and sympathizers.[19]

17. *FEER*, November 8, 1974, item by M. Pillai, and *South China Morning Post*, June 21, 1975.

18. Government of Malaysia, *The Path of Violence to Absolute Power*, pp. 28–30.

19. *Wall Street Journal*, June 15, 1975, and *NYT*, June 23, 1975.

Urban guerrilla activity in the spring of 1976 carried out by the MCP(M-L) was of greater immediacy to the government because for the first time since the early 1950s there appeared to be a growing base of support for the insurgents in the towns and cities that did not simply consist of sympathy, but included providing hiding places, caches, and intelligence. A number of bomb-throwing incidents, sabotage, and selected assassination of police officials contributed to a growing climate of anxiety, resulting in stringent new security measures and government awareness of the seriousness of the situation. In mid-1975 the government promulgated a set of Essential Regulations that, without actually declaring a state of emergency, give sweeping powers to the authorities, including the abrogation in some cases of the rules of evidence.[20] The Essential Regulations also provide for the establishment of a scheme called *Rukun Tetangga* ("neighborhood association," or community self-reliance groups, wherein all males between the ages of eighteen and fifty-five are compelled to participate in local security patrols) and the organization of a vigilante group known as *Rela*, or the People's Volunteer Corps. Other internal security measures instituted to meet the guerrilla menace include strict press censorship, increasing the size of the police force, resettlement of squatters and relocation of villages in "insecure" rural areas, and house-to-house sweeps for arms in urban areas. Some indication of the cost of security precautions can be seen in the 1976 budget,[21] presented to the federal parliament in November 1975: out of a total federal expenditure of $M5,341,000, the defense share amounted to $M1,026,000, or 20 percent—a high figure for a country engaged in an ambitious new economic program that involves considerable social cost. Although the federal government is paying careful attention to the increase in guerrilla operations, no state of emergency has been declared, no doubt both to avoid stimulating the fears of the populace (leading to an increase in ethnic antipathy) and to avoid scaring away much-needed foreign investment. By mid-1977, Malaysian security forces

20. *FEER*, October 3, October 10, and December 26, 1975, series of items by K. Das. One draconian measure, bitterly assailed by Malaysian lawyers, include placing the onus of innocence squarely on the person of the accused.

21. Figures taken from *Suara* (Newsletter of the Federation of Malaysian Students, North America), 1 (December 1975), 6.

had succeeded in substantially reducing the guerrilla threat.

If the MCP is ultimately to succeed it must organize itself horizontally, across ethnic cleavages; its image as a Chinese party must be broadened to include substantial numbers of Malays if it is to find a friendly sea in which to swim. But despite the MCP's limited successes with Malays in the border region (more because of the militancy of Thai Malay irredentism than specifically Malaysian conditions), the party may not be able to win significant Malay support in areas away from the northern and remote Malaysian districts in the predictable future. In the existing circumstances of severe socioeconomic competition between Malays and non-Malays, sharpened as always by language, religious, and cultural differences, there seems little chance of establishing horizontal linkages across ethnic boundaries between dissatisfied Malays, Chinese, and Indians. Any Malay discontent arising out of the failure of their expectations directed against the government is likely to pull toward the right, that is, to become even more pro-Malay "nationalistic," whereas the non-Malay revolutionary pattern in Western Malaysia is set irrevocably on the left.

In Sarawak, Communist guerrillas have long posed a threat to government stability. The history of Communism in the state has never been fully examined except in official White Papers and press releases, and its organization and support remain shadowy. Whatever its form, Communism in Sarawak has never been organizationally linked to the MCP inasmuch as the latter does not recognize the existence of Malaysia as a legitimate political entity and continues to treat Sabah and Sarawak as territories outside of its political purview. In the 1950s and 1960s the Communists in Sarawak utilized various farmer and youth groups as organizational bases, at the same time increasing their political influence through various figures in the SUPP. But the SUPP, much as the PAP in Singapore, with the assistance of the government's security services, has come under the influence and control of the party's "moderate" faction, and its leftist proclivities have been halted. In 1969 and 1970, a new Communist organization appeared in the public eye, calling itself the North Kalimantan Communist Party (NKCP, Kalimantan being the Indonesian name for Borneo), finding its main support in the Chinese population but including some Ibans in its ranks. The NKCP instigated numerous incidents involving armed force in the early 1970s, killing a number of civilians and ambushing Malaysian security forces.[22] The Malaysian government viewed the rising tide of armed insurgency in Sarawak with alarm and reinforced its troops on the ground in order to effect counterinsurgency operations.[23] These and other suppressive measures obviously resulted in success, for in October 1973 surrender talks were held at the residence of Sarawak's chief minister, and some time later the top NKCP guerrilla leader surrendered to the government with 481 of his followers. They brought with them only a meager collection of homemade weaponry, which has raised the possibility that some arms may have been hidden in the forest. The government has estimated that another 200 guerrillas remain secluded in jungle camps in Sarawak,[24] but if so they have been quiet for the past four years.

Militarily the Communist movements in Eastern and Western Malaysia so far have been able to offer only a moderately serious challenge to the government's authority. Politically, however, their potential remains a threat, for the issues that sustain revolutionary hopes still exist. Economic policies that discriminate against Chinese and Indian workers and small shopkeepers (although that is not their official intent), the lack of land made available to Chinese farmers and peasants, the dim employment prospects for non-Malay youths from poor families, and the erosion of non-Malay cultural traditions because of the effects of the government's educational and language policies continue to haunt the government's decision makers in Kuala Lumpur, themselves entrammeled by the strident pressures emanating from Malay ultranationalists unhappy at the slow rate of Malay socioeconomic betterment. In the final analysis, like so many other problems in Malaysia, and in common with civil strife in many other countries in the world, the revolu-

---

22. Michael B. Leigh, *The Rising Moon: Political Change in Sarawak* (Sydney: Sydney University Press, 1974), pp. 156–159.
23. The effectiveness of the counterinsurgency operations was enhanced by a high degree of cooperation between Malaysian and Indonesian forces in the border region.
24. *FEER*, April 4, 1975. Unofficial estimates put the figure as high as one thousand guerrillas still in the jungle.

tionary movement in Malaysia is definable in ethnic as well as in ideological terms.

Finally, the effect that the stepped-up MCP guerrilla activities have had on official Indonesian thinking is worth considering. In recent years the Indonesian and Malaysian governments have moved closely together; especially at the military elite level they have woven strong ties of cooperation. There is some evidence (garnered from private but reliable sources) that Indonesian army generals look upon the Malaysian government's war against guerrilla Communism as their own front line, as it were, in the struggle to contain Communism generally. If the MCP succeeds in mounting a genuinely serious threat against the Kuala Lumpur government and if existing authority stands in danger of being toppled, a scenario can easily be envisaged in which Indonesian forces find themselves compelled to intervene militarily on the side of their Malay allies across the Straits of Malacca.

Foreign Policy

The problems of state integration and of Communism lead naturally to the question of foreign policy, which in recent years in Malaysia has assumed a singularly homemade flavor. This had not always been the case. The colonial experience severed traditional patterns of contact between the Malay states and their neighbors (although the Malay states had never acted in concert prior to British intervention), and for almost a century ties between the Malay Peninsula and the outside world consisted solely of an elongated relationship with Britain as the metropolitan power. The sultans and their state governments were never required to perform foreign policy roles; all decisions were made by Britain, and indigenous leaders were rarely, if ever, consulted. When the new Malayan leaders began to exercise their own policy-making initiatives in the arena of international relations after 1957, they were encumbered by a set of psychological impedimenta inherited from the colonial experience. Because of their lack of experience in foreign affairs prior to independence, Malayan politicians and civil servants were thereafter constrained by the myth that for many years to come they would be forced to rely upon the protection of the British for external security—a state of mind that obviously hindered closer regional cooperation to replace Britain's strategic umbrella. Simultaneously with the granting of independence, Malaya entered into a defense agreement with Britain that committed the latter country to come to Malay's aid in the event of external aggression, and to this end British and Commonwealth troops continued to be stationed on Malayan soil.

Malaysian foreign policy determinants underwent a radical reappraisal in 1966, when the British Labour government decided to attenuate Britain's international commitments by withdrawing most of her forces "East of Suez." On assuming power, Edward Heath tried to reverse this policy and promised to maintain some sort of "military presence" in Southeast Asia after 1971. Obviously Malaysian leaders have seen through the hollowness of this premise, for Britain is militarily impotent in Southeast Asia given the geographical distances and the paucity of her resources. Australia and New Zealand formally moved in to share the burden of Malaysia's defense needs, and there exists today a Five-Power Agreement involving Britain, Australia, New Zealand, Malaysia, and Singapore in which military cooperation and assistance are promised in case of aggression. The United States is not a participant in this agreement, and it has no military security pact with Malaysia.

The current period might be called the postcolonial age of Malaysia's foreign policy. At first the perceived threat of aggression from the PRC still hung over the jungle and towns of Malaysia with miasmic persistence, as the Malaysian foreign minister, acknowledging that the power vacuum left by the British withdrawal had yet to be filled, warned that a "giant outside power, the People's Republic of China, seems bent on a long-range programme of expanding its power and influence through its proxies in Southeast Asia. [Since 1965] Peking has threatened Thailand, Malaysia and Singapore with so-called People's Wars to be launched by local communist movements against these three countries." The time was ripe therefore, the foreign minister concluded, for a strong regional organization, a community of Southeast Asian states, "banded together in the common pursuit of peaceful development . . . harnessing all the talent and resources of the diverse peoples who make up Southeast

Asia."[25] A new set of foreign policy considerations, based on regional cooperation and the neutralization of Southeast Asia, gradually came to dominate Malaysian thinking. The ascent of Tun Razak to the position of prime minister in 1970 gave a fresh impetus to this revitalized approach.

In 1971, Tun Razak reacted quickly to an apparently distinct shift to the right in China's foreign policy, later confirmed by Richard Nixon's visit to Peking in all of its ramifications. The prime minister outlined Malaysia's attitudes in a speech in April 1971: China had often been "erratic" in her policy toward Malaysia, the Tun said, but her actions now appeared to be based upon a "more sober and realistic acceptance of international order." The Tun recognized that China had legitimate interests in the region; these were "commensurate with her importance and dignity as a major power and the right to expect that the countries of the region do not act in ways that adversely affect her." The Tun felt that China's policy toward Southeast Asia was crucial to the region's neutrality—that is, any concept of neutrality demanded that the PRC must agree that interstate relations be based on the acceptance of the Southeast Asian states' independence, on the integrity of their international borders, and on noninterference in their internal affairs.[26] (By 1971, China was Malaysia's fifth largest trading partner, and hopes were growing that the volume of trade would expand rapidly.) Malaysia thus moved rapidly in the direction of improved relations with China, supporting the admission of China to the United Nations and eventually establishing full diplomatic ties—the first "nonaligned" Southeast Asian state to do so.

Tun Razak reiterated Malaysia's foreign policy, based on the twin planks of regionalism and neutralism, in a major speech to parliament in July 1971. In his view, Southeast Asia was in a state of flux because of the withdrawal of British military forces, the gradual disengagement of the U.S. from Indochina, the growing power of Japan and her interests in the region, and, above all, the new posture in Chinese foreign policy. The Tun believed that stability in Southeast Asia, under these circumstances, could "only be safeguarded by

25. Speech by Tun Ismail in Kuala Lumpur, June 23, 1966, reported in *FAM*, Vols. 1 and 2, 1966.
26. Speech in Germany, April 21, 1971. See *FAM*, 4 (June 1971).

a policy of neutralization which will ensure that this region will no longer by a theatre of conflict for the competing interests of the major powers." Recognizing the threat posed by militant Communism within Malaysia's own borders, Tun Razak emphasized that the active suppression of the MCP did not minimize his commitment to peaceful coexistence; although Malaysia would remain anti-Communist in her attitudes toward internal threats posed by the MCP's operations, external affairs would be conducted regardless of the ideology of the other states concerned.[27]

The neutralization policy is predicated upon the assumption and the fear that conflict between the major powers in the furtherance of their interests in the region will lead, as in Vietnam and Cambodia, to destruction and disaster. In pursuit of their own goals, Malaysia believes, "the major powers will tend to continuously examine the international situation [in Southeast Asia], probing areas and markets and sources of raw materials and seeking to extend their respective influence in order to gain an advantageous position in relation to the other powers."[28] Malaysia, therefore, has sought to establish a new international order in Southeast Asia, a zone of peace, freedom, and neutrality through which the region may be free of and isolated from violent intervention by external powers. As the prime minister said in 1971, "The essence of neutralization must be the recognition and accommodation of the legitimate interests of all powers concerned in the area."[29] To this end a genuine partnership between the economically developed and developing states is to be pursued as a basis for establishing peace and perchance prosperity in the region. The neutralization concept may be envisioned at two levels. The first focuses upon regional cooperation, excluding a common regional defense posture, and the second assumes that the long-range goal is for all foreign powers to guarantee, through a joint treaty or other such written instrument, that they will not intervene with military force in Southeast Asia, thereby excluding the region from the global power struggle. In the light of these hopes and ideals, Malaysia has embarked upon a course of nonalignment,

27. *ST* July 27, 1971.
28. Malaysian Minister of Information, "Key to Peace in a Region of Constant Turmoil," *NN*, September 14, 1971.
29. Speech to the UN in New York, in *ST*, October 2, 1971.

of recognizing and dealing with any government, regardless of its ideology, that in turn acknowledges Malaysia's territorial integrity and refrains from interference in Malaysia's internal affairs in an atmosphere of peaceful coexistence. In short, as Tun Razak told the Malaysian parliament in July 1971,

Our commitment to the concept of neutralization [is] the best permanent solution to ensure the security and stability of Southeast Asia. We are naturally aware that this is a long-term solution and it requires to be accepted by the super powers as well as by the countries of the region themselves. It requires that we should resolve sources of tension and conflict within the region, and that we should develop stronger ties of cooperation and solidarity among countries in Southeast Asia.

It also requires the support of the super powers which can only be secured when we can demonstrate that this arrangement provides a guarantee that their respective interests will not be adversely affected.[30]

In pursuance of the new neutralism, Malaysia has strengthened her ties with Communist countries while maintaining old connections with other world blocs. Kuala Lumpur recently concluded trade agreements with the Soviet Union and other Eastern European countries, established diplomatic offices in Moscow and Kuala Lumpur, and allowed a limited number of Malaysian students to study in Moscow. The most interesting development has taken place with Peking. From 1971 onward state-to-state relations between Malaysia and the PRC, previously conducted on a rigidly adversary basis, began to change. The level of anti-Malaysian propaganda issuing from Peking and the Suara Revolusi, a clandestine MCP radio broadcasting from Southern China, diminished to an appreciable degree, and in May 1971 a Malaysian trade mission went to Peking. In late 1973 and early 1974 a series of quiet negotiations were held as a prelude to further progress; these concerned an abatement of Peking's support for the MCP (which in any event had only been verbal), the cessation of broadcasts from Suara Revolusi, and the issuance of an explicit statement from Peking disavowing the old KMT Chinese policy of *jus sanguinis* toward Chinese resident in Malaysia who did not hold Malaysian citizenship.[31] Tun Razak

30. *ST*, July 27, 1971.
31. Stephen Chee, "Malaysia/Singapore: The Political Economy of Multiracial Development," *Asian Survey*, 14 (February 1974), 183–191.

journeyed to Peking in May 1974, and an agreement was signed on May 31 formalizing diplomatic relations between the two countries. Simultaneously Malaysia informed the KMT government in Taiwan that she was severing diplomatic ties with Taipei. The Malaysian government clearly took a calculated risk in promoting state-to-state relations with Peking. On the one hand, Kuala Lumpur believes that a genuine neutralism in Southeast Asia can never be achieved without the benevolent cooperation of China. Conversely, however, the presence in (or near) Malaysia of militant Communist organizations, complete with armed and uniformed wings and mainly Chinese in ethnic content, has long caused residual fears that diplomatic recognition of the PRC might result in an upsurge of prestige and morale within the ranks of the Communists. Malaysia at present assigns primary importance to the former of these two considerations (hoping that the establishment of diplomatic relations with Peking will forestall the possibility of the PRC offering more concrete assistance to the MCP, thereby undercutting Malaysian Communist hopes), but in the long haul Malaysian relations with China must continue to be influenced by the presence within or on her borders of an armed Communist organization and by the fact that the ethnic makeup of her population is almost 40 percent Chinese, many of whom are disenchanted with current Malaysian domestic policies.

The premises upon which the Malaysian neutralization policy is founded may seriously miscalculate Chinese interests. In the first place, the assumption is made that there is to be a convergence of interests in Southeast Asia, that the indigenous states and the major world powers (particularly the U.S., the USSR and the PRC) all have interests in the region that are mutually compatible. This is a dangerous inference. There is every indication that China looks upon the Soviet Union as the principal "contradiction" standing in the way of Marxist socialist goals, and Peking is hardly likely to cooperate in any neutralization project that envisages the recognition or the legitimization of Soviet interests in Southeast Asia, let alone those of the United States except as a buffer to Soviet encroachment. Furthermore, Malaysia's participation in the Five-Power Agreement, no matter how much she protests its short-term, purely defensive character, together with the presence of Com-

monwealth troops on Malaysian soil, may not be expected to persuade the Chinese leadership that Malaysia's neutralization proposals are much more than pious platitudes. In view of the overwhelming dependence of the Malaysian economy on foreign
capital from and foreign markets in the non-Communist world
(despite great efforts to expand trade with China, the USSR, and
Eastern Europe), it must also be asked whether a genuine political
neutrality can ever have any real meaning.

Regionalism in Southeast Asia is nothing new. It spluttered
ineffectively in the early 1960s in the shape of Maphilindo (Malaya,
Indonesia, and the Philippines) and the Association of Southeast
Asia, but both these groups soon disappeared.[32] In their place
in 1967 arose a new and expanded organization called the Association of Southeast Asian Nations (ASEAN), comprising Thailand,
Singapore, Malaysia, the Philippines, and Indonesia. The ASEAN's
main thrust was intended to lie in the direction of economic and
cultural cooperation, but today attempts are made, with increasing
success, to arrive at a political consensus and a joint foreign policy.
Within the economic context, the ASEAN has not proved to be a
shining example of regional cooperation. Attempts to promote
closer economic integration have failed dismally, and the possibility
of forming an ASEAN common market are as remote today as they
were a decade ago. The differentiated rates of economic growth
among the member states, the uneven quality of the infrastructure
on which the various economic systems are constructed, and the
conflicting pulls of bilateral agreements against a regional mul-
tilateralism all militate against the growth of a unified set of
economic policies. There are also politically motivated suspicions
that still pervade the regional atmosphere. One commentator has
summed up the political problems that beset the ASEAN member
states as follows: (a) the status of the Muslim provinces and the
continuous operations of MCP guerrillas in southern Thailand (as
well as the encouragement given by right-wing Malay nationalists in
Malaysia to the Thai Malay irredentists); (b) the deep-rooted suspicions and rivalry existing between Malaysia and Singapore; (c) the

32. The membership of the ASA was not identical to that of Maphilindo. ASEAN
later combined the membership of these two earlier organizations, with the addition
of Singapore.

status of the Malacca Straits (the Malaysian and Indonesian governments have proposed to deinternationalize the Malacca Straits and to impose their own joint controls, a move opposed by Thailand and Singapore); (d) the possible (if improbable) construction of a canal through the Kra Isthmus in southern Thailand, which would pose an economic threat to Malaysia and Singapore; (e) the Philippine government's suspicions of Malaysian interference over her treatment of the Muslim minority in southern Philippines (it is probable that Tun Mustapha in Sabah, who has his own strong contacts among Philippine Muslims, was used as the conduit for arms and ammunition sent to the Muslim rebels from Libya and her eccentric "strong man" Qaddafi—an operation that finally angered a central authority in Kuala Lumpur, which, under its new Prime Minister Datuk Hussein, has become more concerned over long-range foreign policy goals of regional cooperation); and, finally, (f) the long-standing claim by the Philippines regarding her territorial rights over Sabah.[33] (The Philippines' claim at long last appears close to resolution: President Marcos announced formally to the ASEAN summit meeting held in Kuala Lumpur in August 1977 that the claim would be dropped, presumably as a quid pro quo for Malaysian protestations of nonintervention in the Muslim insurgency in the southern Philippines.)

By 1970 the concept of an ASEAN common market had been quietly discarded in favor of less ambitious phrases like "economic cooperation" and "trade cooperation." The ASEAN summit of August 1977 made similar gestures toward joint economic ventures, but little real progress has been made. It is obvious that because of the similar economic base of four out of the five ASEAN members—Singapore being the exception—they are all selling the same primary products (tin, rubber, rice, palm oil, and the like) in competition with each other, and clearly a common market is of little benefit. In terms of industrial production, too, obviously Malaysia with her efficient infrastructure can manufacture a particular article at a far cheaper price than, for example, can Indonesia, which is encumbered by a creakingly corrupt and inefficient bureaucracy. In

33. Dick Wilson, "Economic Cooperation within ASEAN," *Pacific Community*, 5 (October 1973), 80–96.

its economic aspects, then, despite the establishment of a large
number of committees, officials admit that little of economic consequence has been achieved.[34] Nevertheless, the fact that the ASEAN
has held together for a number of years, despite the centrifugal pulls
of the member states' own divergent interests, is a cause for optimism, and the Malaysian government continues to subscribe to its
goals. As Tun Razak remarked in 1971, the outside powers will be
able to see that regional cooperation is a factor in instilling a sense of
self-reliance in the region.[35] Economic cooperation, nevertheless,
remains impaired by individual interests. The 1973 energy crisis
gave an example of the fissiparous nature of the ASEAN, for when
the shortage adversely affected the economies of Singapore, Thailand, and the Philippines, the two oil-producing states of the
ASEAN did little to help. The Philippine government proposed that
the ASEAN partners should adopt a common oil policy under which
the producers would aid the consumers, but neither Malaysia nor
Indonesia reacted favorably. As a major United States newspaper
remarked after the February 1976 ASEAN consultations in Thailand, a number of important economic disagreements can still be
discerned. Jealousy of Indonesia and her potential for political
hegemony, coupled with economic nationalism, prevents the
emergence of little more than rhetorical economic unity.[36]

Politically the ASEAN has been more successful and mutual
policy making over a large range of issues is now apparent. ASEAN
member states regularly meet before the holding of major international fora—the United Nations General Assembly, the United
Nations Committee for Trade and Development, the Group of 77 (a
group of lesser-developed countries that wishes to bring about a
more equable distribution of wealth between North and South
countries), the nonaligned movement, and the like—to work out
common approaches. In the process there is a tremendous inter-
change of views at the top and middle levels of the various bureaucracies, and this is slowly but discernibly helping to bring about an

34. Speech by Tunku Abdul Rahman at the ASEAN Foreign Ministers' meeting
at Cameron Highlands, reported in *FAM*, 4 (March 1971).
35. Speech at Commonwealth Prime Ministers' Conference, Singapore, reprinted in *FAM*, 4 (March 1971).
36. *NYT*, February 11, 24, 1976.

awareness of common problems and a sense of political solidarity. There is no doubt that in these terms the ASEAN is a real force for regional stability.

There remain, however, intra-ASEAN political disagreements, chiefly with regard to the approach to Communist states. Malaysia's inclusion of leftist nations in her foreign policy of neutralism has not been matched by reciprocal approaches from Singapore and Indonesia, which adopt cautious and conservative stances against recognition of Chinese Communist and Soviet interests in the region. In May 1975, ASEAN ministers met in Kuala Lumpur to discuss Malaysia's proposals to create a Southeast Asian "zone of peace, freedom, and neutrality." These required member states to divest themselves of foreign military bases and to refrain from entering into defense pacts with outside powers. Foreign bases already in existence would be regarded as temporary, to be phased out at some indeterminate date in the future. The meeting ended in disagreement, although lip service was paid to Malaysia's proposals. No joint policy could be reached with regard to the newly victorious Cambodian, Vietnamese, and Laotian governments and to the admission of other Southeast Asian states into the ASEAN.[37]

By 1977 Malaysia's proposed zone of peace, freedom, and neutrality appeared to by dying of its own inertia. Strong attacks on ASEAN as a U.S.-inspired neocolonialist plot by Laos and Vietnam during the 1976 nonaligned movement summit meetings in Colombo seem to have resigned Malaysia to the unrealistic nature—at least at this time—of her neutralization proposals. Malaysia herself, however, continues to maintain correct, if at times cool, relations with Communist states. The basic problem for Malaysia is to equate her small-nation status and relative powerlessness with the conflicting interests of the superpowers as they focus on Southeast Asia, and with the emerging foreign policy interests—as yet undefined—of Vietnam and its abundant arsenal of weapons. A Malay proverb often quoted by Malaysian leaders states that when elephants clash, it is the grass underneath that is crushed. Malaysia thus must ask herself the ultimate question: can she stand nonaligned on her own? The emergence of a regional defense posture under the aegis of the

37. *NYT*, May 12, 14, 16, 1975.

ASEAN is unlikely because of Vietnamese and Laotian suspicions. Bilateral arrangements for defense cooperation with states such as Indonesia, Singapore, and Thailand are feasible, but it is doubtful, in long-range terms, whether these will be sufficient to provide regional security.

Economic Problems

Through the long-term implications of the Second and Third Malaysia Plans, the government's economic managers have made it clear that they wish to erase unemployment and other forms of economic deprivation from all ethnic communities in Malaysia. Espousing the concept of "welfare economics," the planners have proceeded on the principle that the general weal of the country can be promoted only if all races are drawn into the mainstream of economic progress and that it will be diminished if one group is advanced through the retardation (or the impoverishment) of another. The government's goal is to have at least 30 percent of "all aspects" of the economy in Malay hands and under Malay economic management by 1991[38]—yet this is to be achieved without adversely affecting the existing economic status of the Chinese and Indians. Since 60 percent of the major share capital in Malaysia is owned by foreign concerns, and only 20 percent by local Chinese, critics of the plan argue that an increased slice of the pie for Malays must be generated at the expense of foreign profit making. Such a policy, however, clashes head-on with the government's perceived need to attract, not to repel, foreign investment in order to stimulate the rate of economic growth. The contradictions are obvious.

What has been achieved so far? Some industry has been dispersed into areas more accessible to the Malay rural population, and several planned, large-scale agricultural projects have been implemented. In his midterm review of the plan, given in November 1973, Tun Razak claimed that Malaysia was on her way to bringing about both full employment and racial balance in employment, ownership, and management of wealth. This optimistic assessment, naturally, is predicated upon the continuation of economic growth, which in turn is subject to the vagaries of world-

38. *NYT*, October 3, 1973.

wide price and demand fluctuations. The Malaysian economic system, a mixture of laissez-faire capitalism, government-controlled centralized planning, and direct state participation in capital-funded enterprises, is reasonably well equipped to deal with the latter exigency, but the problem is to ensure continued economic growth in the face of increasing population growth.[39] Already there is some evidence that while the Chinese "haves" are not being divested of their economic share, the great importance given to the improvement of the Malay position is resulting in an increasing number of Chinese and Indian "have-nots." That is, many well-educated non-*bumiputera* youths entering the economic system are being deprived of equal economic opportunites. Unemployment among Chinese youths in Penang, to give one example, was 25 percent and higher in 1971—surely a volatile situation when linked to an undoubted political and ethnic awareness.[40] For added to economic discrimination against young Chinese, whether deliberate or not, is political discrimination to the extent that many Chinese feel that they are treated as less than first-class citizens, that their votes do not count as much as Malay votes (the Malaysian electoral system is heavily weighted in favor of rural area representation), and that they are underrepresented in the decision-making process.

By the end of 1974, the effects of the world recession in rubber and other commodities reverberated in the Malaysian countryside. Many thousands of Malay peasants, who had been encouraged by the government to grow rubber in smallholdings,[41] found themselves gripped by the dilemma of rapidly falling wholesale prices for the rubber they sold and increasing retail prices for commodities they had to buy. Their standard of living fell to a bare level of subsistence, leading to malnutrition among children and other related ills. In November 1974 some twelve thousand Malay peasants in Baling, Kedah, demonstrated over the insupportable conditions, and this was followed by student rioting and violence on

39. Lim Chong-yeh, "Economic Trends," in *Trends in Malaysia,* Seminar Proceedings (Singapore: Institute of Southeast Asian Studies, July 1971). It is too early to say if Malaysia's birth-control program has been effective.
40. Conversations with Malaysian officials in 1971.
41. There are half a million such smallholders in Western Malaysia.

several university and college campuses.[42] The whole picture has been exacerbated by the flow of overly optimistic propaganda from the Department of Information in Kuala Lumpur ever since the Second Malaysia Plan was implemented, although some action was undoubtedly necessary to loosen up the traditional Malay value system. This stream of assertions, exhortations, and predictions may have created in the Malay pesantry too heavy a reliance on the government's ability to improve their lot, diluting in the process the self-confidence and self-reliance needed to promote a sense of being able to manipulate the environment for themselves and for their own improvement—for ultimately if the Malaysian economy is ever to be put into ethnic balance, the Malays need to demonstrate, to their own community and to others, their capacity to participate and to compete on equal terms with the non-Malay sectors of society.

These, then, are the pluses and minuses of the Malaysian economic system. Strong in overall statistical terms (if undergoing temporary setbacks because of international events), possessed of an abundance of natural and human resources (if overly reliant on rubber and tin), monitored by a reasonably effective government planning bureaucracy (retarded by an increasingly enervating corruption), the economy in and of itself can be assessed with some optimism. Yet when seen in ethnic terms, perils lie ahead; the economic sector is beset by the differentiated growth rates of each ethnic community—a factor that if it is not resolved will undoubtedly be transported into the political arena, aggravating an already high level of ethnic distrust.

42. Many of these Malay students had backgrounds rooted in Malay poverty; their presence in the tertiary educational tier reflects the government's policy of giving preference to rural Malays, but at the same time, ironically, it is linking rural dissidence to a new type of leadership and activism, able to articulate long-standing grievances (especially absentee landlordism).

PART III

SINGAPORE

6 | Recent History

Singapore and Independence

British attitudes toward the granting of independence to Singapore were at first qualitatively different from those toward Malaya. In strategic terms Singapore was considered to be an integral part of Commonwealth security as a vital geopolitical link between Britain, Australia, and New Zealand. Because of its trade relations with and economic dependence on the hinterland of the Malay Peninsula, the British did not envisage that the island could ever become a viable independent state, nor, because of its large Chinese majority population, could it be absorbed into the Federation of Malaya without upsetting the delicate balance of Malay political supremacy. Singapore was therefore separated from the other Straits Settlements and Malaya in April 1946 and established as a Crown Colony. The new administrative system was conducted through a governor as supreme administrator, supported by an appointed executive council and an appointed legislative council, both bodies composed of official and unofficial members.

The first elections ever held in Singapore, in 1948, were irrelevant to most of the populace, since the electorate was confined to British subjects. Only about twenty-two thousand voters were registered, of whom 63 percent voted. The two parties involved[1] were conservative in hue and were geared almost exclusively to the maintenance of the status quo. Merger with Malaya was discussed by some political figures—notably in the newly formed Singapore UMNO

1. The so-called Progressive and Independent parties. Most eligible Chinese voters boycotted the elections and those that followed in 1951. See L. A. Mills, *Malaya: A Political and Economic Appraisal* (Minneapolis: University of Minnesota Press, 1958), pp. 117–119.

(SUMNO)[2]—but no serious movement emerged until several years later. A second series of elections were held in 1951, but again only a minute portion of the population participated.

In 1953 the Rendel Commission report[3] recommended reforms that wcre implcmcntcd in 1955 and considcrably incrcascd thc number of voters (thereby encouraging the growth of more popularly based parties) as well as increasing the size of the legislative assembly. The most important political party that emerged during this period, which has dominated Singapore's politics ever since, was the People's Action Party, the PAP. The party was formed in late 1954; its founders came from the ranks of the trade unions and the legal profession and included journalists and teachers. The intellectual content of the new party was high, and the leadership was aggressive, cerebral, and self-confident—qualities the party has consistently demonstrated down to the present. Although the PAP was officially welcomed by the British, who at this time were seeking to establish the basis for internal, parliamentary self-rule (presumably having sniffed the eager air of the winds of change), the flavor of the party's policies was left wing; British distrust of the PAP and its left-leaning platform soon progressed into an adversary relationship. In fact, as the Singapore journalist Pang Cheng-lian has shown, the PAP was composed of two distinct factions—the allegedly pro-Communists led by Lim Chin-siong and the "moderates" led by Lee Kuan-yew.[4] This split was to remain papered over for some years behind a united anticolonial facade, only to erupt later as the movement for independence approached fruition. The two major planks in the PAP's inaugural platform were (a) merger with Malaya and (b) a common nationality and equal rights for all (that is, no Malay special privileges). These two points have remained at issue.

New elections were held in April 1955, with the PAP offering only four candidates for the twenty-five assembly seats. Other new parties, occupying various positions on the political spectrum, were

2. At this stage the SUMNO's activities were largely concerned with events in the federation and the preservation of Malay rights in that country.

3. Government of Singapore, *Report of the Constitutional Commission 1954* (Singapore: Government Printer, 1954).

4. Pang Cheng-lian, *Singapore's People's Action Party: Its History, Organization and Leadership* (Singapore: Oxford University Press, 1971), chap. 1.

formed to contest this election. Despite an influx of money from the world of traders, entrepreneurs, and compradores in support of conservative parties, the moderate democratic socialist Labour Front, under the flamboyant but principled leadership of David Marshall, emerged victorious—even though it had to form a coalition with the SUMNO-MCA Alliance in order to rule. The PAP was also surprisingly successful, three out of four of its candidates gaining seats. Upon assumption of office, the new chief minister, David Marshall, led an all-party delegation to London in April 1956 to urge Britain to grant early independence. The British, however, were willing to allow only a measure of internal rule, with the metropolitan country retaining control of internal security (the fear of Communism was still strong) and external affairs. Marshall had staked his prestige upon the success of the talks, and when they broke down he returned to Singapore and resigned. His colleagues in the Labour Front government did not, however, and a new coalition government was formed under Lim Yew-hock as chief minister. The events of this period, the political interplay between the forces led by David Marshall, Lim Yew-hock, and Lee Kuan-yew, are too convoluted to be described in detail here. The PAP at first seemingly cooperated with the government in power, but eventually undermined its authority and forced its downfall. The disarray in which the PAP's opponents were left following the struggle for power meant that non-Communist opposition to Lee Kuan-yew had little resilience to organize itself after Lee's assumption of power in 1959.

Meanwhile, the PAP gained in strength, especially in the trade unions and among militant Chinese leftists. A number of violent strikes and riots were fomented, not necessarily by the PAP, although the British blamed that organization. In 1956 and 1957 the British, in concert with a seemingly reluctant Labour Front government, utilized the stringent emergency, or public security, regulations to arrest and detain, without trial, considerable numbers of Chinese, Indian, and Eurasian labor leaders, PAP members, school-teachers, students, and the like, as the bogey of a Communist Singapore continued to exercise British officials.[5] Undaunted by the

5. See Government of Singapore, *The Communist Threat in Singapore, Command No. 33 of 1957* (Singapore: Government Printer, 1957).

arrests, the PAP garnered even more popular support, and in the City Council elections of 1957 the party elected its own candidate for mayor, albeit with a minority of votes cast. All was not rosy within the PAP, despite electoral and other successes, as rival internal factions maneuvered for dominance. An outright split again was avoided, but a scenario was being constructed for further acts in the drama. With the tacit support of the Labour Front government, several leaders from the PAP's "extremist" group were arrested and detained, just as the struggle for control of the PAP's Central Executive Committee (CEC) was joined. After a series of Byzantine machinations, including many further arrests of key left-wing PAP leaders, the moderate bloc finally gained control of the CEC.[6]

Notwithstanding the political turmoil that existed on the island during this period, the British continued to move ahead with plans for self-rule. A second London all-party conference was held from March to April 1957, attended by Lee Kuan-yew[7] among others, and this time compromise on most issues was reached—the one exception being the PAP's strong opposition to a British proposal barring persons involved in "seditious" activities from standing as electoral candiates. This controversy did not prevent agreement on some points, however; specifically, decisions were made that a parliamentary system of government would be based on popular elections by a broadened Singapore citizenry, external affairs and defense matters would remain under the control of the British, and responsibility for internal security would be shared among Singapore, Britain, and Malaya.[8] The Singapore legislative assembly approved the new proposals in May 1957.

Following its success in the 1957 City Council elections, the PAP embarked upon an ambitious program of local government, stressing then, as it does today, elimination of corruption and increased bureaucratic efficiency. Although the party aroused the ire of many British colonial officials and of English-educated local Chinese bureaucrats by the direct (some said arrogant!) methods by which its

6. See Pang Cheng-lian, *Singapore's People's Action Party*, pp. 3–5, for an account of these events.

7. The PAP's left wing by this time had taken a stand strongly opposed to independence through merger with Malaya.

8. See Great Britain (Colonial Office), *Report of the Singapore Constitutional Conference Held in London in March and April 1957* (London: H.M. Stationery Office, 1975).

elected officials fulfilled their responsibilities, its policies were refreshingly successful in many fields. The PAP was enabled to widen its support among Singapore's multiethnic population, attracting many Malays and Indians to its ranks by the vitality of its programs and its "multiracial" ethos—particularly since during this period the SUMNO was both riven by internal dissent and smeared with the taint of corruption derived from its association with the scandal-ridden Lim Yew-hock regime.

The 1959 State Assembly (or parliamentary) general elections saw the PAP and its policies reach full political maturity and power, at least on the surface. The intention of the elections was to install the first government[9] ever elected into power by popular franchise. Fifty-one assembly seats were contested by several parties, with the PAP, the Singapore People's Alliance (SPA), the Liberal-Socialists, and the SUMNO (in association with the MCA-MIC) predominant. The SPA had been formed from the remains of the Labour Front, which had been struggling along in power since 1957 under the vapid leadership of Lim Yew-hock. Standing for each of the fifty-one seats, the PAP successfully attacked the corruption of the Labour Front government and its successor party, the SPA,[10] and was able, through an efficient and dedicated campaign organization, to capture 54 percent of the vote and forty-three out of the fifty-one seats contested. (The seeming disparity between the percentage of the votes and the number of seats won stems from the divided nature of the opposition, in which the anti-PAP right-wing vote was split.) With almost complete dominance in internal political affairs, the PAP seemed poised for an unopposed period of time in office with which to implement its policies. A political manifesto, *The Tasks Ahead*,[11] outlined in detail the future course the party intended to take, involving a series of progressive proposals that attracted much support from a politically aware population chafing under the restraints of colonial rule.

9. The British still retained control over external affairs and defense policy, while internal security, as before, remained shared by British, Singaporean, and Malayan members of the Internal Security Council (ISC).

10. One PAP candidate called the SPA the "Semua Poket Aku" party, or "Everything Goes into My Pocket" party!

11. The People's Action Party, "The Tasks Ahead: The PAP's Five Year Plan" (a series of parts issued by the party during 1959).

But internal disruptions were at work within the PAP leadership, and in 1960 the first overt split occurred—not between extremists and moderates at first, but on an ad hominem basis. Ong Eng-guan had been elected mayor of Singapore in the City Council elections in 1957, and, although a moderate, he was urged by his followers and by his own vaulting ambition to mount a challenge to Lee Kuan-yew's leadership. For reasons of its own, the PAP's left supported Ong, but when the CEC expelled him, left-wing leaders were not yet prepared for the ultimate confrontation. Only a few hundred members deserted the party with Ong, and when Ong founded his own United People's Party he was unable to shape it into a coherent political force, despite one resounding success in a by-election.[12] Ong and his party soon faded into obscurity. Lee had purged the PAP of an ambitious rival within his own moderate faction, but the more serious, ideologically defined struggle still simmered in the intense political heat of the PAP kitchen.

The final chapter in this internecine strife was written in 1961, when Lee Kuan-yew dismounted from the back of the left-wing tiger. Faced with the exigencies of having to rule and administer a government, the PAP under Lee marched to different imperatives than those stimulated by an anticolonial headiness. The PAP preached an ideology of "democratic socialism," but its leadership, faced with the economic realities of a Singapore possessing few resources other than those derived from its own human endeavors, was forced to follow along the lines of what might be termed democratic capitalism. Lee Kuan-yew's slowness in implementing the more radical policies outlined in the original PAP manifesto (although under his leadership the PAP did succeed in instituting a great deal of much-needed and progressive social legislation) had created resentment among the party's left; the proposal to achieve independence through merger with Malaya in a new federation of Malaysia, made in May 1961, proved to be the catalyst that brought about the ultimate rift.

Other factors, too, contributed to left-wing dissatisfaction,[13] but

12. See Pang Cheng-lian, *Singapore's People's Action Party*, pp. 8–11, for details of these convoluted events.
13. These included the continued detention of left-wing figures, a lukewarm official policy toward Chinese-language education, the taming of the trade unions to

the merger issue was paramount. The MCP, the so-called Peking-Jakarta axis, and the left-wing group within the PAP all considered the Malaysian proposals to be a neocolonial plot, contrived by the British and the right-wing Malay government in Kuala Lumpur as a geopolitical obstacle standing between Indonesian and Chinese unity. The months of June and July 1961 saw another tapestry of Machiavellian weavings as each faction of the PAP tried to exert its dominance over the other; failing this, both sides determined upon an open break. This came on July 16, 1961, when thirteen PAP assemblypersons crossed the parliamentary floor to the benches of the opposition, where they formed a new left-wing party entitled Barisan Sosialis (a Malay name meaning the Socialist Front).[14] In retrospect, it appears that those defecting from the PAP to form the Barisan constituted a majority of PAP members, yet the moderates under Lee were able to maintain control of the government and of the party's formidable organization, even though the latter had been crippled by the exodus of the dissenters. Why should this be so? First, the PAP immediately embarked upon a strenuous program of reorganization and persuasion, re-enlisting many previously lapsed members, and second, nonleftist opposition parties in the State Assembly extended temporary support. Nevertheless, Lee and his coleaders in the PAP were badly shaken by their proximity to the brink of defeat. Never again would the PAP allow rival factions to gain control of any of the various party structures; in the future, entrance to the PAP would be strictly scrutinized; the identity of party cadres would be kept a close secret; and the CEC (dominated in every sense by Lee Kuan-yew and his associates) would exert constant oversight of all party activities. Whatever intraparty democracy had existed before was stifled once and for all: the PAP had learned a bitter lesson. With this rather tumultuous backdrop, the stage was now set for Singapore's short-lived membership in the Federation of Malaysia.

---

make them conform to the PAP's economic policies, the existence of the Internal Security Council, and the arrogant, dictatorial attitudes of Lee Kuan-yew and his associates.

14. See Pang Cheng-lian, *Singapore's People's Action Party*, pp. 11–16, and Milton Osborne, *Singapore and Malaysia*, (Ithaca, N.Y.: Cornell University Southeast Asia Program, Data Paper no. 33, 1964), pp. 16–22.

Singapore: The Formation of Malaysia

Since its inception the PAP in Singapore had advocated merger with Malaya on grounds of both economic and political stability. PAP leaders felt that Singapore could not survive as an economic entity on its own (that is, devoid of the hinterland upon which its entrepreneurial economy was based); later, following the "moderate-extremist" split within the PAP, Lee Kuan-yew and his associates believed, in view of a rising ground swell of strikes and civil disorder, that only merger with the stronger and firmly anti-Communist Malaya to the north could ensure an atmosphere conducive to their continued rule and a form of economic development underwritten by foreign investment. Notwithstanding this firm desire for union with Malaya, PAP leaders intended that it be carried out on their own terms. In fact, so demanding and abrasive were they in the negotiations concerning a common Malaysian market and control over customs duties and other revenues that the seeds of disintegration were sown even before the new federation had time to flower. In exchange for certain economic concessions to Singapore's unique position in the federation (and perhaps also to "insulate" her politically) [15] Singapore was allotted only 15 out of 159 seats in the proposed federal parliament—an unfavorable ratio disproportionate to population percentages.

As well as facing these bitter struggles between the PAP and the central government in Kuala Lumpur, the PAP also had to convince the Singapore populace of the desirability of joining Malaysia. No doubt realizing the infeasibility of a process along the lines of the Cobbold Commission (which would have ignited serious civil dissent), the PAP leadership decided to hold a referendum on the subject. The party leadership, shrewdly assessing the strengths of anti-Malaysian feelings organized by Barisan forces, offered the population not a straightforward "yes" or "no" referendum, but one that allowed a choice on three different types of merger. It was in reality a staged, "Catch-22" referendum, since no alternative to entrance into Malaysia was granted. The Barisan

15. See R. S. Milne, "Singapore's Exit from Malaysia," *Asian Survey*, 6 (March 1966), pp. 175–184.

tried to persuade its followers to cast blank votes in protest, but the PAP was able to circumvent this ploy by ruling that all blank votes cast be construed as an indication of approval of the PAP's policies! The results of the referendum were, naturally, a resounding triumph for the PAP, although 25 percent of the votes turned out to be blank. Singapore merged with the federation of Malaysia with much fanfare and rejoicing, only to find, after a few brief months, that the new-found federalism did not allow Singapore either the political or the economic latitude that her leaders found themselves driven to pursue.

The Secession of Singapore

In August 1965, after only two years of merger, Singapore withdrew (or was expelled) from the federation and became an independent republic standing on her own. The reasons that informed this decision are complex and have been well described elsewhere.[16] In retrospect the break was inevitable, given the issues and the personalities involved. From the outset Singapore had been a very uncomfortable, and uncomforting, partner in the ambitious political venture, even though the economic factors that secured her entrance were as real as ever. These economic considerations had never been properly settled during the negotiations that preceded merger, and they were to remain in contention afterward.[17] Singapore was interested in the rest of Malaysia as a common market for the products of her own rapidly developing industries, but the government in Kuala Lumpur made little attempt to move ahead with the implementation of a common market, probably because of her own industrial ambitions. Thus the nonrealization of a Malaysian common market removed one of the main reasons for Singapore's entrance into the federation. Other financial considerations were at stake, such as defense costs and the proportion of Singapore's revenue that should go to the central government, but the common market was the major concern.

16. Nancy McH. Fletcher, *The Separation of Singapore from Malaysia* (Ithaca N.Y.: Cornell University Southeast Asia Program, Data Paper no. 73, 1969).
17. The rift was sharpened by personality conflicts between Lee and his Finance Minister, Goh Keng-swee, and the more conservative central Finance Minister, Tan Siew-sin.

Political matters were to prove even more disputatious than economic affairs, and it may, I believe, fairly be stated that these focused on Malay-Chinese animosity—although there was, to be sure, also an ideological rift along progressive-conservative lines. At issue were two different approaches to the resolution of ethnic conflict in Malaysia. The PAP campaigned for a "Malaysian Malaysia,"[18] that is, a policy of "multiracialism" that afforded no one ethnic community a privileged status, promising "the democratic socialist way to a more equal and just society, making an appeal to both Malay and non-Malay have-nots with a more effective way of raising their educational and living standards."[19] This policy was, naturally, a direct threat to the privileged status of the Malays embodied in the Malaysian Constitution; in the view of the federation Alliance Malays needed special treatment because of their socioeconomically deprived position so they could catch up with the other, economically secure, ethnic communities. The Tunku expressed his fears in this respect: "Malaysian Malaysia, in particular, suggests that the Malaysia we now have is bad, for it gives all the advantages to one race while depriving others of their rightful place in our society."[20]

These differences were obviously irreconcilable, given the unwillingness of both sides to compromise. As the situation became more heated, each party became involved in the internal affairs of the other's territory—the UMNO in Singapore and the PAP in the Malaysian peninsula. In Singapore, the SUMNO, with much guidance and leadership from the UMNO in Kuala Lumpur, tried to rally the Singapore Malays to the Kuala Lumpur position, while the PAP countered with its own attempts to win over the latter group. Demand was met by rejection, insult by insult, and the Malay press ran heated editorials accusing the PAP of repressing the Singapore Malays. Simultaneously with these events, the PAP "intruded" into the Malaysian elections of 1964 by entering nine candidates in races against MCA candidates. (It is commonly believed that the

18. See Lee Kuan Yew, *Towards a Malaysian Malaysia* and *The Battle for a Malaysian Malaysia*, both published in 1965 by the Ministry of Culture, Singapore.

19. Republic of Singapore, *Separation* (Singapore: Ministry of Culture, 1965).

20. Tunku Abdul Rahman, *Singapore Breakaway* (Kuala Lumpur: Department of Information, 1965).

PAP wished to replace the MCA in the Malaysian Alliance, although there is no hard evidence to point to this ambition.) The Tunku and other Alliance leaders were distressed at this political incursion into their territory, especially since they believed that Lee had pledged not to participate, but the PAP pressed forward.[21] Right-wing members of the UMNO (Lee called them the "mad Mullahs") were especially incensed and mounted a virulent campaign against Lee and the PAP. The Alliance gained a smashing triumph in the 1964 elections, only one PAP candidate winning his seat, but nevertheless the PAP announced plans to establish branches at various centers throughout the peninsula, thereby escalating the stakes even higher.

Matters came to a head in July 1964, when serious race riots erupted in Singapore between Malays and Chinese—probably instigated by Malays.[22] A recrudescence of the violence occurred in September of the same year, and although these events sobered up both sets of protagonists the dispute simmered on. To make matters worse, in early 1965 the PAP organized a so-called Malaysian Solidarity Convention in Singapore in an attempt to coalesce an anti-Alliance, but pro-Malaysia, all-party opposition, including parties from Sarawak and Sabah. The ethnic composition of this body is interesting, for although the MSC endeavored to attract as many Malays as possible to its ranks, it ended up by being a largely non-Malay group. The PAP-Alliance dispute, inside and outside of parliament, became more and more venomous, with UMNO "ultras" (right wingers in the sense of being "Malay Firsters") calling publicly for Lee's arrest and detention as a traitor to the cause of Malaysia. Clearly the quarrel could not continue without further and even bloodier communal violence, and in August 1965, following a secret meeting between Lee and the Tunku, arrangements were made for Singapore's exit from the federation as amicably as possible given the fever pitch of the conflict.

21. Fletcher, *Separation of Singapore*, p. 36.
22. See Michael Liefer, "Communal Violence in Singapore," *Asian Survey*, 4 (October 1961), 1115–1121.

7 | The Contemporary Setting

The Economy

The modern Singapore is an artificial creation born out of imperial economic expansion, and down to the present economic affairs dominate political realities, both in terms of internal policies and relations with the surrounding region. After Raffles founded a new Singapore in 1819, the island port rapidly became the entrepôt center for most of Southeast Asia, fulfilling the role of a large free-trading warehouse, the economic "middleman" or entrepreneur for its neighbors nearby and for the colonial power, its raison d'être staunchly mercantilist. An efficient commercial and administrative infrastructure soon grew up, controlled by the colonial government, European agency houses, and Chinese businessmen, and able to exploit the natural hinterlands of the Malay Peninsula and the Indonesian islands to import raw materials (rubber, oil, copra, palm oil, pepper, coffee, timber, rice) for re-export to industrial countries elsewhere in the world. From these industrial processing countries Singapore obtained bulk supplies (consumer goods, textiles, tractors, motor vehicles, and other manufactured products) for redistribution throughout the region. The Singaporeans, especially the Chinese, conducted their economic affairs (and still do) with neighboring Malaya and Indonesia through a network of Chinese businesses and trade associations, intertwined in a mutually profitable symbiotic relationship.

Singapore's separation from Malaysia signaled the demise of hopes for a regional common market, upon which Singapore's economic plans for the future had been based. Henceforward the new republic's economy had to be steered in significantly new directions, and the population mobilized to that end. Dr. Goh

Keng-swee, then the finance minister, reflected upon his feelings the morning that separation occurred:

> The problems of the future loomed in awesome and intimidating proportions. Here we were, an island trading post, with its economic hinterland in other countries. . . . Even the water we drank had to be mostly imported. We had no natural resources other than a diligent and enterprising people. At 10:00 A. M. news of the separation was announced over the radio. It was greeted by the firing of crackers in Chinatown. I thought this a light-hearted response to a grave situation.[1]

Having no natural resources—other than human—of her own and possessing an economy based mainly on entrepreneurial relations with an unstable regional hinterland, the republic moved into an era of rapid industrialization. Because of the lack of domestic resources, foreign capital, with its attendant demand for improvement in technological skills, needed to be attracted, which in turn necessitated a long period of political stability and labor tranquillity. The new economy would remain of an "emporium" character; Raffles' description of Singapore as the Emporium of the Southern Seas would be expanded into the Emporium of the Seven Seas. Singapore would become, economically, a global city no longer dependent on regional resources, seeking world markets and adjusting to them accordingly.[2] Singapore's tenuous future at this time was given a further jolt by the British government's decision to withdraw the bulk of Britain's military forces east of Suez by 1970.[3] The PAP government thereafter adopted policies designed to organize the population into a tautly controlled, efficient, and achievement-oriented society. The new "politics of survival" (the government's own phrase) envisaged the mobilization of a "rugged society," innovative and technological in outlook: "What is required," wrote a PAP leader, "is a rugged, resolute, highly-trained, highly-disciplined community."[4]

1. Goh Keng-swee, *Decade of Achievement* (Singapore: Ministry of Culture, 1970), p. 9.
2. Economic directions outlined by George Thomson, a senior Singapore government official, in *FEER*, August 21, 1969.
3. Approximately 10 percent of Singapore's population derived their income from local employment in and other economic spin-offs from the British military bases in Singapore.
4. PAP, *12th Anniversary Souvenir Magazine, PAP District Eight* (Singapore: PAP, 1966), p. 9.

Since 1965 the government has been singularly successful in developing the state's industrial and commercial potential. Foreign capital has been lured in large amounts and many foreign-owned factories have been established through the government's policies of affording tax breaks for "pioneer" industries and of repressing any form of labor unrest whatever the issue. New industrial estates have sprung up under the direction of well-managed government planning units, the economy expanding especially well in the fields of electronics, shipbuilding and repairing, and petroleum processing. (From 1965 to 1974 the economy grew at an annual rate in the double digits.) By the early 1970s Singapore was the world's fourth largest port, had a booming industrial sector with almost full employment, had developed into the region's most important financial center, possessed large oil refineries and ancillary services for the petroleum industry, and generally had the highest level of per capita income and production anywhere in Asia outside of Japan. The educational system had been completely revamped, with a substantial number of students channeled into technical and vocational streams to satisfy the demands of the new technology.

Singapore's economy is now a mixture of public and private enterprise, with the government moving more and more into the realm of state capitalism and direct control of certain sectors of the economy, owning percentages of private companies (foreign and local), and moving in the direction of an ever-expanding, bureaucratically managed state: "The government is the most important entrepreneur in the Singapore economy. The government conglomerate has extensive ownership in diversified industries, ranging from shipbuilding to tourism, lotteries to country-club operations. Small wonder it has sometimes been called Singapore Incorporated."[5] The political implications of the government's policies are obvious and will be examined later.

The Society

Singapore, like Malaysia, is afflicted with the problems of competing ethnic identities, although the dimensions of the equation

5. Tan Chwee-huat, "Developing Singapore Incorporated," *FEER*, August 9, 1974.

are quantitatively different, as the population figures given in Table 10 indicate.

Table 10. Singapore population, 1970

	Numbers	Percentages
Malays	311,379	15.1
Chinese	1,579,866	76.2
Indians	145,169	6.9
Others	38,093	1.8
Total	2,074,507	100.0

SOURCE: P. Arumainathan, *Census of Population, 1970, Singapore, Interim Release* (Singapore: Department of Statistics, 1970), Table 1.

Under normal circumstances, the small size of the minority groups, Malay and Indian, in relation to the overwhelming Chinese majority population would mean a lesser degree of ethnic conflict than in a state such as Malaysia, where ethnic communities are almost equal to each other numerically. But the Malays of Singapore are not a minority when viewed from a regional aspect; geographically and historically they live at the core of the "Malay world" and have easy access to cultural and political influences emanating from Malaysia and Indonesia. To this extent their cultural attributes tend to be continually reinforced and therefore permanent, and it has proved difficult for the PAP to redefine Malay values and behavior along lines consistent with the party's long-range policy objectives. Experiences while part of Malaysia, too, have imposed further strains on Singapore's state-building process; that is, although for a long time the Malays were politically unaware of their socioeconomic backwardness as a community, entrance into Malaysia in 1963 heightened consciousness of their position in Singapore vis-à-vis their Malay brethren to the north and generated new demands on the Singapore political system. So the construction of a cohesive state in Singapore is not focused merely on the composition of and interactions between the constituents of the state itself; the PAP leadership has to look outward, across territorial boundaries, for centrifugal forces. In this respect, Singapore's tenuous relationship with her Malaysian and Indonesian neighbors means that the PAP is obliged to handle the Singapore

Malay minority with special care, for any violent or vociferous alienation of the latter would undoubtedly probe deeply into the nerve endings of a residual anti-Singapore (or anti-Chinese) sentiment abroad in Malaysia and Indonesia.

What are the PAP's policies toward Singapore's multiethnic society and what are the mechanisms employed to create a Singapore identity? There is no "Singaporean person" in the historical or cultural sense with whom to identify; appeals for state unity cannot be based on deep-rooted attachments to kinship or territorial ties—to blood or to land—but only on the less heady calls of common citizenship, economic achievement, and pride in the government as an efficacious, problem-solving institution. This is a flimsy foundation on which to build, for should the state fail to supply the material and psychological needs of its people, there is no legitimacy, no symbolism, on which to fall back. Prior to merger with Malaysia in 1963 and during the merger period, the PAP made every attempt to impart a veneer of "Malayness" to Singapore; Malay was recognized as the "national" language (if only one of four "official" languages), a Malay was installed as the first ceremonial head of state, and Malay acculturation generally was promoted—even if mainly in a symbolic form—in order to demonstrate to the Malay political leadership in Kuala Lumpur that Singapore was ready to become a true and loyal partner in the Malaysian adventure.[6] These policies, plus the act of merger itself, filled the Singapore Malays with hope, made them feel secure politically and culturally.

Separation changed the scene dramatically. The PAP now had to cater to a more narrowly based set of constituents. Lee Kuan-yew has had to manipulate and control Chinese-educated Chinese, English-educated Chinese, Indians, Malays, and others, all within a specifically Singaporean context. The PAP could not create a Chinese Singapore, for this would not be acceptable to the Malay world around, long suspicious of Communist ambitions in the region. The present PAP leadership is concerned, too, lest the maintenance of a Chinese cultural identity would ultimately facili-

6. Michael Leifer, "Politics in Singapore: The First Term of the PAP, 1959–1963," *Journal of Commonwealth Political Studies*, 2 (May 1964).

tate adherence to Chinese Communist political ideology. Nor could the PAP construct a Malay Singapore, for this would immediately expose the party's political underbelly to a fatal attack from the more chauvinistic elements of the Chinese-educated population. So the PAP has, perforce, sired a new Singaporean person, one whose main language is English but who will also be fluent in his or her mother tongue and possibly even another language. A new merit-oriented society is being constructed, in which ethnicity, religion, old traditions, and other impedimenta are to be thrust to the side. The government's priorities are urban in nature—rapid industrialization, modern education, bureaucratic efficiency, urban resettlement, and social mobility. Stable conditions are vital to the success of this program. and to this end an uncompromising "multiracialism" is stressed as the basis of society. No one race is to be afforded special privileges; each and every person is to make it on his or her own merit as a Singaporean, not as a member of any particular ethnic bloc.

The economic aspects of these policies have not presented as many problems to the Chinese, most of whom have been able to adjust themselves to the new environment—although it must not be forgotten that thousands of Chinese live in circumstances of poverty, however inconspicuous they may seem to the casual observer.[7] Politically and culturally, however, certain Chinese elements present a continual threat to the PAP's policies and political ascendancy. The Chinese population is not a socially coherent, homogenous unit, but is rigidly stratified into English and Chinese-educated segments, as well as into the various dialect groups. The English stream of education has a long history; substantial numbers of Singapore Chinese are unable to speak and an even greater number unable to write the Chinese language. This linguistic dichotomy has produced in turn a divergence of values and interests that is made manifest in several ways, including the political. English-educated Chinese have a distinct advantage in relation to existing PAP policies, finding occupational oppor-

7. See Iain Buchanan, *Singapore in Southeast Asia: An Economic and Political Appraisal* (London: George Bell, 1972), chap. 6, "The Problem of Poverty in Singapore." Buchanan estimates that between 20 and 25 percent of Singapore's population lives at a definable level of poverty.

tunities at every level in the government service and in the private sector. The PAP's main problem, along with that concerning the Malay community, lies with the Chinese-educated populace, many of whom are at the bottom of the socioeconomic ladder and who inhabit the crowded city slums of Chinatown and the vast public housing estates. These Chinese-educated persons, in my view, are becoming increasingly disaffected with the PAP government and provide a potent reservoir of support for left-wing, anti-PAP forces. They are uneasy about the increased cost of living and taxes, about the inability of the insipid trade-union movement to bargain on their behalf for a more equable share of the state's economic rewards, about the decline of traditional Chinese culture, and about the PAP's clear if tacit encouragement of all these circumstances. (On this latter issue they are joined by many wealthy Chinese merchants, also traditional as regards their cultural legacy.) The Chinese-educated group fear that they will be relegated to the status of second-class citizens in a society of the future envisioned by Lee Kuan-yew and his associates—a society mainly English-educated, elitist, and technocratic in orientation and subscribing to universalistic values of modernity not related to any single cultural tradition. Other sources of dissatisfaction stem from the massive urban renewal programs that involve large-scale squatter and slum clearance, land acquisition schemes in which many feel that they have been cheated of their land and inadequately compensated for it, and compulsory military service.

The Malays are a special case.[8] They are immigrants to the island from the Malay Peninsula and the Indonesian archipelago, but the bonds of a similar language, culture, and especially religion, coupled with the stress of living in the middle of new and alien cultures, have stimulated the emergence of a definable Singapore Malay community. Malays coming to Singapore have not been "detribalized" into atomized groups of Javanese, Menangkabau, Bugis, Malacca Malays, and the like—rather they have become "supertribalized"[9] and have evolved into the Singapore Malay

8. The information contained in the following paragraphs is based on my "The Singapore Malay Community: The Politics of State Integration" (Ph.D. dissertation, Cornell University, 1974).

9. The term is taken from I. M. Wallerstein, "Ethnicity and National Integration

community; the weakening of geographical ties to their place of origin has not wrought a corresponding decrease in their awareness of being Malay. The Malays of Singapore, like those in Malaysia, have been inhibited by environmental and cultural factors from participating on equal terms in the state's rapid economic development. The PAP's policy toward them, nevertheless, has not been to grant special privileges in the Malaysian sense. The Singapore Constitution recognizes that the Malays are the indigenous people of Singapore, and as such are in a special position, but this recognition has not been translated into special attention except for certain free educational benefits. When the PAP assumed power in 1959, its leadership announced a new policy for Malays: no longer were they to be sheltered by a humiliating set of privileges, and all Malays were to be educated and socialized to take their place in a meritocratic society. Stultifying traditions were to be swept away, and in the not too distant future the Singapore Malay community would emerge from its socioeconomic backwater to take its rightful place in a new and progressive Singapore society. That at least was the PAP's stated intention. Ever since 1959, strenuous efforts by PAP Malay cadres and senior Malay government officials have been made to steer Malay values away from the old, inhibiting traditions toward a set of norms more in step with the government's policies. A clash between competing sets of values was inevitable.

In the years since 1959 the PAP's progressive policies toward the Malays have not been transformed from rhetoric into reality, for in the mid-1970s there is a perceived crisis within the Malay community, derived from two essential problems that must retard the PAP's attempts to build a state. These are, first, the extent of socioeconomic backwardness, and second, the question of cultural and political identity, both of which overlap and interact. There can be no doubt that measured by any economic indicator, the Singapore Malays are not taking part in the economic sector at the same level as other ethnic groups. Two unassailable facts emerge from statistics available: the types of jobs open to Malays are still in the low

in West Africa," in Harry Eckstein and David Apter, eds., *Comparative Politics* (Glencoe: Free Press, 1963), p. 666.

prestige and income levels of occupational categories, and Malays have the highest rate of under- and unemployment in the state. One factor that previously exacerbated the unemployment scene was the government's unwritten but real policy of not calling up Malays for military service or recruiting them into the police force. Malays dominated these two organizations in the past (up to 80 percent of the total strengths under the British), and obviously no government can be expected to tolerate the dominance of its security forces by a minority (and potentially suspect) group. In practical terms, however, the government's policy was severe, for it closed a previously important avenue of employment and social mobility to the Malays and increased the already large pool of Malay unemployed. It was difficult for Malay youths to get jobs after leaving school because they could not produce the requisite certificate of completion of national service—which the government could not give them because it was reluctant to publicize openly its disinclination to accept Malays into the military and the police. By not enlisting Malays for national service the government introduced two impediments into its integrational endeavors, in addition to the problem of unemployment. First, Malay youths were denied the opportunity of passing through an important phase of socialization just at a time when they were beginning to challenge the government's motives toward the Malays. Second, the government's actions made many young Malays suspect that they were not trusted as responsible citizens by the government to whom and by whom they are constantly exhorted to be loyal. Given the historical Malay reliance on the police and military as a means of livelihood, suddenly to exclude Malays from their ranks is almost tantamount to preventing Chinese from entering the world of commerce. To embark on such action, many Malays believe, without providing any alternative, makes a mockery of all PAP pronouncements concerning multiracialism and meritocracy. (The policy was finally ended in 1973, after a mounting surge of complaints.)

Under all these circumstances, the concept of meritocracy and multiracialism may result in the institutionalization of Malay economic backwardness, and poverty may become self-perpetuating, as two senior Singapore Malay civil servants pointed out in a seminar in 1970:

Multiracialism and meritocracy by themselves can very well be a negative and sterile policy; and with industrialization and modernization gaining momentum day to day, the gap between the Malays and the non-Malays could in due time become unbridgable. . . . We feel a policy be committed to actively helping . . . the Malays wherever and whenever such privileges, whether economic, political or educational, are needed. It must be borne in mind that aids rendered to the Malays . . . should not be construed as something that will remain forever; rather they should be regarded more like temporary crutches for the handicapped.[10]

The socioeconomic disparities that exist between the Malay and non-Malay communities are not simply the result of the PAP's policies, but stem from a multitude of historical and social facts, such as the paternalistic and ultimately divisive policies of colonial rule, the competitive and aggressive ethos of non-Malay migrants, the residues of a traditional, rural past, and culturally reinforcing residential patterns. The danger is that the PAP's rhetoric, promising early solutions to the ills that for so long have beset Malay society, may have come full circle, and Malays are attributing their continued disappointing status to the failures of the government's policies.

Here it must be fairly stated that the Singapore government is the most efficient in Southeast Asia, and its services—health, education, and welfare—rank among the most progressive anywhere in the world. The PAP's control over all activities is complete, and the government with which it is synonymous has, from 1959 onward, constructed a set of institutions designed to penetrate into every level of society and to organize the state's population in directions consonant with the leadership's vision. The educational system has been restructured, both as a means of serving the demands of new economic policies and as a weapon in the socialization process. Officially there are four equal streams of education—English, Chinese, Malay, and Indian—but in reality the English-language stream offers the greatest socioeconomic re-

10. Athsarni Karni and Ridzwan Dzafir, "Singapore Malays and Employment Opportunities," in Sharom Ahmat and James Wong, eds., *Malay Participation in the National Development of Singapore* (Singapore: Eurasia Press, 1971), p. 19.

wards, and the government is inexorably persuading students to enter this stream. As a result, an increasing number of Malay, Chinese, and Indian parents are sending their children to English-language schools.[11] Over the past ten years enrollment figures for the non-English-language streams have decreased significantly, a trend that for Malays may presage the end of Malay education as presently constituted. It certainly has led to much unhappiness among those interested in preserving Malay and Chinese culture. (Indians have not been so vociferous in maintaining Indian-language schools, where enrollment has dropped to an insignificant number.)

Another major PAP social program is concerned with urban resettlement and renewal. Housing programs were born of two desiderata: (a) to satisfy demands arising out of an acute shortage of land and an increasing population, exigencies that transcend the bounds of politics,[12] and (b) to build physically integrated residential areas (thereby eradicating culturally isolated ethnic enclaves such as the Malay stronghold of Geylang Serai) that will act as instruments of social and political integration: by living in the same block of flats in an enforced ethnic mix, the modern Singaporean of the immediate future will live in a minimultiracial milieu, the ideal Singapore in microcosm, in which it is hoped that life will become "a daily discipline of communal tolerance and understanding."[13] Middle-class and poor Malays, Chinese, and Indians will live together in close proximity, shop and attend school together, and gradually become Singaporeans.[14]

On the face of it the vast new public housing estates are monuments to the efficiency and dynamism of Singapore's PAP leadership. But in the construction of 150,000 new public housing units

11. For Malays the pattern among uneducated parents is to send males to English schools, while females enter either religious or Malay-language schools; many Malay conservatives still are not convinced of the validity of secular education for females.

12. By 1979 it is estimated that 80 percent of the population will live in public flats in order to accommodate the demands of commerce and industry. In 1971, 85 percent of the total population lived on twenty-eight square miles of land—a high density with little room for lateral expansion for residential purposes.

13. Speech by the Minister for Home Affairs, reported in *ST*, December 6, 1971.

14. For an account of housing in Singapore, see Robert E. Gamer, *The Politics of Urban Development in Singapore* (Ithaca, N.Y.: Cornell University Press, 1972).

between 1960 and 1970 (a mammoth physical achievement) the stress was placed on quantity, and the social needs of those resettled have been somewhat neglected: "There is growing feeling among certain groups of people that the conditions of living in an HDB [public housing] estate are so appalling that these areas are fast becoming the source of major social ills in Singapore. . . . It is undeniable that there is more to public housing programmes than the provision of dwelling places."[15] The Singapore Master Plan envisages that the bulk of the populace eventually will reside either in the city proper or in industrial satellite towns built around the periphery to form a pattern of ring cities connected to the central core by a network of expressways. In the satellite towns planning has focused on the "neighborhood principle"; markets, schools, shopping centers, community centers, banks, government services, and so on are to be built in each town center, and it is intended that workers will commute only a short distance to their place of employment. Many of the estates already are crime-ridden, have drug and gambling problems, are dirty and noisome in the elevators and corridors, and are noisy and lack privacy. One Singapore researcher has commented that there is every reason to fear that the estates will come to "resemble the slums which the authorities are trying to eradicate."[16]

The Malays, again, are especially affected by the change to public housing. The government hopes that the removal of Malays from the solidary motifs of the urban ghetto into ethnically integrated public housing will result in new psychological configurations, in which Malays will no longer have to glance backward over their shoulders, fearful of the approbation of their peers and neighbors, should they wish to break away from parochially defined norms of behavior. But many Malays feel sadly out of place in the anonymous concrete corridors of the housing estates. Their new flats are too small to accommodate the ritual and ceremony integral to their culture, they have been taken out of an extended family system into

15. Speech by the Minister of Education to the Singapore Institute of Planners, reported in *The Mirror*, 9 (March 12, 1973).

16. Rita Cheong Wai-fong, "Rehousing in a HDB Estate: A Case Study of Internal Migration in Singapore" (Academic Exercise, Department of Geography, University of Singapore, 1968).

a nuclear setting, and, most important, there are no mosques or Malay coffee shops through which to express their Malay identity. Rental in the housing estates is more expensive, they cannot rear ducks and chickens as in their ghetto houses, and the smell of pork being cooked next door in a Chinese flat is an affront to their nostrils. Because of the lack of an adequate income, many parents living in the flats let their children drop out of school to earn money for the family's upkeep, and so the back-breaking wheel of poverty goes on. Middle-class, better-educated Malays, on the other hand, find the transition to the housing estates advantageous. They tend to have smaller families, have an income sufficient to meet rental requirements, and their wives, also better educated, are happy to escape the gossip and traditionalism of the Malay ghetto, or *kampong*. But thousands of poor Malays still await resettlement, and it is too early to predict the ultimate results of the government's policies; once again, however, many Malays are pessimistic and remain fearful of the long-term effects on their cultural identity.

Apart from its education and resettlement programs, the PAP has established a set of mass organizations with which to socialize the population and mobilize it in new directions. The first structure of importance is the Community Center, an adjunct of the PAP-controlled People's Association. There are now 184 Community Centers throughout the island, sponsoring a varied set of recreational, vocational, cultural, and educational activities. The products of the mass media (all of which are controlled, one way or another, by the government) are fed into the centers; television, radio, newspapers, propaganda pamphlets, and state-produced films all are available. Formal membership is not required, and the centers are open to everyone. An equally vital function of the Community Centers is their role in combating political opposition; indeed, they were organized in the early 1960s primarily as a means of counteracting the leftist elements of Singapore society, which were then very strong at a grass-roots level. My own research suggests that the Community Centers do reach the Chinese-educated and help to draw them into some form of civic participation. For those who take part in center activities there are genuine utilitarian benefits to be obtained, and in Chinese areas the centers tend to be crowded. But generally speaking the English-or Malay-educated sectors of the population tend to avoid participation, on class and ethnic grounds respectively, and to this extent the effectiveness of the Community Centers as part of the integrative structure is diluted.

Another PAP-dominated mass organization is a series of Citizens' Consultative Committees, one of which is set up in every electoral constituency. Each committee consists of a number of persons drawn from the local area—local community leaders selected (or approved) by the PAP—who work in conjunction with their member of parliament. The committees are designed to act as intermediaries between the government and the people; complaints and demands from the people are intended to be channeled upward, and government policy is interpreted downward through the member of parliament concerned. Ideally, the committees are supposed to act like a New England town meeting, but in reality they are nominated by and are responsible to the PAP leadership (although the PAP denies its control over them). The committees also serve as a channel of recruitment within the PAP, and young political activists are often absorbed therein as apprentices for future political roles. Technically designed to be above partisan politics, in fact they are tightly controlled by the PAP—another legacy of the days of savage infighting with the Communists and their allies. The committees tend to be dominated by Chinese members, and the language used in committee meetings is often Chinese. This creates problems, insofar as the Malay-, English-, and Indian-educated are sometimes excluded from active participation in the committees, lessening their effectiveness to the PAP.

Other socialization structures include a number of uniformed organizations that proliferate in Singapore (the Vigilante Corps, school army cadet corps, volunteer police reservists, cadet corps, and others), a cowed and subservient mass media,[17] and the trade

17. The government's stringent control over all aspects of the mass communications media is reflected in Lee Kuan-yew's idea of their role: "The mass media can help to present Singapore's problems simply and clearly and then explain how if they support certain programmes and policies these problems can be solved. More important, we want the mass media to reinforce, not to undermine, the cultural values and social attitudes inculcated in our schools and universities" (speech to the International Press Institute in Helsinki, following the controversial enforced closure of the *Singapore Herald*, reported in *ST*, June 10, 1971).

unions. The present trade-union movement and the PAP's policies toward it result from the experiences of the critical days of the 1950s and 1960s, when labor unions were a vital part of left-wing forces. In those days unions organized riots, economic boycotts, strikes, and several times came close to crippling the government of the day. Lee Kuan-yew was intimately associated with left-wing unions in the anticolonial period, but when he and the PAP came to power he moved against them. Most unions were deregistered, their funds sequestered, and many of their leaders imprisoned and detained without trial. In their place the PAP established its own set of unions, under the aegis of the National Trade Union Congress (NTUC), which although nominally independent is in reality firmly administered by leading PAP cadres, its strength a countervailing force on behalf of the workers emasculated. Strikes are outlawed on the grounds that the state's economy cannot afford them at the present stage of the economic take-off. NTUC unions are now an intrinsic part of the state-building process, helping to inform workers of the government's policies. Most union leaders are also PAP members of parliament, and unions are in the forefront of the multifarious government and PAP campaigns, from "build a rugged society" to "don't spit on the sidewalks" and "keep Singapore green." In 1971, however, the NTUC had a membership of only 118,000—a relatively small percentage of the total work force—and its utility as a socializing agent is therefore circumscribed.

The population of Singapore is a society in transition. The government's endeavors to transform society are slowly bringing about results, as more of the republic's citizens pass through the English stream of education, undergoing a change in values and behavior as a consequence. There are, nevertheless, residual strengths in the Chinese and Malay cultural traditions that are not susceptible to political manipulation and social engineering—for the Malays, especially, the undoubted efficiency of the PAP's state-building operations is continually submerged by the persistence of ethnic sentiment—and the question of whether a new Singapore identity, in the PAP's image, will ever emerge cannot yet be determined.

8 | The Political Process

The Constitution

In 1966, when Singapore embarked upon its first full year as an independent republic, the government appointed a Constitutional Commission with a mandate to make recommendations regarding the protection of linguistic, racial, and religious minorities. The commission found that "the future of the nation lies in a non-racial approach to all problems under a form of government which would enable the growth of a united, multiracial, free and democratic nation in which all of its citizens have equal rights and equal opportunities."[1] Because in the new Constitution "the principle of equality before the law and equal protection of the law for all persons" would be categorically provided for, special privileges for Malays were not included. Most of the commission's recommendations were adopted by the government and ratified in parliament in 1967. The new Constitution included the following provisions: (a) creation of a Presidential Council as a nonelected advisory body with the function of offering well-informed criticism of measures proposed by the government that concerned minority groups[2] ; (b) creation of a unicameral parliament consisting of fifty-eight members elected by a simple majority in single-member

1. Republic of Singapore, *Report of the Constitutional Commission* (Singapore: Government Printer, 1966).
2. The Presidential Council was to become very much a creature of the PAP. David Marshall, one of its appointed members, resigned from the council in 1970, claiming that the secrecy of its proceedings, the limited character of its powers (a bill enacted in 1970 enabled the Prime Minister to bypass the council in respect of any bill passed by parliament), and its composition, dominated by PAP ministers and PAP permanent secretaries, meant that there could never be a vote against any measure passed by parliament. *SH*, November 24, 1970.

districts. The prime minister and his cabinet are also members of, and thus responsible to, parliament. The legislature sits for a period of five years, unless dissolved earlier. The head of state is the president, elected by the parliament for a period of five years; his duties are ceremonial, real power being wielded by the prime minister; (c) creation of an independent judiciary, under a chief justice and a Supreme Court. Appeals may lie to the Privy Council in London. The PAP abolished the jury system in 1970, and care is taken to ensure that judges and magistrates are appointed who are sympathetic to the PAP and its policies. (The PAP denies this emphatically, but the fact remains that in major cases involving the PAP's authority the courts have always ruled in favor of the government.) The Preservation of Public Security Ordinance enables the government to arrest and detain, without trial, any person whose actions are deemed to be inimical to state security, so that fundamental liberties and rights, although guaranteed by the Constitution, can be circumscribed at the whim of the government; (d) Singapore was to be a secular state, with freedom to practice any religion guaranteed to all; (e) recognition of the special position of the Malays as indigenous to the island and therefore to be granted certain educational privileges.

The PAP

Since its inception in 1954 the PAP has proclaimed its ideology as one of "democratic socialism," although in its present form the party, as the government, can be said to be democratic in form only, and socialistic hardly at all.[3] Indeed, the Singapore economy is based on an admixture of foreign and local investment capital combined with state capitalism; the "socialist" aspect of the PAP's pronounced ideology is based solely on the provision of excellent social services (health, housing, education, welfare, and the like, which the government has undoubtedly produced) and on creating avenues of social mobility for all through a meritocratic, multiracial state. The PAP's policies are based less on ideology than on

3. A PAP member of parliament, Dr. Augustine Tan, told an audience in 1971 that "a widening in inequality of incomes in a country leads to greater economic growth," provided that inequality did not arise from exploiting the working classes! (*ST*, July 8, 1971). This is hardly socialist doctrine.

pragmatic expediency, designed to adjust to any political or economic situation as it evolves, either internally or externally.

The various structures established by the PAP to penetrate and control the society over which it rules have been described in a previous chapter. The motivations behind the PAP's policies have been based, as I have said, on assessments of the republic's economic future; all the party's efforts, all its remarkable dedication, have been directed to create a stable political climate in which economic development could proceed. A look at the values the PAP promotes is sufficient to underline this assumption: ahistorical symbols that stress the future and not the past, meritocratically rewarded hard work, individual discipline within a framework of the rugged society, technology, innovation, and the eradication of ethnic traditionalism where it clashes with PAP policy.[4]

To create this identity the PAP has striven with a single-minded intensity of purpose. In Singapore the two normally parallel lines of party and government have been blurred to a degree where they are impossible to separate. Domestic politics as exercised by political parties have diminished to an almost meaningless ritual performed during the quinquennial elections, which are preceded by a few allocated days of political campaigning. As the only party represented in parliament the PAP today enjoys total control over politics, which it has translated into total power over most major socioeconomic institutions inside the state. Appointments to and promotions within the civil service and the various statutory bodies (the Harbour Board, the Economic Development Board, the state tourist agency, the state airline, the utilities, and so forth) are made on the basis of loyalty to the PAP as well as on merit; there are no promotions within the bureaucracy for any person identified with an opposition party.[5] The PAP thus maintains its tentacles of command not only through an efficient party machinery, but also through the institutions of the government (including community

4. Chan Heng-chee and Hans-Dieter Evers have described Singapore's identity orientations in "Nation-building and National Identity" in S. N. Eisenstadt and S. Rokkan, eds., *Building States and Nations*, 2 vols. (Beverly Hills and London: Sage Publications, 1973), II, chap. 10.

5. Pang Cheng-lian, *Singapore's People's Action Party: Its History, Organization and Leadership* (Singapore: Oxford University Press, 1971), p. 78.

organizations), the judiciary, and the trade-union movement, the whole being carefully scrutinized by the all-pervasive and efficient Internal Security Department (ISD, formerly the police Special Branch) with its unlimited powers of arrest and detention. The PAP itself is a tightly disciplined, elitist party, monitored by a small authoritarian leadership and supervised through a cadre system, the identity of whose members is kept a close secret. Rumors are bruited around from time to time concerning splits in the PAP between English-educated and Chinese-educated factions, but if these do exist they are kept out of the public forum and have not affected the party's performance, nor, indeed, its continued solidarity.

The result of the PAP's long period in office without serious opposition in recent times has been an inevitable lessening in the level of politics. Elections are held when required by law, but the effectiveness of opposition parties has been undercut so that election campaigns hardly cause a ripple on the even surface of Singapore's political process. The republic's future as an industrialized global city, as it appears in the PAP's vision, has meant a high degree of government management of the economy ("Singapore Incorporated"), and insofar as management of the economy is best left to managers rather than to politicians, the PAP leadership has transferred real power in the state out of the political arena into the hands of the PAP-controlled bureaucracy. Chan Heng-chee, a political scientist at the University of Singapore, has described this process cogently in a recent article in which she calls Singapore "an administrative state" and asks the question "where has the politics gone?" Chan Heng-chee characterizes the depoliticization of Singapore's citizenry that has occurred over the past ten years, pointing out that because of the intensive pace of economic development it has been necessary to transfer power to the bureaucratic and administrative sector, which in turn has meant that the role of the PAP politician (outside of the PAP central leadership) has been downgraded to one of "mobilizer." PAP members of parliament are now expected to act simply as intermediaries in the government system of communications, transmitting and explaining policies and reporting on dissatisfaction among the populace where it is made manifest. The PAP at present, Chan concludes, exercises a "style of governance [which] looks for the elimination of politics, disdains the need for conciliation and trusts in the expertise and the judgment of the leadership to plan and implement with complete and irreversible power."[6] Under these circumstances the Singapore parliament has no decision-making autonomy of its own, acting primarily as a legitimator of executive proposals. Government measures are "debated" in parliament, and occasionally PAP back benchers endeavor to voice complaints from the public on what are generally matters of minor import, but in view of the lack of any opposition in the Singapore legislature its principal function continues to be that of the rubber stamp.

Opposition Parties

It is not to be assumed from the foregoing that opposition parties do not exist, for some fourteen parties are officially registered, though not all of them are active. Their effectiveness, however, remains limited in proportion in some instances to their own incompetence and in others to the PAP's ability to interfere with the proper performance of their political role. The most important party outside of the PAP, and the one that retains some residual if decreasing support among the workers and the Chinese-educated, is the Barisan Sosialis. The Barisan was formed in July 1961 following a split within the ranks of the PAP and the subsequent breakaway of thirteen former PAP assemblypersons. For the next two years the Barisan was able to pose a constant threat to Lee Kuanyew's leadership, but from 1963 onward the party began to lose its efficacy, as its more competent leaders and organizers were arrested and detained under the appropriately named Special Branch operation "Cold Store." The Barisan's ineptness over the question of merger with Malaysia, its statement that the separation of Singapore from Malaysia had resulted only in an artificial independence for Singapore (an issue with deep emotional significance for Singaporeans of Chinese descent, who felt a sense of relief and pride at Singapore's disengagement from Malaysia), and its decision later to boycott Singapore's parliamentary elections all helped

6. Chan Heng-chee, "Politics in an Administrative State: Where Has the Politics Gone?", paper delivered at a seminar on Trends in Singapore, November 24, 1974, sponsored by the Institute of Southeast Asian Studies, Singapore.

to erode the Barisan's support among the masses and to bring about dissatisfaction inside the party. The elections boycott, particularly, was bad strategy, for it denied the party a chance to give its policies a public platform, even for a brief period. In 1966, the Barisan went one step further; its remaining members of parliament resigned, claiming that the party could best pursue its objectives by extraparliamentary means—a process the Barisan leader, Lee Siew-choh, called "street democracy." This turned out to be yet one more disadvantageous decision, for it gave the government further grounds for repressing party activities and arresting party members. Surely, the government proclaimed, if the Barisan was unwilling to work within constitutional means, then it must have decided to subvert the system and should it not be treated accordingly?

The Barisan, basically a Chinese party with only minimal Indian and Malay support, is the repository of left-wing radicalism and pro-Communist sympathies, and indeed it makes no secret of its leanings. With the MCP it steadfastly opposes the concept of Malaysia, and its party line generally supports the People's Republic of China.[7] The degree to which the Barisan has organizational ties with the MCP is not known, but most Singaporeans assume that they do exist. Nor is it known whether the Barisan's strategy of "street democracy" is responsible for the series of minor bomb and arson outbreaks that have occurred in Singapore from time to time, but in any case the government has conducted mass arrests of Barisan leaders and members whenever the occasion seemed to demand it (many Barisan figures were arrested, for example, prior to the Commonwealth Prime Ministers' Conference held in Singapore in 1971, but were released afterward). Barisan support in left-wing trade unions was very strong in the heady days of the anticolonial struggle, but when Lee Kuan-yew consolidated his power he moved to exorcise them of their militancy; by the mid-1960s most left-wing Barisan unions had gradually been deregis-

7. The Barisan's publication, *The Plebeian*, in 1971 exhorted its readers on the front page of every issue as follows: "Malayan People Unite, Defeat US-British Imperialists and Their Razak-Lee Kuan-Yew Puppet Regimes. Crush 'Malaysia,' Crush Phony 'Independent Republic of Singapore.' Struggle for a Genuinely Independent Democratic United Malaya."

tered, many union leaders had been placed under detention, and union funds sequestered.[8] (One or two Barisan-supported trade unions still exist, but they are kept under constant supervision and are not effective.) With its power base partially atrophied because of its long abstinence from public politics, an absence that left the arena clear for the PAP to construct its own impregnable fortifications, and increasingly embarrassed by the rightward turn in China's foreign policy (which in 1972 was moving to a gradual recognition of Malaysia and the establishment of state-to-state relations—a Malaysia whose very existence the Barisan had denied), in March 1972 the Barisan announced that it would contest the forthcoming 1972 Singapore parliamentary elections. In making the announcement, Lee Siew-choh claimed that the decision had been made in response to the wishes of the party's rank and file and that the parliamentary struggle would march hand in hand with "street democracy"; there were signs, however, that a faction inside the Barisan opposed the new strategy,[9] presumably those who saw that the parliamentary road to power was a delusion.

On the right of Singaporean party politics stands the SMNO—the Singapore Malay National Organization, also known as Persatuan Kebangsaan Melayu Singapura (the Malay National Union of Singapore) or PEKEMAS and formerly known as SUMNO.[10] The SMNO was formed as the Singapore branch of the UMNO as part of the grand Malay opposition to the Malayan Union proposals of 1946, and perhaps because of the nature of its external genesis, the SMNO has never been as successful organizationally as its counterpart in the federation, even though it was able in the 1950s to tap—almost by default—the residual core of Singapore Malay ethnic sympathies because of the UMNO's continuing success in the peninsula. From its outset the SMNO was plagued by a shortage of party funds and by seemingly endless intraparty dissent and personal jealousies. Before Malaya and Singapore became two independent territories, the SMNO was dependent upon UMNO headquarters in Kuala Lumpur for policy decisions, and senior UMNO

8. Michael R. Stenson, *Industrial Conflict in Malaya* (London: Oxford University Press, 1970), pp. 236–251.
9. *ST*, March 25, 1972.
10. Not to be confused with the PEKEMAS party in Malaysia.

leaders frequently had to intervene in the SMNO's internal squabbles. In the late 1950s, when the PAP attracted many Malay members away from the SMNO,[11] Tunku Abdul Rahman criticized its weak and divided leadership, undue attention to personal interests, subversive elements (that is pro-PAP) within the party, and hostile, disruptive elements outside.[12] The SMNO's dilemma then (and to a lesser extent today) was the necessity to work politically within a specifically Singaporean context and at the same time to give the appearance of complete independence from Malay influence emanating from the federation. Another factor enervating the SMNO is the generation gap between younger, better-educated Malays and the traditional elders in the party, as a result of which many of the younger Malays have left the SMNO, dissatisfied with their inability to obtain a proper hearing and thereby to influence decisions.

In 1959 the SMNO was able to elect three Malay members to the Singapore legislature, but in the 1963 elections all SMNO candidates were defeated, a bitter blow to the party's hopes. At the time the SMNO was split by its usual internal dissension, and its appeal to the Singapore Malays was undercut by the PAP's own program for entrance into Malaysia and by PAP proposals for improving the status of the Malays in Singapore, ideas that in 1963 had not yet lost their appeal to many Malays. The SMNO has never regained enough electoral support to be translated into parliamentary seats, a process hastened if not actually caused by electoral reapportionment. The party is also deprived of adequate channels of recruitment to leadership positions. Because of economic configurations in Singapore, most educated Malays are obliged to enter government service to seek their livelihood, and once they are so ensconced their ability to work politically (or socially) for the improvement of their community is severely constrained, unless they do so within the ambit of PAP-approved organizations. Singapore Malays repeat-

11. The SMNO's chairman claimed to me in a personal interview (1971) that the PAP enticed SMNO members away by offering them positions in the PAP. A non-Malay PAP member of parliament also cited to me several instances in which SMNO leaders were offered positions of responsibility inside the PAP provided they switched their allegiance. Certainly a number of PAP Malay members of parliament today were previously members of the SMNO.

12. *ST*, September 21, 1959.

edly informed me in 1971 that any Malay government officials who attempt to identify themselves with the SMNO would face sanctions from the government in one form or another for their acts.

What, then, is the SMNO's future? Its membership today is composed of a mixture of Malay-Arab businessmen, schoolteachers, fishermen, journalists, religious teachers, small shopkeepers, clerks, office peons, and a handful of nongovernment Malay professionals. As an active organization, the SMNO has moved away from the parliamentary political arena for obvious reasons and is concentrating its endeavors in the social and cultural spheres, organizing such events as religious competitions and seminars, picnics, cultural shows, and kindergarten classes. The SMNO regards itself as the repository and guardian of Malay culture and the Islamic religion in Singapore, and its stand on these matters is generally of a conservative hue. SMNO leaders complain of the constant ISD surveillance imposed on their activities and of PAP pressure exerted on the mass media to play down their operations. Despite the SMNO's poor showing in the 1972 elections the party remains an active (if politically inarticulate) voice of the Malay community in Singapore, serving as a rallying point for conservative and pro-Kuala Lumpur Malays and therefore representing another barrier in the way of the PAP's state-building policies.

Other political parties include the Workers' Party (WP), the United National Front (UNF), and the People's Front (PF). All three espouse an inchoate, non-Communist–cum-leftist orientation toward politics and have been unsuccessful in attracting sufficient votes to gain any parliamentary seats. All three parties campaign on an anti-PAP platform, avowing that they would restrict government power in almost every field should they come to power. The WP secretary-general, for instance, accuses the PAP of possessing "total and complete control over all forms of activity in the state" and of "undermining the civil service, robbing it of its security and harrassing its members so that they no longer feel secure in the service nor pride in their work."[13] The multiracial leadership of the WP comes from a cross section of the community and includes lawyers, teachers, and businessmen, but it has so far been unable to construct

13. *ST*, September 23, 1971.

a broad grass-roots organization.[14] The UNF was registered in March 1970 from the remnants of the old Singapore Chinese party (previously the Singapore branch of the MCA), plus two Malay groups, and it has mixed Chinese, Indian, and Malay leadership. The UNF calls for the construction of a genuine multiracial Singapore and for the reunification of Malaysia and Singapore. It entered candidates to contest two of the five by-elections announced by the PAP in 1970, five PAP members having resigned to make way for new blood. The UNF, under its secretary-general R. Vetrivelu (a veteran of a number of other political parties in Singapore and Malaysia), has displayed distinctly eccentric leadership qualities and, like the WP, has been unable to establish any apparent party organization. In the 1970 by-elections the UNF campaigned on an obvious anti-PAP protest platform, appealing especially to the non-English-educated sector of the population.[15] Despite poor organization and the short period granted by the PAP for the actual campaign, the UNF surprised everyone by obtaining 37 percent of the total vote in the two by-elections in which it took part; it was generally agreed, however, that this figure was more an indicator of anti-PAP dissatisfaction than of pro-UNF sentiment.

The People's Front was launched on its stormy journey in March 1971, again not on any particular platform of its own but on the basis of anti-PAP rhetoric: "Come forward courageously and join the forces of the People's Front," proclaimed a PF official, "so that you do not remain under the dictatorial, bureaucratic and iron rule of one-party government."[16] At first successful in attracting a number of well-known professionals and intellectuals (including several former PAP and Barisan figures) to its ranks, the PF soon faltered in a sea of internal conflict. After a few months in office, the PF secretary-general resigned amid a welter of rumors following the departure of a Malay PF leader who had been identified in public by

14. By November 1971 the WP had been able to establish only two branches (*Arena*, November 7, 1971).

15. In 1971, Vetrivelu accused the PAP of trying to turn Singapore into a Westernized city on Asian soil, saying that "we have to maintain our Asian culture, if possible at the expense of the English language" (*ST*, October 25, 1971).

16. Quoted in editorial, *ST*, March 29, 1971.

Lee Kuan-yew as a former government agent.[17] Several months later, in November, more of the PF's leadership left the party in a second crisis. The PF lingers on almost moribund (it participated in the 1972 elections) under an unstable party leadership "bugged by fears," one observer has written, "perhaps not altogether ground-less, that the PAP has planted its own 'stooges' among them."[18]

Electoral Reapportionment

The PAP has always feared, with good reason, violence resulting from politics conducted along ethnic lines, and it constantly attacks parties whose raison d'être is communally based. In 1967 the government delineated new electoral divisions[19] that had the ef-fect—not, of course, stated explicitly—of diluting the Malay vote by dispersing it in several constituencies where its impact was coun-terbalanced by the non-Malay population.[20] The government's rationale for reapportionment was the uneven economic develop-ment among the various constituencies and their abnormally large population ratios, but a close investigation of the delineation report reveals that the stated reasons were at best contrived. Clearly there was a need for reapportionment because of the disparate popula-tion ratios, but the section of the report concerning the uneven level of development is, to my mind, invalid. Singapore's economic development is controlled by a highly centralized process in which all development decisions are made and implemented at a state level. The makeup of electoral constituencies *qua* constituencies is not a factor involved in the planning process, for Singapore is so small that it is more advantageous and logical to make economic de-cisions on an islandwide basis. Many constituencies are small in area

17. *ST*, July 2, 3, 1971. The PF leadership was also split over the decision to proceed with the implementation of "a unified Malayan democratic republic includ-ing Singapore" (*NN*, July 7, 1971).

18. Willard Hanna, "How to Win a Clean Sweep in Free Elections," American Universities Field Staff, Field Staff Reports, Southeast Asia Series, 20 (1972).

19. Republic of Singapore, *White Paper on the Report of the Electoral Boundaries: Delineation Committee on the Review of the Boundaries of the Present 51 Parliament Electoral Divisions*, Command 22 of 1967 (Singapore: Government Printer, 1967).

20. One leading PAP Malay figure, who had been involved with the Delination Committee's *Report*, admitted privately to me that this was actually the PAP's intent.

Singapore

and inextricably integrated in both geographical and social terms with adjoining constituencies; to devote part of the planning process to them as separate units would be ludicrous. The inescapable conclusion is that reapportionment was carried out for reasons of political expediency, to ensure, as far as the Malays were concerned, that ethnically oriented candidates (such as those from the SMNO) would find it nigh impossible to become elected—given the assumption that very few non-Malays would ever vote for a Malay candidate standing on a communal platform and, conversely, that at least some Malays would vote for the candidate of a PAP-style multiracial party. The SMNO's reaction was bitter, and the party's chairman claimed in a letter to the press that there had been no opposition representative on the delineation committee and that most of the constituencies that had been readjusted were predominantly Malay areas.[21] Certainly the main Malay residential enclaves were included in reapportionment, as well as several non-Malay areas, and the government's measures dealt a severe blow to the future of the SMNO as an electoral party standing on its own—or, for that matter, to the future of any other exclusively Malay communal party.

The 1972 General Elections

The PAP went into the 1972 election campaign exuding confidence, secure in the knowledge that the party was in an unassailable position. A few remarks were made by PAP leaders to the effect that a "loyal" opposition in parliament would be a useful step in the democratic process, but their actions before, during, and after the 1972 elections showed them to be as politically ruthless as ever, determined to crush all opposition. The 1968 elections, in which the PAP had swept the board, gaining all fifty-eight seats,[22] saw the PAP opposed only by two WP candidates and five independents—other parties, including the SMNO and Barisan, having boycotted the process. In 1972 the PAP was opposed by the Barisan, SMNO, WP, UNF, and PF, plus two independents, and this time the combined opposition was able to garner 31 percent of the total vote. A shaky coalition of parties of the left—the Barisan, UNF, and PF—

21. *ST*, November 17, 1971.
22. Another seven seats were added in time for the 1972 elections, making a total of sixty-five.

emerged to contest the elections, while the SMNO and WP looked for electoral assistance from other opposition parties where it could be found, but in the main the opposition lacked both cohesive campaign organizations and the financial wherewithal necessary to operate them. As one commentator points out, "Most of the parties were in fact patched together or re-patched together just barely in time to nominate candidates."[23] The opposition may have been unprepared for a 1972 campaign (the PAP could have held off until 1973 had it so wished), and the brevity of the campaign (a mere nine days between nomination and polling days, a frequent PAP electoral tactic) gave little time to construct the requisite level of campaign organization, but the campaign passed without violence or disorder. The PAP conducted its electoral operations on a platform of its own solid accomplishments in the material field, combined with attacks on Malay and Chinese chauvinism, political "communalism" long anathema to PAP doctrinists. PAP leaders also assailed opposition parties for accepting financial assistance from unspecified foreign sources. The party cleverly raised the specter of potential interference from outside if the electorate failed to vote loyally, claiming that a vote for the PAP was a vote for Singapore. The foreign minister, Sinnothamby Rajaratnam, played upon the voters' fears:

Vote on Saturday in a way that all the superpowers may know that, whether you are Chinese-educated, English-educated, or bilingual, or whether Indians or Eurasians, you are voting as Singaporeans. . . .

A lot of people [that is, outside interests] are interested to see whether the Malays will vote for the Malays, how the Indians will go . . . and so on.

Naturally the Malaysians and Indonesians, being close neighbors, they would like to know what the breakdown is between loyal Singaporeans and those who are not.[24]

The PAP's famed intolerance toward the press and suspicion of non-PAP intellectuals is shown by the following allegation, also made by Rajaratnam (himself a former journalist):

All the bright students go into engineering, the sciences, medicine, economics and so on. The not-so-bright go to political science and sociology. When they cannot get a good job they go on to journalism. We are supposed

23. Hanna, "How to Win a Clean Sweep," p. 5.
24. *ST*, August 30, 1972.

to have freedom of the press. Their analysis of the PAP is often completely wide of the mark. They do not know the basic data of men and politics in Singapore, that politics here literally mean life and death.[25]

For its part the opposition collectively chastised the PAP for its performance—for continuing compulsory national service, for its garrison-state mentality, for its stringent citizenship laws, for arrest and detention without trial, for its strict control over trade-union activities, for stifling free speech and dissent, for no longer giving equal treatment to all four educational language streams, for "graceless" and "crass" materialism, for neglecting the Malays, and for not striving for reunification with Malaysia—all to no avail,[26] as the PAP won all sixty-five seats despite a combined opposition vote of 31 percent.

Once again the PAP had fulfilled its constitutional responsibility and held parliamentary general elections, winning in the process another five-year mandate from the people in apparently free elections.[27] But even though the 31 percent opposition vote had not resulted in any opposition parliamentary seat, it stimulated the PAP leadership to announce even more draconian measures to control the electoral system; it proposed, for example, to enact legislation requiring all political parties to reveal their campaign contributions to government inspectors in order to determine whether "outside" sources had made financial donations. (During the campaign Rajaratnam had cited what he called the "proxy technique" of infiltration by foreign interests, whereby internal political parties and newspapers stood proxy in Singapore for external and subversive organizations.[28] There is no real proof for such allegations, at least none has been revealed.) After the elections the PAP prosecuted a number of opposition candidates for

25. Ibid.
26. The opposition's campaign was not helped by the PAP's release of adverse information relating to several opposition candidates; the secretary-general of the UNF was in arrears in his rent, the public was told, four candidates (two from the UNF, two from the WP) had criminal records, and the PF secretary-general was on the verge of bankruptcy.
27. I say "apparently" because over the years numerous people and groups have attacked the electoral system as not being secret. Voting is mandatory by law, and each ballot carries upon it a registration number. It is therefore possible, if tedious, for the government to discover who are opposition voters.
28. *ST*, August 31, 1972.

alleged election abuses, the PF secretary-general (who is also a novelist of the "protest" genre) being sentenced to one month in prison and a substantial fine. When, however, in October 1974 the WP sued the government-controlled radio station and a PAP member of parliament for libel and slander (for falsely alleging that the WP had received $250,000 in contributions from foreign sources), the Singapore attorney-general, acting as defense counsel for Radio Singapore, argued that the radio station was privileged because it was only reporting what had been said at a public meeting.[29]

Despite the many difficulties placed in their path by the PAP, opposition parties live on in Singapore if in some disarray. Subject to constant ISD harrassment, denied the right to own a newspaper as a forum for opposition views, inadequately reported by a mass media (press, radio, and television) completely subjugated or directly controlled by the government,[30] adversely affected by the reapportionment of electoral constituencies, and otherwise discriminated against, their very existence is a miracle. It will be many years before opposition parties, under the present system of politics and the PAP's methods of overkill, are able to mount any serious political alternative to the PAP government unless external conditions, such as the state of the international economy, result in the deterioration of the domestic economy to crisis or near-crisis proportions.

The Military and the Police

After separation in 1965, the new Republic of Singapore was forced to reappraise its thinking on defense and security matters, a process that was accelerated when the British announced in 1968 that they would withdraw all their forces east of Suez. Singapore now had to become self-reliant, to define new and potential enemies, and to reconstitute the armed forces and police accordingly. The plan finally drawn up was "to develop a small, well-

29. *NYT*, October 15, 1974.

30. Lee Kuan-yew, in one of his many attacks on the press, at a Press Club speech in 1972 warned the media that when they "pour out a daily dose of poison, I say I put my knuckle-dusters on as the first stage. If you still continue, then I say here are the stilettos. Choose your weapons" (*NYT*, November 26, 1972).

equipped, highly trained and mobile defense force comprising a small nucleus of regulars backed up by a large part-time volunteer citizens force—the People's Defense Force."[31] To implement this goal, in 1967 compulsory national service was introduced for all able-bodied males above the age of eighteen, who were required to serve for two years in the armed forces, the Vigilante Corps, or the police Special Constabulary. After completing this service, the men would become reservists (with yearly training periods) for another ten years or up to the age of forty, whichever came later, so that at all times Singapore would have a reservoir of trained, disciplined men on whom to call should an emergency arise. The idea has been, apparently, to turn Singapore, with its citizens' army, into another Israel, and indeed Israeli advisers were quietly brought to Singapore to work with the new military forces. (They were afterward withdrawn as the result of too much publicity.) By 1971, Singapore had raised and trained six full-time infantry battalions, plus support groups including a large armored unit complete with tanks and a pool or organized reservists. A small but efficient air force and navy have also been formed.

Two indications of the high priority assigned to the military build-up were (a) the transfer of Goh Keng-swee, Singapore's most efficient administrator-politician, from his post of finance minister to that of defense minister, and (b) the increased allocation of state expenditures for defense purposes, which in 1970 had reached 33 percent of the total budget.[32] The government plans by 1980 to have a total of at least eighty thousand trained men in the armed forces, including reserves,[33] a high proportion of the male population in such a small island republic. The objective of the militarization program, as it may be called, is not simply military in scope; the government's policy is to use the training period consciously to create a "rugged" state identity through a common experience, to build, in the government's words, "a multiracial, multilingual and multireligious community committed to Singapore and to the

31. Republic of Singapore, *Singapore '71* (Singapore: Government Printer, 1971), p. 100.
32. Iain Buchanan, *Singapore in Southeast Asia: An Economic and Political Appraisal* (London: George Bell, 1972), p. 293.
33. *ST*, October 15, 1971.

well-being of its citizens. It follows the directions begun in schools, where an integrated community is educated together, where young people of all races study together, to forge a national identity."[34] The possibility of a military coup is remote in Singapore as long as the present convergence of interests and values between the military and the regime continues.

The police force, as in Malaysia, bears primary responsibility for the preservation of public security and falls under the control of the Ministry of the Interior and Defense. A large and efficient unit is maintained for the suppression of riots and other forms of public unrest, and in recent cases of serious disturbances it has acted impartially,[35] treating all ethnic groups alike. (In the race riots of 1964, for instance, police riot squads took equally firm action against Malay mobs and Chinese secret society thugs.) According to government figures, in 1970 the police force reached a strength of 7,100 regular personnel, supported by ancillary units including the Vigilante Corps and the Special Constabulary. Service with the police and the police cadet corps, too, plays a part in the socialization programs of the government: "When National Service was introduced in 1967, it included part-time service in the Special Constabulary and the Vigilante Corps, both of which came under the Police National Service Command. To encourage a greater interest in the police among schoolboys and girls, the Police Cadet Corps organization was extended to almost all the secondary schools, and is now part of the National Cadet Corps."[36]

Other Interest Groups

The roles of the press as watchdog of the public interest and of the trade unions as independent representatives of the working class have been radically curtailed by the activities of the PAP so that they can no longer fairly be called interest or pressure groups, as has been remarked elsewhere in these pages. The two universities, Nanyang and the University of Singapore, have in the past acted as

34. Republic of Singapore, *Singapore '71*, p. 104.
35. This has not always been the case. Under the British, when the police was 80 percent Malay, in a number of instances squads of Malay police discriminated against non-Malays or refused orders to act against Malay mobs.
36. Republic of Singapore, *Singapore '71*, p. 108.

annoying mosquitoes buzzing around the PAP's rump, but the PAP's policy toward them has been one of inexorable control and infiltration, so that apart from minor and sporadic outbursts of indignation by small numbers of courageous students and faculty the university campuses remain dormant, fulfilling the function of service stations for the state's economic policies and as recruiting grounds for the PAP's cadre system.

The single most influential interest group is the Chinese Chamber of Commerce (CCC), whose leaders have the ear of the PAP's top councils. The CCC has been active in politics for many years, at one time publicly supporting right-wing groups like the Democratic Party in 1955. Generally it acts as a spokesbody for Chinese cultural traditions, especially the continued use of the Chinese language, as well as for Chinese commercial interests. In both of these areas the CCC has been able to exert influence on the PAP with varying degrees of success; because it represents a vast amount of Chinese investment capital in Singapore, Lee Kuan-yew is obliged to court its support, but he and his party are more ambivalent about the CCC's role as the protector of traditional Chinese culture with its implicit backdrop of the hated Chinese "chauvinism."

The bureaucracy is now an interest group in itself, as it has become the pre-eminent arm of government operations. The bureaucracy is divided into two: the civil service proper and the statutory boards and government companies. The latter nominally retain a measure of autonomy, but there is much overlapping of functions between the two branches, and the PAP remains in real control. Chan Heng-chee succinctly sums up the political role of the bureaucracy:

The growth of government activities through the statutory institutions and private companies has increased the scope of the power of the civil servants who are placed in charge of the statutory boards and as members of the Board of Directors of the companies. In any real life situation, the tra-ditional dichotomy between politics and administration is academic. Ad-ministrators are politicians in their own way. They do not merely serve, they also wield decision-making power without the mandate [that is, the vote]. In Singapore, the division between the administrator and the politi-cian is particularly blurred because it is unstated official policy to politicise the administrators and to entrust them with major power in decision-making in the government's enterprises. The Head of the Civil Service . . . has reiterated on several occasions in public that the civil servant must possess—above all qualities—political alertness. . . . The civil servant who succeeds and is entrusted with responsibility must be both "red" and "expert."[37]

Other small interest groups exist, most in an adversary relationship with the PAP. They include specifically communal groups such as the Malay Schoolteachers Union and other Malay community groups that are striving, outside of the government's own multiracial structures, to improve the socioeconomic status of the Malay community. Pro-Chinese-language and Chinese cultural groups, from Chinese-language schools and other associations, also endeavor to exert some pressure. One more interest group that monitors government activities in the area of the physical environment is the Singapore Planning and Urban Research Group (SPUR), formed in 1964, that consists of an association of nonpartisan, multiracial architects and other professionals who have criticized the PAP on occasion for placing material development over human well-being. The SPUR has met with scathing counterattacks from the PAP, but the quality of the group's membership at least makes the government sit up and listen.[38] On the whole, however, Singapore is not a pluralist society as the term refers to the role of government as an aggregator of diffuse group interests and allocator of rewards. The PAP does not seek active participant citizens or citizen groups. Its communications system is designed to inculcate an informed acquiescence; its decision-making machinery is narrowly and tightly based, and criticism from outside is not lightly endured, no matter how informed.

37. Chan Heng-chee: "Politics in an Administrative State: Where Has the Politics Gone?" (Singapore: Institute of Southeast Asian Studies, 1974), pp. 19–20.
38. The SPUR's philosophy can be read in its publication '68–'71 SPUR (Singapore: SPUR, 1971).

9 | Major Problems

Singapore's problems are different in some respects from those of Malaysia, similar in others. The republic does not have in its midst an armed and organized Communist revolutionary force, although politically Communism poses a menace to the PAP's version of the status quo—far less of a menace, perhaps, than the PAP would have its citizens believe because the government has been able to emasculate political parties and groups sympathetic to Communist ideology. Yet Singapore's population is 76 percent Chinese, and their feelings toward Communism cannot but be colored by a residual Chinese chauvinism and pride in the PRC's accomplishments. These attitudes will diminish as the PAP's socialization policies take root in the younger generation and its successors, but in the meantime the potency of pro-PRC sentiments remains a factor. More important contemporary problems, however, are those focusing on the economy, on foreign relations, on the Malay minority, and on the effects of the PAP's policies and activities in general.

Economic Problems

In one sense the Singapore government has met and overcome its major economic challenge—that of adjusting to the island's status as an independent political and economic entity. By the dedication of her public servants, the farsightedness of her economic planners, and the industry of her population, Singapore has been able to create an economic base of her own with which to alleviate the pressures resulting from separation in 1965 from her natural geographic hinterland. Pursuing policies of granting liberal concessions to foreign investors and of creating a stable, skilled, and undemanding (as yet) work force, the government has succeeded in attracting substantial amounts of investment capital represented by a growing number of foreign commercial and industrial enterprises. The republic was fortunate enough to undergo her economic crises at a time (1965–1970) when the international economic situation was favorable, enabling the new economic policies to take root and flourish. By intelligent anticipation of regional needs Singapore has been able to establish herself as a center for service industries (especially in petroleum exploration and production), for financial transactions, and for tourism, at the same time holding onto a goodly portion of the previous entrepreneurial, or entrepôt, trade with her neighbors.[1] In this sense, when one considers the number of multinational corporations based in Singapore, the republic has become a true global village.

There are, however, inherent weaknesses in Singapore's economic system which the government will find difficult to counter. No matter how well her efficient policy makers succeed in constructing a large industrial sector, several factors must affect the rate of growth and the level of stability in the economy. By becoming a global village Singapore now has to participate, in less than advantageous terms, in the global economic system and therefore is subject to the periodic vacillations of that larger market, possessing virtually no countervailing resources of her own (such as a significant agricultural sector) with which to survive major economic shocks. The only cushion between the whims of the international economic system and economic disaster for Singapore lies in the continuance of her regional entrepreneurial role, that is, interport trade with her immediate neighbors and reliance on them for a major share of her raw materials, including food and water. Should this trade fail—and Singapore's relations with her two most important neighbors, Malaysia and Indonesia, have always been fragile—the island's economic landscape will become bleak.

A further threat to the republic's economic stability is represented by domestic problems. At present her work force remains docile

1. For political reasons, the government deliberately underplays the importance of these latter transactions (most of which are regarded as smuggling by Indonesia), refusing to make available figures for trade with Indonesia because of its illegality in the eyes of Jakarta.

because of a good record of full employment in the past. Government restraints on the ability of workers to organize themselves for the purposes of job action (strikes, slowdowns, picketing, walkouts, and so on) have kept labor unrest to a minimum (despite overt signs of conspicuous consumption by Singapore's wealthy and their children), providing foreign and domestic employers on the island with a pool of cheap, disciplined, and skilled labor. But the industrialization process is creating a large corpus of workers, many of them employed in sizable factories—the makings, in short, of an industrial proletariat. In the past the government has been able to placate and control the workers through emotional appeals for solidarity in the face of a series of real crises and because of relatively low commodity prices. This is no longer the case. The energy and monetary crises of recent years have had their inevitable repercussions in Singapore, where prices have risen sharply in conformity with the international economic situation. Workers' wages have not increased proportionally, however, and complaints against the raging surge of inflation are increasing.[2] The government thus has to grapple with an unenviable predicament: it needs to keep foreign investors happy (by maintaining wages and labor unrest at an acceptable minimum) so that they will not remove their operations to other countries with even cheaper labor, and it must not allow worker discontent to burgeon to such an intensity that it attempts to organize itself in a more militant, anti-PAP direction. How long the PAP will be able to tread this precarious path is not entirely within the PAP's own ability to decide.

Foreign Policy

Singapore's view of herself in the world is necessarily moderated by her geographic and strategic position at the core of Southeast Asia, by her own lack of economic resources, and by a recognition of her basic "alien"—that is, Chinese—character lying between Malaysia and Indonesia. The republic is only too aware that events in

2. The consumer price index rose almost 30 percent in 1973, and in 1974 thousands of workers were retrenched because of recession. For a highly critical view of Singapore's policy toward her workers, see Chou See Ahlek, "In Lee Kuan-yew's Singapore, Prosperity Rides on the Rails of Repression," *Harvard Crimson*, May 13, 1975. See also Yeo Toon-joo, "Grumbling But Little Action," *FEER*, August 9, 1974 (Singapore '74 Focus).

these two countries, where anti-Chinese sentiments have welled up periodically among their rulers and their indigenous peoples, may well reverberate in Singapore; race riots in Malaysia, for example, could easily spill across the causeway into Singapore. On the economic side, far from participating in an ASEAN common market, both Malaysia and Indonesia have individual ambitions of their own that run counter to Singapore's pronounced economic policies. Already pressures from Kuala Lumpur and Jakarta have forced several multinational corporations (especially the oil industry) to transfer their service operations from Singapore to the country whence the product concerned actually originates, and attempts are continuing to bypass Singapore as the middleman in the exporting of primary products and the importing of other commodities. These attempts have been only marginally successful to date, given the overwhelming superiority of Singapore's port facilities (Singapore is the world's fourth largest port) and her other efficient service and entrepreneurial infrastructures, but they will surely increase in the future.

In view of these obvious circumstances, it is difficult to understand the reason for Singapore's abrasive foreign policy attitudes toward Kuala Lumpur and Jakarta following separation from Malaysia in 1965. For several years Singapore adopted a posture of what can only be termed arrogance toward her neighbors, caring little for their national susceptibilities and decrying their attempts to manage their economic affairs.[3] Singapore naturally had been angered by her virtual expulsion from Malaysia and by Sukarno's confrontation policies, but the stridency of Singapore's verbal attacks on Malaysia and Indonesia—no matter the provocation—seems in retrospect to have been counterproductive. The republic had nothing to gain thereby and everything to lose. Since 1970, however, Singapore has tried desperately to improve her relations with Kuala Lumpur and Jakarta, with some limited success. Visits by Lee Kuan-yew to Jakarta (Suharto reciprocated with a visit to Singapore in 1974) and Kuala

3. In 1968 the Singapore government executed, by hanging, two Indonesian marines who had been captured during "Confrontation" following a successful and violent act of sabotage, despite pleas for clemency from all over the region and the world to save the lives of the two marines. Anti-Singapore animosity in Indonesia remained high for several years afterward.

Lumpur (Tun Razak visited Singapore in 1973) have been followed by smoother diplomatic and economic transactions, but suspicions and jealousies remain.

Singapore is now conducting her relations with her two closest neighbors on the premise that both countries are, for the time being, stable and even if rivals are at least in the same political and economic camp as Singapore.[4] As Goh Keng-swee, the minister for defense, pointed out in 1970, Singapore has a vested interest in the economic success of Malaysia and Indonesia; the more the two countries achieve a degree of political stability and economic rationality the easier it will be for Singapore to find a meaningful role in Southeast Asia. For, Goh continued, if the gap in the relative standards of living widens in the future, foreign relations will suffer correspondingly.[5] For the past several years, therefore, the Singapore government has urged local capitalists to invest in Malaysia and Indonesia. In 1971, for instance, Singapore was the largest single investor among foreign countries in pioneer companies in Malaysia, and between 1968 and 1971, Singapore businessmen invested S$60 million in industrial ventures in Indonesia.[6] Joint economic cooperation between Malaysia and Singapore was also strengthened in 1971 by the signing of an agreement between the government-operated trade corporations of Malaysia and Singapore concerning the exchange of overseas market information, the acting of export agents for each other, and cooperation in third-country trade.[7] It is obviously to Singapore's benefit to sustain amicable ties with Malaysia and Indonesia for as long as feasible.

Singapore's attitudes toward ASEAN and regional cooperation are tempered by her perspectives on big-power rivalry and by her fears of Communist expansionism, although the PAP leadership is not as much concerned with PRC ambitions in Southeast Asia as with those of indigenous Communist organizations. On economic mat-

4. When Indonesia's new "Cabinet of Technocrats" was appointed in late 1971, Singapore's business and political leaders believed that "Singapore [would] reap economic gains if the new Cabinet, committed towards accelerating economic growth, succeeds in promoting a prosperous Indonesia with its healthy 'spill over' effects in the region" (*ST*, September 16, 1971).

5. Speech in a forum, "Singapore in the 1970s," *ST*, November 23, 1970.

6. *ST*, May 22, 1971 and *SH*, March 13, 1971.

7. *ST*, October 13, 15, 1971.

ters Singapore is willing to cooperate in ASEAN projects—she has more to gain in this respect than her primary producing neighbors—but quietly refuses to join with Malaysia (and now Thailand and the Philippines) in a policy of regional nonalignment and neutralization. Singapore, like Malaysia, was not a member of the Southeast Asia Treaty Organization (SEATO), but is, with Malaysia, a participant in the Commonwealth Five-Power Agreement, on which she places more reliance than does a lukewarm Malaysia. (Lee Kuan-yew was unhappy at Australia's decision to withdraw her infantry forces from Singapore in mid-1973, perhaps viewing their presence as a buffer against outside aggression—including that from Malaysia.) On gaining independence in 1965, Singapore's leaders assiduously courted Third World countries in Asia and Africa, with some success, as the prime minister and other cabinet ministers toured these countries seeking recognition and support. In these early days Lee openly scoffed at alignment with Britain (or with the United States), but gradually perceptions of Communist encroachment, generated by the various revolutions taking place in Indochina and by the desire to retain and protect foreign investments, forced a policy change. Singapore realized that Britain was no longer a possible bulwark against external interference in the region, and so looked to the United States as the new defender of the anti-Communist faith. In the early 1970s, at the height of the U.S. commitment in Vietnam, high-ranking U.S. military officers frequently were welcomed in Singapore as were naval vessels and their crews; Singapore became one of the service centers for U.S. operations in Indochina, and Lee Kuan-yew consistently supported the U.S. position to all who would listen, even though there were, and are, no direct defense agreements between the two states.

Now that the United States has been expelled from the Indochinese amphitheater, the Singapore government's fears of the Communist revolutionary potential in Southeast Asia have been enhanced. Lee Kuan-yew reportedly is unhappy at the decision by Thailand, the Philippines, and Malaysia to establish diplomatic relations with the PRC, believing that state-to-state ties will not inhibit local Communist insurgency; on the contrary, Lee asserts, "by Peking recognizing the existence of contrary regimes [that is,

Thailand, the Philippines, and Malaysia] and seeming to abandon the fraternal parties, the parties become less and less the creation of China and, therefore, become stronger." Singapore thus believes that it is Peking's "calculated strategy to give pro-Peking insurgencies the *appearance* of independent strength."[8] Now that Vietnam has achieved its independence as a member of the Communist bloc, Lee also feels that once the Vietnamese have consolidated their internal position, they could set their country up as an arsenal for regional insurgency movements. For these reasons Singapore has urged the United States to maintain a strong presence in Southeast Asia, in Lee's words, "to maintain the security balance between the great powers so we are not caught by too rapid a desire by the Soviets or China to pre-empt on each other for influence in the region."[9] Singapore is willing to trade with China, the Soviet Union, and other Communist countries (the USSR has an embassy in Singapore and vice versa) and has allowed Soviet naval vessels to call at Singapore, but she has consistently refused to establish formal diplomatic ties with the PRC. In this decision the PAP is influenced by the ethnic composition of her population, for apart from external considerations the ruling party undoubtedly does not wish to impart any legitimacy to existing Chinese chauvinism in Singapore, nor does it wish to allow a PRC presence in Singapore (which recognition would entail) to extend a potential fillip to the attractions of Chinese Communist ideology.

The Singapore Malay Community

The obvious differences between the Malays of Singapore and those of Malaysia is that the former are a distinct numerical minority and do not command any effective political power. They can exert leverage only vicariously, through the knowledge that they are part of the geographical Malay world in Malaysia and Indonesia and thus protected from overt discrimination. It is difficult for the Singapore government to counteract the centrifugal cultural (not to say political) pulls issuing from her two Malay neighbors, for the Singapore

---

8. Quoted in an Evans and Novak syndicated column, by-lined in Singapore and appearing in the *Providence Journal*, July 17, 1975. The authors of the column had been granted an interview with Lee.
9. Ibid.

Malay community, like the rest of Singapore's inhabitants—apart from a small number of literally indigenous Singapore Malays, descendants of those few whom Raffles found on the island when he arrived—is comprised of immigrant stock that has settled in Singapore over the past 150 years. Many Singapore Malays have kinship, cultural, and other solidary ties to Malaysia and Indonesia, and the Singapore government's policy of molding the whole of the republic's population into a new Singaporean society is rendered more difficult by these external linkages. The situation is compounded by the fact that the isobars of socioeconomic backwardness generally coincide with those defining the Malay community, a fact in no way attributable to the PAP's policies (which cannot be expected to have reached fruition after only fifteen years), but to the grinding mills of history, that is, to the cultural residues of the Malays' rural past and to the benign neglect of the colonial era. The danger to the government is that because of the plethora of promises and rhetoric directed at the Malay community in the early days of the PAP's accession to power, stimulated by a desire to enter Malaysia, Malays may have come to blame the PAP government solely for their inability to escape from their perceivably unhappy lot. As long as the PAP leadership insists on a policy of multiracialism and meritocracy—ideal policies in themselves provided all groups set out from identical startingblocks—and refuses to afford Singapore Malays meaningful, special treatment (even if only on a temporary basis), the potential for communal disorder will endure.

Malays in Singapore are faced with two challenges. First, they have to grapple with the question of their own political and cultural identity: are they Malays or are they Singaporeans? (It seems that the PAP is reluctant to let them be both.) Second, they have to adjust to the problems of modernization (including, in a real sense, urbanization), which is the foundation upon which the present-day Singapore is constructed. Both problems are, of course, interrelated. The ultimate results of the government's resettlement schemes (together with other socialization processes) may be the emergence of a new type of Malay who is integrated psychologically as well as physically with his neighbors. New role patterns, taken from the Chinese and the Indian work ethos, may help to generate new values more compatible with conditions in urban, industrializing Singapore.

Change is taking place in the Singapore Malay community, some filtering across from Malaysia through osmosis, as it were: what the Second Malaysia Plan demands of *bumiputeras* in the federation is not significantly different from what the Singapore government wants of its own Malay population. In Singapore today many Malays, including women, are working efficiently in factories; *rezeki*, while still of religious import, is no longer seen as a mind-enervating "fate," but can be influenced by individual effort. Groups of younger, well-educated Malays (often, alas, under the too careful scrutiny of the Internal Security Department) are moving out into their communities and working positively toward change; this generation is far better educated than its parents and has a greater level of awareness of the problems that must be grappled with and resolved. There are optimistic as well as pessimistic signs. Finally, however, valuechange among the Malays cannot be a simple unilateral process. Implicit in the Singapore government's outlook toward the Malays is the assumption that the solution to the minority problem lies in the adaptation of the Malays to the new and evolving Singaporean identity. But race relations, which are at the core of Singapore's multiracial, meritocratic policies, cannot be understood and solved by reference only to the minority group. In the Singaporean experience, the non-Malay population (the Chinese), which exercises political and economic control, needs to examine its own structures with regard to the betterment of the Malay minority— and here the socioeconomic equation is of primary importance. Unless a greater attempt is made to afford the Malays genuine access to the economic sphere and unless steps are taken to ensure the preservation of the Malay language and cultural tradition, loyalties extending outward beyond the territorial borders of Singapore may exert contrary impulses.

The PAP: Promise and Fulfillment

Any person who has lived in Singapore cannot but be impressed with the efficiency of the state and with the PAP's remarkable accomplishments in its one and a half decades in office. Hundreds of millions of dollars have been attracted in foreign investment, and by any economic indicators the republic enjoys the second highest (next to Japan) standard of living in Asia. Over one-third of the population live in what are, on the surface, clean and bright public housing estates. The state bureaucracy is one of the least corruptible in the world and is staffed by dedicated officials. The system of education is of excellent quality and, generally speaking, is available to all who wish to use it; the nice balance between "formal" education and vocational and technical training, too, means that the state is not—unlike so many other countries—turning out a pool of overeducated youths whose employment prospects do not correspond with their expectations.

But cracks are appearing in the façade of success, as some disillusionment with the PAP begins to show and people look for something deeper than material achievements. An inherent contradiction lies in the difference between the PAP's rhetoric, in the view of itself that it tries to project to the public, and its activities. Through its various socialization agencies the PAP espouses an image of the party and the government as bulwarks of social justice and upholders of a democratic socialism in which liberal ideas are esteemed—adapted, of course, to Singapore peculiarities. Social consciousness in Singapore is high, and the PAP's goals, values, and attitudes are well known. More and more people, especially the young and better educated, are beginning to see a gap between rhetoric and social reality and to be repelled by what many perceive as a growing repressiveness. Newspapers are closed down arbitrarily in a supposedly free society, students are denied a university education unless they possess a "suitability certificate" approved by the political police, detention in prison for long periods without trial is implemented frequently, the right to trial by jury has been ended, and the right of habeas corpus is denied to those arrested for "political" offenses. In other words, Lee Kuan-yew's ever-increasing arrogance of power, the erosion of civil liberties guaranteed by the Constitution, the rapid and often savage crackdown on any form of dissent are inimical to the set of values the PAP theoretically is committed to construct. The party in a way has become satiated by its own success and seems reluctant (or unable) to modify means that have proved successful in the past to the ends of the present and the future. The PAP leadership in the 1950s and 1960s was immersed in a life or death struggle with dissidents, and the intensity of the conflict, although it proved successful, has hardened the leadership so that it is perhaps no longer susceptible of reform from within. Critics of the PAP who attack the leadership for the suppression of civil liberties are assailed by the party for being influenced by Western values that, the party claims, are often not reducible to Singapore peculiarities. It may be, however, that some freedoms, some civil liberties, represent universal values, striven for (if not always achieved) throughout the world and no more the product or the exclusive property of the West than is philosophy itself. The PAP undoubtedly produces material goods and services for its people in a remarkably able and dedicated manner; whether this efficiency will be able, over the long haul, to offset demands for a greater degree of cultural and political freedom has yet to be decided.

PART IV

THE SULTANATE
OF BRUNEI

10 | History and Future Status

History

The future of the tiny sultanate of Brunei,[1] 2,225 square miles in size with a population of around 130,000,[2] is unpredictable. Its relationship with Britain, though strong in the past, is now tenuous at best; but for the presence of its sizable oil resources and its increasingly important liquid natural gas, it would probably have become part of Malaysia in 1963. When the British withdraw, as they undoubtedly will over the next few years, covetous eyes will be cast in its direction and it is not likely to remain immured in its current state, an anachronistic if benevolent relic of Southeast Asia's feudal past.

Brunei's early history is difficult to piece together from the sparse record available. Trade and tributary contacts with China go back to the Sung dynasty, and there are early records of commerce with voyaging Arab merchants. It became the first Muslim state to emerge in Borneo (this name for the island as a whole is derived from the word "Brunei"), being converted as a consequence of its trade relations with Malacca. As in Malacca, Islam soon became a major force, shaping the directions of Brunei society and its politics down to the present. After the Portuguese capture of Malacca, Brunei became even more important as Muslim merchants migrated from Malacca to the sultanate. Brunei influence—in con-

1. The definitive study on Brunei is Donald E. Brown, "Sociopolitical History of Brunei, A Bornean Malay Sultanate" (Ph.D. dissertation, Cornell University, 1969).
2. In 1970, Brunei's population amounted to 130,260, of which 54 percent were Brunei Malays, 16.5 percent other indigenes, 26 percent Chinese, and 3.5 percent others.

junction with that of Islam—spread rapidly round the coastal areas of most of Borneo and up into the southern Philippines; once the sultan's agents even briefly captured Manila.

Brunei's expansionism and dominance of the region lasted approximately one hundred years, until the coming of Western explorers—Spanish, Portuguese, and Dutch at first, and finally the British. Gradually Brunei's outlying vassal and semisubordinate states were swallowed in the seventeenth century by the Dutch, and at the end of the eighteenth century the British opened trading stations in the northeast of Borneo, further eroding Brunei's influence. By the nineteenth century the splendor that was Brunei had almost entirely disappeared, and the arrival of the first of the Brooke family in 1839 completed the process. By manipulating to his own advantage the court intrigue, rebellion, and piracy that had become endemic to the sultanate, Brooke was able to have himself installed as rajah of Sarawak in 1841. By 1853, Brooke had established hegemony over the state of Sarawak, now completely independent of Brunei sovereignty.

Further portions of Brunei territory were whittled away by the Brooke rajahs and later by the North Borneo Chartered Company. By the end of the nineteenth century, the sultanate had shrunk to its present two small enclaves on the coast. The British government, having first taken the island of Labuan as a colony, declared the sultanate to be a British protectorate in 1888. The British reinforced their control in 1906 by an agreement similar to that imposed on Malay states in peninsular Malaya: the authority of the sultan was restricted to matters pertaining to native customary law and the administration of Islam. Thereafter, although due deference was paid to the person of the sultan, the British Resident exercised real power through a small bureaucracy headed by British civil servants seconded from Malaya. The Resident himself was administered by the government of the Straits Settlements, the governor of which also acted as the British high commissioner to Brunei.

The importance of Brunei underwent a sharp transformation in the 1920s with the discovery of oil in the sultanate and in neighboring Sarawak. Thereafter Brunei affairs of state became irretrievably enmeshed in the politics of oil. European and Asian administrative and technical personnel, together with numbers of manual workers from nearby territories, were brought in by the Shell Oil Company to exploit the new oil fields. New skills and new education were demanded, and soon at least part of the population acquired a new sophistication. Underneath this veneer of modernity, however, most Brunei Malays remained outside of the new society. A conservative royal Brunei family, with its court of Malay ruling families, was reluctant to expose the Brunei Malay peasants and fishermen to new influences that might erode their traditional loyalty and adherence to old customs. In a sense Brunei became a miniscule replica of British Malaya. Two separate societies evolved: one composed of an ascriptive Brunei Malay elite, supported by a Chinese entrepreneurial class and locked into a profitable symbiotic relationship with the oil company and its bustling world, the other comprised of Brunei Malay peasants and fishermen, sheltered from modern influences by the determination of their rulers that they remain unsullied by the unsettling winds of change. A few thousand non-Muslim indigenes still live in what for Brunei passes as the hinterland. Their isolation from modern life is best summed up by their reaction to the gift by the government of some color television sets, complete with generators, that were installed in remote longhouses and rural schools. As an Associated Press report put it: "Descendants of headhunters sit on reed mats in their traditional longhouses, taking in some of the wonders of the 20th century for the first time. A few older tribesmen, after watching 'The Virginian,' remarked that they had never realized that there were so many horses in Brunei. Other Iban and Murut tribesmen were baffled by such space-age fantasies as 'Voyage to the Bottom of the Sea.' "[3]

The Modern Era

Not until well after the end of World War II did nationalism and an indigenous politics emerge. The British returned after the surrender of the Japanese and reconstituted Brunei as British-protected territory. Slowly some measure of local government was introduced. Elections for local municipalities were proposed for

3. *NYT*, October 28, 1976.

1957 and then postponed. Finally a new Constitution was promulgated in 1959, in which provision was made for the election of sixteen of a thirty-three-member Legislative Council, the remainder being appointed by the sultan, and this proved to be the stimulus that gave voice for the first time to an indigenous, nontraditional nationalism. Prior to the proclamation of this new Constitution, the authority of the state was vested in the sultan-in-council, in which the sultan presided over a State Council of eleven members, all nominated by the ruler, plus the British Resident who remained responsible for general government administration. Leading positions in the sultanate, apart from those occupied by British civil servants, were filled almost exclusively by members of the Brunei Malay aristocracy.

A political party, the Brunei People's Party or Partai Rakyat, was organized in 1956 as a manifestation of nonaristocratic Brunei Malay sentiment. The 1959 Constitution and the elections it produced gave the new party an opportunity to demonstrate its popular strength. This it did in convincing fashion, winning all sixteen of the elected seats in the Legislative Council in the first elections ever held in Brunei in August 1962. The Partai Rakyat was socialist in orientation, with close links to eminent left-wing Malay politicians in Malaya, including Ahmad Boestaman of the Malayan Partai Rakyat and Dr. Burhanuddin of the PMIP, and to the SUPP in Sarawak. The leader of the Partai Rakyat was A. M. Azahari, a strange, driven figure, reputedly of Arab descent and possessing strong pro-Indonesian sympathies. Under Azahari the Partai Rakyat proposed that the three British Borneo territories become independent in one single political entity, governed by a democratically elected legislature that would be led by the sultan of Brunei as a constitutional monarch. Azahari and several of his fellow leaders, however, undoubtedly had plans for closer links with Indonesia.

After the elections of August 1962 the battle lines were clearly drawn: the militantly nationalistic and anti-British Partai Rakyat on the one hand, and the sultan, the Brunei Malay aristocracy, and the British on the other. No other political party had any popular support. The arena was delineated in July 1962, when the sultan announced tentatively that Brunei would participate in the projected new country of Malaysia. The Partai Rakyat immediately took the line previously adopted by the SUPP in Sarawak, the Barisan Sosialis in Singapore, and the Socialist Front in Malaya: it announced its strenuous objection to the formation of the new state and Brunei's participation in it.

The overwhelming victory of the Partai Rakyat in the elections held the next month caused the sultan to mute his intentions of joining Malaysia. There were other reasons, of course, for Brunei's reluctance and subsequent refusal in 1963 to join Malaysia: personality clases between the sultan and leading royal and secular personages in Malaya, disagreement over the sultan's prerogatives under the royal protocol of the proposed state, and, most important, dissatisfaction over revenue-sharing plans for Brunei's vast oil profits.

The Partai Rakyat nevertheless remained suspicious of the sultan's plans regarding Brunei and Malaysia, and in December 1962 suspicions were translated into armed rebellion. About three thousand armed rebels simultaneously attacked police stations and oil installations throughout Brunei and in contiguous areas of North Borneo and Sarawak. The insurgents' plans called for the liberation not only of Brunei but also of North Borneo and Sarawak. The sultan barely escaped capture: rumors prevalent at the time suggested that he was aware of the rebellion beforehand and that he acquiesced in its goals, seeing in them an excuse for staying out of Malaysia and a means of restoring some of Brunei's lost territory. After the initial flush of success, however, the insurrection was quickly put down by police from North Borneo and British troops from Singapore. Azahari, surprisingly, repaired to Manila immediately before the revolt broke out, whence he issued grandiose statements of intention, including the creation of a revolutionary government of northern Borneo.

There were indications that several of the rebels had received training in, if not logistic support from, Indonesia, and certainly many of them fully expected Indonesia to give direct and immediate military support. Indonesian complicity is difficult to determine, however, and reports that it was the major instigator ignore the internal reasons for the revolt, not the least of which was the sultan's intransigence in denying Brunei Malays an opportunity for social and economic betterment and a voice in the affairs of their state. British reports at the time laid the blame for the simultaneous uprisings in adjacent areas of North Borneo and Sarawak on years of neglect by the colonial regime: too many district officers, who should have been out in the villages catering to the needs of the isolated rural peasantry, were confined to their offices by the dreary weight of administrative detail that the government demanded of them.

A great deal of bitterness remains to this day, and the Partai Rakyat has never been allowed to regain its popular position inside the borders of the sultanate. Its leaders either fled to other countries or were imprisoned without trial; several still remain under detention. Mass arrests were also carried out in Sarawak, Singapore, and Malaya. In Brunei the rule of the sultan was strengthened, and the quickening spirit of participatory democracy was extinguished. In addition to his other reasons, the sultan used the revolt as a demonstration of Brunei Malay resistance to merger with Malaysia and withdrew from the London talks on Malaysia in July 1963. The Indonesians were able to point to the Brunei revolt as the first manifestation of popular rejection of the Malaysian concept and pledged their undying support for the freedom fighters of Azahari's revolutionary army. Brunei was thus the overture to "*konfrontasi,*" and the Brunei Partai Rakyat finally died insofar as its activities inside Brunei were concerned when it became clear that Sukarno's attempts to establish his regional leadership had failed.

The Contemporary Scene

If nothing else the Brunei revolt persuaded the sultan to embark on a major campaign to improve the welfare of his subjects. Hospitals and schools were built, roads constructed, and comprehensive welfare schemes introduced to better the social and economic standards of the population. The wealth of the country is such that impressive achievements have been made, so that overt discontent has been kept to a minimum. A British journalist reported in 1968—and nine years later the scene is largely unchanged—"Money is being spent if not lavishly at least freely. After slow years of indecision Brunei is embarking on a development boom that could make it a model state. More, much of this money has filtered

down to the rice roots level, as it were, and the people have bene-
fitted. There is no unemployment. . . . Living standards have risen
markedly. Education is free and so is medical attention, carried by
flying doctor services to every part of the state."[4]

The flow of money from oil and liquid natural gas will continue
for the foreseeable future, and the resultant economic well-
being—the Shellfare state, as some call it—should suffice to rec-
ompense for the lack of any significant political freedoms as long
as it is permitted to trickle down to the level of the peasants and
fisherfolk. Ironically, however, different problems may arise because of the superabundance of wealth. In 1972, as a result of the
expanded educational system, approximately one-third of the total
population was in school, which in the near future will pose famil-
iar questions: what will happen to these educated youths? Will they
have employment opportunities compatible with their qualifications and, more important, their ambitions? A militant,
nationalistic Islam is stirring in the sultanate, partly because an
increasing number of young Brunei Malays are receiving a Middle
Eastern education. A ban on the public sale of liquor is only one
instance of the intense nationalism and religious fervor among
Brunei Malays. Can this process be reconciled to the need to
maintain an integrated, multiracial state? There are signs that the
Chinese population is becoming uncomfortable under certain aspects of Brunei rule, and this, of course, will increase when the
British finally leave. In 1970, for example, the government decided
to cut back on financial aid to Chinese schools and to impose stricter
surveillance and controls.

In 1967 the old sultan, who had personally dominated the affairs
of state for seventeen years, suddenly, and for reasons of his own,
abdicated in favor of his twenty-one-year-old son. The latter has
continued to follow the cautious policies of his father, who remains
a real power behind the throne. The Legislative Council, provided
for in the 1959 Constitution, had been dissolved during the state of
emergency declared at the time of the revolt; it was reconvened
briefly in July 1963 and then "reformed" in 1964 when direct
elections were introduced for ten out of its new chamber of

4. *ST*, August 7, 1968.

twenty-one members. In 1970 the council was dissolved again following elections in which a newly formed opposition party secured all the elected seats—whereupon it was replaced rapidly with a chamber appointed in its entirety by the sultan.[5] The state of emergency still exists, and in practice the sultanate is administered by royal decree. What press there is in Brunei is tightly controlled, if not overtly censored, and no matters of internal controversy appear in the newspapers. Attempts to revive the concept of political parties since the revolt have failed; politics today is largely meaningless, and parties are banned.

Brunei and the British

The British still retain much influence in Brunei. British officers dominate the police force and army, and British civil servants still effectively control most portions of the state's bureaucracy even though much is made publicly of their replacement by qualified Bruneians. A battalion of Gurkha troops from the British army are stationed on Brunei soil to guarantee the sultanate's territorial integrity. This mantle of defense, strongly redolent of Britain's colonial past, does not lie lightly on British authorities, and for several years they have sought an effective formula whereby they could withdraw gracefully from their responsibilities. The sultan pays all the expenses of the British presence, but this is not enough to induce a promise to provide an indefinite strategic umbrella.

In 1971 a new agreement between the sultan and the British led to a diminution of the role of the high commissioner. No longer does the latter offer "advice" on internal matters, which are now strictly the sole responsibility and prerogative of the sultan. The high commissioner was henceforward to be the representative of the British government and was empowered only to offer advice on matters of foreign policy and defense. In 1974 the British government announced its decision to remove the Gurkha troops, but the sultan—and presumably the oil company—lobbied effectively for a postponement of this move, and in March 1975 the British reluctantly acceded to his wishes. Talks have been held on a desultory basis ever since, amid periodic noises from the British that the

5. *NYT*, October 15, 1970.

withdrawal of the Gurkhas would not pose a threat to Brunei's security. In the words of Lord Goronwy-Roberts, minister of state in the Foreign and Commonwealth Office, "Our view is that there is no inherent or real threat to Brunei . . . [even though] it is not for me to deny that the Sultan is apprehensive about the security of his state."[6]

The British have reasons for their disquiet over Britain's continued role in Brunei. United Nations Resolution Number 3424 was adopted in the General Assembly in late 1975 "affirming the right of Brunei to self-determination and independence, and asking Britain to facilitate democratic elections following the lifting of the ban on political parties and the return of political refugees." In reply to a question on the matter in the House of Lords, Lord Goronwy-Roberts replied that he had transmitted the General Assembly resolution to the sultan, but that "Brunei is a sovereign state in treaty relationship with the United Kingdom. We have no responsibility for its internal affairs, but we have made our view on participatory government known to the Sultan, and continue to do so. A formal review of the treaty is now proceeding at the request of Her Majesty's Government."[7] Talks are due to resume sometime in 1977, but in view of the sultan's suspicions of his neighbors' intentions, their outcome is likely to be contentious.

Brunei and Malaysia

Relations with Malaysia have been deteriorating ever since Brunei's refusal to enter Malaysia in 1963. Brunei did not help matters in 1970, when in a statement issued from the palace the sultan announced that he had a claim, on historical and religious grounds, to the towns of Limbang, Lawas, and Trusan in neighboring Sarawak.[8] Matters were further exacerbated in 1973, when ten of the fifty-nine Partai Rakyat leaders who had been under detention without trial since 1962 escaped from prison and fled to Malaysia, where they were given immediate asylum and enabled to establish a political office. Since then the Brunei Partai Rakyat has

6. Press conference in Kuala Lumpur, *New Straits Times*, January 15, 1976.
7. Debate in the House of Lords, February 24, 1976.
8. *ST*, December 17, 1970.

been active in exile with the connivance if not the direct sponsorship of the Malaysian government.

In April 1975, the Partai Rakyat leadership in exile, presumably operating from Malaysia but with a Brunei address, forwarded a political manifesto to the sultan. A far cry from the party's previous socialist position, this new document is couched in moderate political and economic terms—possibly in deference to Malaysian sensitivites and in recognition of the party's new situation—and what animosity it contains is reserved for the British. In the words of the manifesto's preamble:

> The Association of Southeast Asian Nations (ASEAN) has emerged as a new political force in Southeast Asia. The concept of Neutralism for Southeast Asia, as expounded by the Right Honorable Tun Haji Abdul Razak bin Dato Hussein, the Prime Minister of Malaysia, has received momentum and world support. These changes, just to quote a few, have entirely changed the political pattern of Southeast Asia, and it is under the influence of such radical changes in the politics of this region that the Peoples Party of Brunei readjusts its stand to align itself with the movement for the regional cooperation and universal peace.[9]

The party now wishes to establish an independent Kingdom of Brunei with the sultan as constitutional head of state and with political sovereignty vested in an elected parliament. The state ideology is to be founded on the three concepts of belief in Islam, nationalism, and democracy. In the future economic ventures, the exploitation of natural resources, are to be "evaluated on the basis of equal and just partnership with local control," with a substantial amount of public revenues devoted to the funding of indigenous projects. Finally, the manifesto stresses the essential "Malayness" of the proposed new state and its need to maintain strong ties to the Malay world round about:

> Since culture is the basic foundation of a nation, it shall be the duty of the Malays to retain and exalt the value of Malay Culture. In order to safeguard our culture and at the same time to ensure that the people are not influenced by yellow culture, Malay culture has to be intermingled with the Islamic Culture. This shall immunise the Malay Culture against moral decadence and make the Malays more faithful to the teachings of Islam. . . . Here, the teaching of Islam will be made compulsory in schools

9. The manifesto was published under cover of a Partai Rakyat letter dated April 16, 1975.

throughout the Sultanate of Brunei. The Malays of the Sultanate of Brunei have strong cultural ties with the Malays in Indonesia, Malaysia and the Philippines, and it is therefore essential for the Kingdom of Brunei to strengthen its cultural ties with these countries.

Since their daring escape from detention, Partai Rakyat exiles have pursued their cause in the corridors of the United Nations, in Middle Eastern nations, and in the Islamic Conference. In 1973 the Committee of Twenty-four in the United Nations—the so-called decolonization committee—refused to recognize the self-governing status of Brunei and passed a resolution in the United Nations necessitating the sending of a team of observers to Brunei to investigate the situation. This request was refused by the sultan, and in May 1975, Partai Rakyat exiles presented a petition to the United Nations calling for immediate independence from Britain and asking that the party be entrusted with the formation of a new Brunei government. The sultan thereupon charged that a "foreign power"—clearly referring to Malaysia—was interfering in the internal affairs of his sultanate. The Malaysian newspaper, the *New Straits Times*, often the source of Malaysian government opinion, responded in an editorial:

Malaysian concern arises out of our commitment to decolonialisation, and our concern over the future of a neighbor whose present political maturity and future stability are in doubt and which is ill-prepared for the independence and the popular participation in government that must come. . . . Malaysia does not consider pursuit of its commitment to UN Resolution 1514(XV) on [Brunei] decolonialisation (a cornerstone of our foreign policy) and actions such as its co-sponsorship of the UN Resolution on Brunei earlier this month as "interference." . . . We have a legitimate right in wanting Brunei to be free.[10]

Malaysia has not relaxed its efforts to keep the Brunei issue alive in the United Nations. In his speech to the UN General Assembly on October 6, 1976, the Malaysian foreign minister again referred to Brunei's status:

There still remains an area in Southeast Asia where this august body at its last session has called upon the administering power to facilitate expeditiously the holding of free democratic elections by the appropriate authorities in accordance with the inalienable rights of the people to self-

10. *New Straits Times*, December 31, 1975.

determination and independence. I refer to the territory of Brunei. Malaysia would urge the responsible authorities to respond positively as early as possible to General Assembly Resolution 3424 so that the people of Brunei will not be denied their inalienable right.

Another neighbor, Indonesia, supported Malaysia in sponsoring another draft resolution, submitted to the UN in November 1976, once again calling for Brunei's independence.[11] Generally speaking, however, Indonesia seems content to permit Malaysia to maintain momentum on the issue, no doubt wishing to downplay the Indonesian role because of embarrassment over the annexation of the former Portuguese colony of East Timor.

Conclusion

Once the Gurkha battalion has been withdrawn, as it probably will in the near future, the sultanate's isolated and sheltered position will surely be exposed to the buffeting streams of political change. Brunei's oil and natural gas reserves are too rich a prize to remain forever in the hands of a quasi-feudalistic royal family. Whether change comes from within or from without, change there will be. The likelihood is that Brunei, in one form or another, will become part of Malaysia within the next one or two decades.

11. *Angkatan Bersenjata* (Jakarta), November 20, 1976.

Suggested Readings

Historical Background

Brimmell, Jack H. *Communism in Southeast Asia.* London: Oxford University Press, 1959. An overview, written by a former British official, which contains a good, if somewhat one-sided, section on the Communist Party of Malaya.

Chapman, F. Spencer. *The Jungle Is Neutral.* London: Chatto & Windus, 1951. One of the most gripping accounts to come out of World War II. Written by a British army officer who stayed behind in 1942 to fight the Japanese, this superb book is indispensable to students of MCP guerrilla history.

Cowan, Charles Donald. *Nineteenth Century Malaya: The Origins of British Political Control.* London and New York: Oxford University Press, 1961.

Emerson, Rupert. *Malaysia: A Study in Direct and Indirect Rule.* New York: Macmillan, 1937. A classic look at the way the British ruled prewar Malaya and the way the country's inhabitants reacted to the British presence.

Gullick, J. M. *Indigenous Political Systems of Western Malaya.* London: University of London Press, 1968. An excellent historical study of Malay society and government prior to the arrival of the British.

Hall, D. G. E. *A History of South East Asia.* 3d ed. London: Macmillan, 1968. The standard history of Southeast Asia, detailed and comprehensive.

Han Su-yin. *And the Rain My Drink.* London: Jonathan Cape, 1956. Well-written, realistic novel of the Emergency period in general and life in a New Village in particular. Han was married to a British Special Branch officer at the time she wrote this book, and it contains many insights.

Hanrahan, Gene Z. *The Communist Struggle in Malaya.* New York: Institute of Pacific Relations, 1954. The most compelling study of the origins of the MCP and the early days of the Emergency.

Parmer, Jess Norman. *1960 Colonial Labor Policy and Administration: A History of Labor in the Rubber Plantation Industry in Malaya, c. 1910–1941.* Locust Valley, N.Y.: J. J. Augustin (Monographs of the Association for Asian Studies, 9).

Pringle, Robert. *Rajahs and Rebels.* Ithaca, N.Y.: Cornell University Press, 1970. The best treatment so far of the Brooke rajahs in Sarawak and the effects of their rule on society.

Purcell, Victor. *Malaya: Communist or Free.* Stanford: Stanford University Press, 1955. A controversial but compelling study of the social underpinnings of the Emergency and the measures taken by the British.

Rauf, M. A. *A Brief History of Islam with Special Reference to Malaya.* Kuala Lumpur: Oxford University Press, 1964. An interesting analysis of the way Islam came to Malaya, written by a Malayan Muslim theologian.

Roff, William R. *The Origins of Malay Nationalism.* New Haven: Yale University Press, 1967. One of the most important books on Malaya in recent years and a pioneering study presenting the interplay of an indigenous nationalism, British colonialism, and Islam.

Short, Anthony. *The Communist Insurrection in Malaya, 1948–1960.* New York: Crane Russak, 1975. A retrospective and detailed look at the Emergency which, although flawed, presents a great deal of new material.

Steinberg, David J., et al. *In Search of Southeast Asia.* New York: Praeger, 1971. A first-rate overview of Southeast Asia prior to and after the coming of the West, with special reference to the impact of European encroachment on indigenous tradition.

Wheatley, Paul. *The Golden Khersonese.* Kuala Lumpur: University of Malaya Press, 1961. A most sophisticated, literate, and erudite investigation into the early history of the Malay Peninsula.

Winstedt, Richard O. *The Malays: A Cultural History.* London: Routledge & Kegan Paul, Rev. Ed. 1950. The standard work on the origins of the Malays and their cultural traditions.

Society

Alisjahbana, S. T., S. T. Nayagam, and Wang Gungwu, eds. *The Cultural Problems of Malaysia in the Context of Southeast Asia.* Kuala Lumpur: Malaysian Society of Orientalists, 1965. A compendium of excellent studies by Malaysian scholars that gives many insights into Malaysia's diverse society and its contemporary problems.

Harrisson, Tom. *The World Within.* London: Cresset Press, 1959. A fascinating account of the author's wartime experiences after being parachuted into Borneo. Also includes an important anthropological perspective on some of the people of the interior of Sarawak.

——. *The Malays of South-west Sarawak before Malaysia.* London: Macmillan, 1970. Perhaps the best work of this well-known scholar of Sarawakian society, this is a penetrating investigation of a Malay community and its cultural evolution.

Lee Yong-leng. *North Borneo: A Study in Settlement Geography.* Singapore: Eastern University Press, 1965. An excellent, concise study of the cultural geography of North Borneo.

Ooi Jin-bee. *Land, People and Economy in Malaya*. London: Longmans, Green, 1963. A short but useful geographical survey.

Purcell, Victor. *The Chinese in Southeast Asia*. 2d ed. London: Oxford University Press, 1965. A sympathetic account, comprehensive and at times controversial, by a former British administrator and Chinese scholar.

Radcliffe, David J. *Education and Primary Development in Malaya, 1900–1940*. Washington, D.C.: U.S. Department of Health, Education and Welfare, 1968. A little-known but important study of education under the British, showing how the system tended to create separate ethnic development.

Swift, M. G. *Malay Peasant Society in Jelebu*. London: Athlone, 1965. An anthropological study of Malay village society, invaluable for an understanding of Malay values and life styles.

The Economy

Buchanan, Iain. *Singapore in Southeast Asia: An Economic and Political Appraisal*. London: George Bell, 1972. An astringent, highly critical look at Singapore under the PAP and its role in Southeast Asia. The author's conclusions are debatable, and his sources often unidentified, but his book is nonetheless thought-provoking.

Kasper, Wolfgang. *Malaysia: A Study in Successful Economic Development*. Washington, D.C.: American Enterprise Institute for Public Policy Research, 1974. A brief, overly optimistic view of Malaysia's economy. It does, however, contain some interesting data.

Lim Tay-Boh. *Problems of the Malayan Economy*. Singapore: Donald Moore, 1956. A series of short essays on various aspects of the Malayan economy. Although somewhat dated by now, it contains useful historical backgrounds.

The Contemporary Setting and Its Problems

Chan Heng-Chee. *The Politics of Survival, 1965–1967*. Singapore: Oxford University Press, 1971. A leading Singapore political scientist effectively analyzes in this brief study the results of Singapore's separation from Malaysia and the way in which the PAP adapted itself to the new conditions.

———. *The Dynamics of One-Party Dominance: The PAP at the Grass Roots*. Singapore: Singapore University Press, 1976. An excellent study of the PAP and the means by which it permeates and controls almost every aspect of contemporary Singapore life.

Esman, Milton J. *Administration and Development in Malaysia*. Ithaca, N.Y.: Cornell University Press, 1972. A first-rate account of the way institutions are shaped in Malaysia's pluralistic society.

Fletcher, Nancy McH. *The Separation of Singapore from Malaysia*. Ithaca, N.Y.: Cornell University, Southeast Asia Program, Data Paper no. 73,

1969. A detailed account—the best so far—of this traumatic event.

Gamer, Robert E. *The Politics of Urban Development in Singapore.* Ithaca, N.Y.: Cornell University Press, 1972. In this thoughtful study the author describes the growth of public housing in Singapore and its relationship to the government's political goals.

Leigh, Michael B. *The Rising Moon: Political Change in Sarawak.* Sydney: Sydney University Press, 1974. This excellent book charts the formation of political parties in Sarawak and their subsequent transformation to a Malaysian pattern.

Means, Gordon P. *Malaysian Politics.* London: University of London Press, 1970. An outstanding, detailed work that analyzes current politics and their immediate origins.

Ongkili, James P. *Modernization in East Malaysia, 1960–1970.* Kuala Lumpur: Oxford University Press, 1972. A concise but effective description of party formation in East Malaysia by a Kadazan scholar who is now a minister in the Sabah government.

Pang Cheng-Lian. *Singapore People's Action Party: Its History, Organization and Leadership.* Singapore: Oxford University Press, 1971. A brief but well-researched and useful look at the formation of the PAP, its ideology, and its structure by a well-known Singapore journalist.

Ratnam, K. J. *Communalism and the Political Process in Malaya.* Kuala Lumpur: University of Malaya Press, 1965. A classic study by a leading Malaysian scholar of the origins of political parties and their roots in Malaya's ethnic diversity.

Ratnam, K. J., and R. S. Milne. *The Malayan Parliamentary Elections of 1964.* Singapore: University of Malaya Press, 1967. An analysis of one particular election that has application to a wider context of Malayan politics.

Roff, Margaret C. *The Politics of Belonging.* Kuala Lumpur: Oxford University Press, 1974. The author chronicles the origins and development of political parties in Sabah and Sarawak.

Stenson, Michael R. *Industrial Conflict in Malaya.* London: Oxford University Press, 1970. A controversial but well-documented account of the origins of the Malayan and Singaporean trade-union movement.

Glossary

adat	Malay customary behavior, often pre-Islamic in origin.
akhirat	Muslim life-hereafter.
Bapa Malaysia	The Father of Malaysia: refers to the first prime minister, Tunku Abdul Rahman.
boneka	puppet.
bumiputera	son (literally prince) of the soil: refers to Malays and other indigenous Malaysians.
derhaka	the Malay sin of treason against the sultan.
Gandjang Malaysia!	Crush Malaysia!: the slogan coined by Sukarno in 1963 to crush the newly formed state of Malaysia.
haj	the pilgrimage to Mecca: one of the five pillars of Islam. *Haji* refers to a person who has performed the *haj*.
imam	Muslim religious official attached to a mosque.
infiltrasi	infiltration: Sukarno's military strategy of infiltrating guerrillas into Malaysia as part of his Crush Malaysia! campaign.
kampong	Malay village or hamlet; sometimes, as in Singapore and Kuala Lumpur, refers to the Malay quarter of a city.
kapitan China	the captain of the Chinese: name given by the British to a Chinese village or small-town headman.
kenduri	ritual, or customary, feast with both Islamic and *adat* significance.
konfrontasi	confrontation: Sukarno's general strategy of opposition to Malaysia.
malu	shame, often used in the sense of loss of face.
masok Islam	enter Islam: to become a Muslim.
masok Melayu	enter Malayhood: to become a Malay, generally refers to becoming a Muslim.
Melayu Rayu	Greater Malaya, sometimes known as *Indonesia Rayu*, or Greater Indonesia: the concept of one political Malay world, encompassing Malaysia, Indonesia, Singa-

	pore, southern Thailand, and the southern Philippines.
merdeka	freedom, independence from colonial rule.
orang asli	the original people: refers to Malaysia's aborigines.
pajak	lease, cede.
panglima	village headman, especially of a coastal or island village and used mainly in Sabah and Brunei.
pasok momogun	son of the soil: Kadazan term used in Sabah to refer to non-Muslim indigenous people.
penghulu	village chief or headman.
pengiran	aristocratic Malay title, used chiefly in Brunei.
rezeki	Islamic term that refers to a divinely determined fate, or lot.
Rukunegara	the Principles of the State: the ideals upon which Malaysia is founded.
Rukun Tetangga	Neighborhood Association: refers today to a system of legally enforced neighborhood patrols to counteract Communist activities.
Suara Revolusi	The Voice of the Revolution: MCP radio station also known as the Voice of the Malayan Revolution, which operates out of southern China.
ummat	the community of Islam.
Yang di-Pertuan Agong	The Supreme Ruler, also known as Malaysia's king: one of the sultans, appointed by all the sultans in council on a rotational basis to act as the constitutional head of state.

Index

Oil industry: Brunei, 99, 108, 257–259, 261, 263, 268; Singapore, 247
Ong Eng-guan, 204
Ongkili, James, 164
Onn bin Jaafar, Dato, 86, 87, 155
"*orang Asli*," 20

PRC (People's Republic of China), 7, 30, 108, 185, 244; foreign policy, 82, 186–189, 250; and Malaysia, 176, 188–189, 249; Sino-Soviet power struggle, 176, 178, 179, 189–190; supporters, 126, 128, 230
Pahang (Malay state), 24, 30, 33
Pang Cheng-lian, 200
Pangkor Engagement, 33, 55, 75
Paramesvara (later Megat Iskandar Shah), 24
Peaceful Coexistence, Five Principles of, 82, 83
Penang (Malay state), 30, 31, 56, 69, 74, 116n, 146, 152, 195; riots in, 116n, 130, 144; status as Malaysian state, 91
penghulu (headman), 27–28
People's Defense Force (Singapore), 240
Perak (Malay state), 30, 33, 51, 146, 152
Perlis (Malay state), 34
Phan Hien, 179
Philippines, 21, 22, 39, 163n, 249; in ASEAN, 190–192; claims to North Borneo, 105, 109–110, 191; opposition to Malaysia, 109
Political organizations in Brunei
Alliance, the, 107
Partai Rakyat, 107, 108, 155n, 260; electoral success of, 261; exiles, 267; political manifesto, 266, 267; suppression of, 262, 265
Political organizations in Malaya, 56–57, 72, 73, 82, 86, 87
AMCJA (All Malayan Council of Joint Action), 89; formation of, 73
Alliance, the, 86–91, 101
IMP (Independence of Malaya Party), 86, 87
KMM (Kesatuan Melayu Muda), 57, 58, 64, 72
KRIS (Kesatuan Ra'ayat Indonesia Semenanjong), 64, 71
MCA (Malayan Chinese Association), 74, 85–89, 100, 126
MCP (Malayan Communist Party), 11, 60–63, 65, 72, 75–76, 80, 85, 128, 166, 187, 188, 205; Central Committee of, 177, 180; DMW (Department of Malay Work), 180; formation of, 60; guerrillas, 20, 75, 81, 168, 176, 179, 180; insurrection by, 77–79, 82, 87, 89; leadership split, 178–181; opposition to Malaysia, 176n, 182, 230; policies, 81–83, 176–178; and trade unions, 76–77
MDU (Malayan Democratic Union), 72, 73
MIC (Malayan Indian Congress), 88–89, 130; in the Alliance, 88, 144; in the NF, 152
MNLA (Malayan National Liberation Army), 176
MNLL (Malayan National Liberation League), 176
MNP (Malayan Nationalist Party), 64; founding of, 72
MPAJA (Malayan People's Anti-Japanese Army), 62, 65
MRLA (Malayan Races Liberation Army), 80–84
Malay Union movement, 56, 57
PETA (Pembela Tanah Ayer), 63, 64, 71
PUTERA (Pusat Tenaga Ra'ayat), 73
UMNO (United Malays' National Organization), 57, 84–85, 95, 115, 144, 147, 151, 155; in the Alliance, 86–88; conflicts within, 156; in the NF, 152; opposition to, 73; in Singapore, 208, 231–232; supporters, 70–72, 74
see also FMS *and* UMS
Political organizations in Malaysia, 151–156
Alliance, the, 115, 144, 145, 148, 151, 152; leaders of, 149, 209; success of, 150, 209; *see also* NF *under* Political organizations in Malaysia
DAP (Democratic Action Party), 144,

Library of Congress Cataloging in Publication Data
(For library cataloging purposes only)

Bedlington, Stanley S., 1928–
  Malaysia and Singapore.

  (Politics and international relations of Southeast Asia)
  Bibliography: p.
  Includes index.
  1. Malaysia—Politics and government. 2. Singapore—Politics and government.
    I. Title. II. Series.
DS597.B42   320.9′595   77–3114
ISBN 0–8014–0910–1
ISBN 0–8014–9864–3 pbk.

DUE DATE

20-6503

Printed
in USA